D0189653

Handbook of
CALIFORNIA BIRDS

With a 1986 revision of the Checklist of Species, Families and Orders.

Vinson Brown ● Henry G. Weston, Jr. ● Jerry Buzzell

To Angela
Laurel
and Roger

Library of Congress Catalog Card Number: 73-6826

Copyright © 1961, 1965, 1973, 1986 Naturegraph
Third Revised and Enlarged Edition,
with a 1986 revision of the Check List of Species.
ISBN 0-911010-16-5

Naturegraph Publishers has been publishing books
on natural history, Native Americans,
and outdoor subjects since 1946.
Please write for our free catalog.

Books for a better world

Naturegraph Publishers
P.O. Box 1047
Happy Camp, CA 96039 USA

TABLE OF CONTENTS

INTRODUCTION

The praises of California's varied topography have been sufficiently sung, so it need only be said that any state whose borders include over a thousand miles of seashore, a humid coast, high mountains, rolling foothills, broad valleys and arid deserts is going to contain an equally varied bird fauna. Of special interest are the Anna's Hummingbird, Nuttall's Woodpecker, Wrentit, California Thrasher and Tricolored Blackbird because they are found primarily in California, while the California Condor and Yellow-billed Magpie are found only in California. Add to these specialties over 450 different species recorded in this state and it is not difficult to see why California offers so much interest to bird watchers.

Handbook of California Birds is an attempt to aid those bird watchers who would like an identification guide wholly concerned with this ornithologically rich state. It is hoped that the beginner will find this book especially helpful because it pares down the number of species you need to look at, and the ones described will lead to less confusion. The more advanced student ought to find it a useful addition to the other fine field guides which cover a larger area.

Several features separate this book from other identification handbooks. Most notable is the arrangement of species. The order of species laid down by the American Ornithologists Union has been altered whenever it was thought that such a change would aid identification in the field. Thus the swifts and swallows, which are not closely related, are placed together because of their like appearances. Likewise many pages would normally separate gulls from the primitive *"Tube-nosed gliders"* which show differences in the hand but look very similar in the field. In this book they are placed close together to aid ease of field identification. Also in this book *"Land"* and *"Water"* birds are put in separate sections to make them easy to find quickly, whereas in most bird books the gulls, terns and related *"Water"* birds are usually sandwiched in proper A.O.U. order between the chicken-like birds and the owls. For the *"purist"* and to help the general reader see the birds in scientific order we furnish a life list of species on pages 8-12 as they appear in the normal A.O.U. order. You can check off birds on this list as you observe them.

It will also be noted that the names of species on the color plates appear at the bottom of the page. This is to enable the reader to go on an armchair field trip, testing his knowledge of identification thoroughly while at home. The names can be conveniently covered for self-testing in identification. In this way familiarity with formerly unknown birds will lead to much less frustration in the field, especially among the more illusive species of the brush and treetops.

Of California birds (including those on offshore islands) 368 species are described in this book. Names are based on the 1957 A.O.U. Checklist of North American Birds, plus its 32nd supplement in 1973 and its 33rd supplement in 1976. All these species are illustrated in color in the book and many are also pictured in black and white to show species qualities such as flight patterns or food foraging behavior. Additional species recorded in the state but considered rare or unusual in occurrence have been listed and briefly described on pages 60-63.

Most of the color plates are shown in groups of two facing pages so you can see in one glance the maximum number of birds possible that are of similar appearance and compare them quickly. The descriptions are on the opposite sides of these color plate pages and emphasize only those colors that are most important in field identification. Important in the descriptions are ranges and habitats (living places) where the birds are found, special behavior patterns of use in identification, and songs and calls. Further details on habits are given in such special chapters as those on flight patterns, food foraging behavior and courtship (see Table of Contents), to all of which you should turn for extra help when you notice bird actions that fit one or more of these categories. Bird study depends on observing small details accurately and listening very carefully for every sound. In time and with practice you will often be able to identify a bird in the distance, too far off to see its colors, simply by the way it acts or the sounds it makes.

The most obvious clue to correct identification (perhaps next to voice) is size. Shown here are comparative sizes of common species which will provide a helpful rule of thumb. Care should be taken to be accurate in size-estimate because bright or contrasting plumage tends to exaggerate a bird's true size.

Shown from largest to smallest: Crow pigeon, robin, sparrow and warbler.

ABBREVIATIONS

♀=female ♂=male   mts=mountains.
imm=immature   med=medium

A. Humid Coast Forest
B. Northwest Mtn. Forest
C. San Francisco Bay Area
D. Inner Coast Range
E. Southern California
F. Colorado Desert
G. Mojave Desert
H. Inyo-Owens Valley
I. San Joaquin Valley
J. Sacramento Valley
K. Sierra-Nevada Mtns.
L. Cascade Mtns.
M. Great Basin

206

ORDER, FAMILY AND COMMON NAME

This book has the birds arranged in groups of similar appearing birds as an aid in identification. The following checklist is arranged by Order, Family and Common Name according to the American Ornithologists Union Checklist of North American Birds, 6th Edition, 1983. For convenience Common Names are arranged alphabetically within each Family. Family Emberizidae has been subdivided because of the large number of species.

This also is a checklist that may be used in checking off each species as you see it in the field, so determining your bird life list. The number following each Common Name is as the bird appears in this book so one can locate it quickly. Former Common Names (used in the text of this book) are in italics after the new offical Common Name (*), which will be used in the next edition.

Order GAVIIFORMES
Family Gaviidae
☐ Arctic Loon (7)
☐ Common Loon (6)
☐ Red-throated Loon (8)

Order PODICIPEDIFORMES
Family Podicipedidae
☐ Eared Grebe (1)
☐ Horned Grebe (2)
☐ Pied-billed Grebe (3)
☐ Red-necked Grebe (4)
☐ Western Grebe (5)

Order PROCELLARIIFORMES
Family Diomedeidae
☐ Black-footed Albatross (108)
Family Procellariidae
☐ Manx Shearwater (113)
☐ Northern Fulmar (109)
☐ Pink-footed Shearwater (110)
☐ Sooty Shearwater (111)
☐ Short-tailed Shearwater (112)
Family Hydrobatidae
☐ Ashy Storm-Petrel (116)
☐ Black Storm-Petrel (117)
☐ Fork-tailed Storm-Petrel (114)
☐ Leach's Storm-Petrel (115)

Order PELECANIFORMES
Family Pelecanidae
☐ American White Pelican (42) *
   (White Pelican)
☐ Brown Pelican (43)
Family Phalacrocoracidae
☐ Brandt's Cormorant (46)
☐ Double-crested Cormorant (44)
☐ Pelagic Cormorant (45)
Family Fregatidae
☐ Magnificent Frigatebird (107)

Order CICONIIFORMES
Family Ardeidae
☐ American Bittern (54)
☐ Black-crowned Night-heron (52)
☐ Great Blue Heron (49)
☐ Great Egret (50)
☐ Green-backed Heron (53) *
   (Green Heron)
☐ Least Bittern (55)
☐ Snowy Egret (51)
Family Threskiornithidae
☐ White-faced Ibis (56)
Family Ciconiidae
☐ Wood Stork

Order ANSERIFORMES
Family Anatidae
☐ American Wigeon (29)
☐ Barrow's Goldeneye (20)
☐ Black Scoter (23)
☐ Blue-winged Teal (31)
☐ Brant (37)
☐ Bufflehead (17)
☐ Canada Goose (36)
☐ Canvasback (13)
☐ Cinnamon Teal (32)
☐ Common Goldeneye (19)
☐ Common Merganser (9)
☐ Fulvous Whistling-Duck (35)
☐ Gadwall (27)
☐ Greater Scaup (15)
☐ Greater White-fronted Goose * (41) (White-fronted Goose)
☐ Green-winged Teal (30)
☐ Harlequin Duck (22)
☐ Hooded Merganser (11)
☐ Lesser Scaup (16)
☐ Mallard (26)
☐ Northern Pintail (28) *
   (Pintail)

☐ Northern Shoveler (33)
☐ Oldsquaw (21)
☐ Red-breasted Merganser (10)
☐ Redhead (12)
☐ Ring-necked Duck (14)
☐ Ross' Goose (29)
☐ Ruddy Duck (18)
☐ Snow Goose (40)
☐ Surf Scoter (25)
☐ Tundra Swan (38) * *(Whistling Swan)*
☐ White-winged Scoter (24)
☐ Wood Duck (34)

Order FALCONIFORMES
Family Cathartidae
☐ American Kestrel (167)
☐ Bald Eagle (141)
☐ Black-shouldered Kite (152) *
  (White-Tailed Kite)
☐ California Condor (150)
☐ Cooper's Hawk (159)
☐ Ferruginous Hawk (148)
☐ Golden Eagle (142)
☐ Harris' Hawk (149)
☐ Merlin (156) * *(Pigeon Hawk)*
☐ Northern Goshawk (158) * *(Goshawk)*
☐ Northern Harrier (153) * *(Marsh Hawk)*
☐ Osprey (140)
☐ Peregrine Falcon (158)
☐ Prairie Falcon (154)
☐ Red-shouldered Hawk (144)
☐ Red-tailed Hawk (143)
☐ Rough-legged Hawk (147)
☐ Sharp-skinned Hawk (160)
☐ Swainson's Hawk (145)
☐ Turkey Vulture (151)
☐ Zone-tailed Hawk (146)

Order GALLIFORMES
Family Phasianidae
☐ Blue Grouse (200)
☐ California Quail (206)
☐ Chukar (209)
☐ Gambel's Quail (207)
☐ Gray Partridge (208)
☐ Mountain Quail (205)
☐ Ring-necked Pheasant (203)
☐ Ruffed Grouse (201)
☐ Sage Grouse (202)
☐ Wild Turkey (204) * *(Turkey)*

Order GRUIFORMES
Family Rallidae
☐ American Coot (63)

☐ Black Rail (57)
☐ Clapper Rail (61)
☐ Common Moorhen (62) *
  (Common Gallinule)
☐ Sora (59)
☐ Virginia Rail (60)
☐ Yellow Rail (58)
  Family Gruidae
☐ Sandhill Crane (47)

Order CHARADRIIFORMES
Family Charadriidae
☐ Black-bellied Plover (69)
☐ Killdeer (66)
☐ Lesser Golden Plover (68) *
  (American Golden Plover)
☐ Mountain Plover (67)
☐ Semi-palmated Plover (65)
☐ Snowy Plover (64)
  Family Haematopodidae
☐ American Black Oystercatcher*
  (70) *(Black Oystercatcher)*
  Family Recurvirostridae
☐ American Avocet (93)
☐ Black-necked Stilt (94)
  Family Scolopacidae
☐ Baird's Sandpiper (77)
☐ Black Turnstone (72)
☐ Common Snipe (174)
☐ Dunlin (82)
☐ Greater Yellowlegs (87)
☐ Least Sandpiper (78)
☐ Lesser Yellowlegs (88)
☐ Long-billed Curlew (91)
☐ Long-billed Dowitcher (86)
☐ Marbled Godwit (92)
☐ Pectoral Sandpiper (81)
☐ Red Knot (123) * *(Knot)*
☐ Red-necked Phalarope (97) *
  (Northern Phalarope)
☐ Red Phalarope (95)
☐ Ruddy Turnstone (71)
☐ Sanderling (80)
☐ Short-billed Dowitcher (85)
☐ Solitary Sandpiper (75)
☐ Spotted Sandpiper (76)
☐ Surfbird (73)
☐ Wandering Tattler (84)
☐ Western Sandpiper (79)
☐ Whimbrel (90)
☐ Willet (89)
☐ Wilson's Phalarope (96)

Family Laridae
- [ ] Arctic Tern (133)
- [ ] Black Tern (136)
- [ ] Black-legged Kittiwake (121)
- [ ] Bonaparte's Gull (122)
- [ ] California Gull (127)
- [ ] Caspian Tern (139)
- [ ] Common Tern (132)
- [ ] Forster's Tern (131)
- [ ] Glaucous-winged Gull (130)
- [ ] Gull-billed Tern (134)
- [ ] Heermann's Gull (125)
- [ ] Herring Gull (126)
- [ ] Least Tern (135)
- [ ] Long-tailed Jaeger (120)
- [ ] Mew Gull (124)
- [ ] Parasitic Jaeger (119)
- [ ] Pomarine Jaeger (118)
- [ ] Ring-billed Gull (128)
- [ ] Royal Tern (138)
- [ ] Sabine's Gull (123)
- [ ] Thayer's Gull *
  (Former subspecies of 126)
- [ ] Western Gull (129)

Family Alcidae
- [ ] Ancient Murrelet (102)
- [ ] Cassin's Auklet (103)
- [ ] Common Murre (98)
- [ ] Marbled Murrelet (100)
- [ ] Parakeet Auklet (104)
- [ ] Pigeon Guillemot (99)
- [ ] Rhinoceros Auklet (105)
- [ ] Tufted Puffin (106)
- [ ] Xantus' Murrelet (101)

Order COLUMBIFORMES
Family Columbidae
- [ ] Band-tailed Pigeon (210)
- [ ] Common Ground Dove (216) *
  (Ground Dove)
- [ ] Mourning Dove (214)
- [ ] Ringed Turtle Dove (215)
- [ ] Rock Dove (211)
- [ ] White-winged Dove (213)

Order CUCULIFORMES
Family Cuculidae
- [ ] Greater Roadrunner (175) *
  (Roadrunner)
- [ ] Yellow-billed Cuckoo (217)

Order STRIGIFORMES
Family Tytonidae
- [ ] Common Barn-Owl (161) *
  (Barn Owl)

Family Strigidae
- [ ] Burrowing Owl (170)
- [ ] Elf Owl (171)
- [ ] Flammulated Owl (169)
- [ ] Great Gray Owl (184)
- [ ] Great Horned Owl (165)
- [ ] Long-eared Owl (167)
- [ ] Northern Pygmy Owl (172) *
  (Pygmy Owl)
- [ ] Northern Saw-whet Owl (113) *
  (Saw-whet Owl)
- [ ] Short-eared Owl (166)
- [ ] Snowy Owl (162)
- [ ] Spotted Owl (163)
- [ ] Western Screech Owl (168) *
  (Screech Owl)

Order CAPRIMULGIFORMES
Family Caprimulgidae
- [ ] Lesser Nighthawk (222)
- [ ] Common Nighthawk (223)
- [ ] Common Poorwill (221) *
  (Poorwill)

Order APODIFORMES
Family Apodidae
- [ ] Black Swift (220)
- [ ] Vaux's Swift (218)
- [ ] White-throated Swift (219)

Family Trochilidae
- [ ] Allen's Hummingbird (294)
- [ ] Anna's Hummingbird (288)
- [ ] Black-chinned Hummingbird (290)
- [ ] Broad-tailed Hummingbird (292)
- [ ] Calliope Hummingbird (291)
- [ ] Costa's Hummingbird (289)
- [ ] Rufous Hummingbird (293)

Order CORACIIFORMES
Family Alcedinidae
- [ ] Belted Kingfisher (174)

Order PICIFORMES
Family Picidae
- [ ] Acorn Woodpecker (181)

☐ Black-backed Woodpecker *
(189) *(Black-backed Three-
toed Woodpecker)*
☐ Downy Woodpecker (185)
☐ Gila Woodpecker (182)
☐ Hairy Woodpecker (186)
☐ Ladder-backed Woodpecker (183)
☐ Lewis' Woodpecker (190)
☐ Northern Flicker (176) *
*(Red-shafted Flicker, Gilded
Flicker, Yellow-shafted Flicker)*
☐ Nuttall's Woodpecker (184)
☐ Pileated Woodpecker (187)
☐ Red-breasted Sapsucker (179b)
☐ White-beaded Woodpecker (188)
☐ Williamson's Sapsucker (180)
☐ Yellow-bellied Sapsucker (179a)

Order PASSERIFORMES
Family Tyrannidae
☐ Alder Flycatcher (240a)
☐ Ash-throated Flycatcher (232)
☐ Black Phoebe (236)
☐ Cassin's Kingbird (233)
☐ Dusky Flycatcher (242)
☐ Eastern Kingbird (231)
☐ Gray Flycatcher (243)
☐ Hammond's Flycatcher (241)
☐ Olive-sided Flycatcher (237)
☐ Say's Phoebe (235)
☐ Vermilion Flycatcher (239)
☐ Western Flycatcher (244)
☐ Western Kingbird (232)
☐ Western Wood Pewee (238)
☐ Willow Flycatcher (240b)
Family Alaudidae
☐ Horned Lark (322)
Family Hirundinidae
☐ Bank Swallow (226)
☐ Barn Swallow (229)
☐ Cliff Swallow (228)
☐ Northern Rough-winged Swallow *
(27) *(Rough-winged Swallow)*
☐ Purple Martin (230)
☐ Tree Swallow (225)
☐ Violet-green Swallow (224)
Family Corvidae
☐ American Crow (192) *
(Common Crow)
☐ Black-billed Magpie (193)
☐ Common Raven (191)
☐ Gray Jay (195)

☐ Pinyon Jay (196) *
(Piñon Jay)
☐ Scrub Jay (198)
☐ Steller's Jay (197)
☐ Yellow-billed Magpie (194)
Family Paridae
☐ Black-capped Chickadee (254)
☐ Chestnut-backed Chickadee (253)
☐ Mountain Chickadee (255)
☐ Plain Titmouse (250)
Family Remizidae
☐ Verdin (261) (moved from family Paridae)
Family Aegithalidae
☐ Bushtit (252) (moved from family Paridae)
Family Sittidae
☐ Pygmy Nuthatch (258)
☐ Red-breasted Nuthatch (257)
☐ White-breasted Nuthatch (256)
Family Certhiidae
☐ Brown Creeper (249)
Family Troglodytidae
☐ Bewick's Wren (261)
☐ Cactus Wren (265)
☐ Canyon Wren (263)
(Cañon Wren)
☐ House Wren (260)
☐ Marsh Wren (262) *
(Long-billed Marsh Wren)
☐ Rock Wren (264)
☐ Winter Wren (259)
Family Cinclidae
☐ American Dipper (267) * *(Dipper)*
Family Muscicapidae
(species moved from Sylviidae, Turdidae, and Chamaeidae)
☐ American Robin (307) * *(Robin)*
☐ Black-tailed Gnatcatcher (248)
☐ Blue-gray Gnatcatcher (247)
☐ Golden-crowned Kinglet (248)
☐ Hermit Thrush (311)
☐ Mountain Bluebird (310)
☐ Ruby-crowned Kinglet (245)
☐ Swainson's Thrush (312)
☐ Townsend's Solitaire (313)
☐ Varied Thrush (308)
☐ Western Bluebird (309)
☐ Wrentit (266)
Family Mimidae
☐ Bendire's Thrasher (296)

- ☐ California Thrasher (298)
- ☐ Crissal Thrasher (300)
- ☐ LeConte's Thrasher (299)
- ☐ Northern Mockingbird (297) *
  (Mockingbird)
- ☐ Sage Thrasher (295)
  Family Motacillidae
- ☐ Water Pipit (306)
  Family Bombycillidae
- ☐ Bohemian Waxwing (304)
- ☐ Cedar Waxwing (305)
  Family Ptilogonatidae
- ☐ Phainopepla (303)
  Family Laniidae
- ☐ Loggerhead Shrike (301)
- ☐ Northern Shrike (302)
  Family Sturnidae
- ☐ European Starling (314) * (Starling)
  Family Vireonidae
- ☐ Bell's Vireo (284)
- ☐ Gray Vireo (285)
- ☐ Hutton's Vireo (283)
- ☐ Solitary Vireo (286)
- ☐ Warbling Vireo (287)
  Family Emberizidae
(species formerly found in Parulidae, Icteridae, Thraupidae, and part of Fringillidae)
  Warblers:
- ☐ American Redstart (273)
- ☐ Black-throated Gray Warbler (279)
- ☐ Black and White Warbler (280)
- ☐ Common Yellowthroat (271)
- ☐ Hermit Warbler (277)
- ☐ Lucy's Warbler (270)
- ☐ MacGillivray's Warbler (275)
- ☐ Nashville Warbler (269)
- ☐ Orange-crowned Warbler (268)
- ☐ Townsend's Warbler (278)
- ☐ Wilson's Warbler (272)
- ☐ Yellow-breasted Chat (276)
- ☐ Yellow Rumped Warbler (281)
- ☐ Yellow Warbler (274)
  Sparrows:
- ☐ Abert's Towhee (368)
- ☐ Black-chinned Sparrow (361)
- ☐ Black-headed Grosbeak (329)
- ☐ Blue Grosbeak (321)
- ☐ Brewer's Sparrow (360)
- ☐ Brown Towhee (367)
- ☐ Chipping Sparrow (359)
- ☐ Dark-eyed Junco (343) * (Gray, Oregon, and Slate-colored Juncos)
- ☐ Fox Sparrow (352)
- ☐ Golden-crowned Sparrow (357)
- ☐ Grasshopper Sparrow (354)
- ☐ Green-tailed Towhee (366)
- ☐ Harris' Sparrow (364)
- ☐ Lapland Longspur (349)
- ☐ Lark Bunting (348)
- ☐ Lark Sparrow (363)
- ☐ Lazuli Bunting (332)
- ☐ Lincoln's Sparrow (381)
- ☐ Northern Cardinal (328) * (Cardinal)
- ☐ Rufous-crowned Sparrow (358)
- ☐ Rufous-sided Towhee (365)
- ☐ Sage Sparrow (363)
- ☐ Savannah Sparrow (347)
- ☐ Song Sparrow (350)
- ☐ Summer Tanager (327)
- ☐ Vesper Sparrow (346)
- ☐ Western Tanager (326)
- ☐ White-crowned Sparrow (356)
- ☐ White-throated Sparrow (355)
  Orioles, Blackbirds:
- ☐ Bobolink (320)
- ☐ Brewer's Blackbird (315)
- ☐ Brown-headed Cowbird (316)
- ☐ Hooded Oriole (325)
- ☐ Northern Oriole (324) * (Bullock's Oriole)
- ☐ Red-winged Blackbird (317) * (Redwing Blackbird)
- ☐ Scott's Oriole (323)
- ☐ Tricolored Blackbird (318)
- ☐ Western Meadowlark (321)
- ☐ Yellow-headed Blackbird (319)
  Family Fringillidae
- ☐ American Goldfinch (339)
- ☐ Cassin's Finch (336)
- ☐ Evening Grosbeak (330)
- ☐ House Finch (337)
- ☐ Lawrence's Goldfinch (341)
- ☐ Lesser Goldfinch (340)
- ☐ Pine Grosbeak (333)
- ☐ Pine Siskin (342)
- ☐ Purple Finch (335)
- ☐ Red Crossbill (334)
- ☐ Rosy Finch (338) * (Gray-crowned Rosy Finch)
  Family Passeridae (Ploceidae)
- ☐ House Sparrow (369)

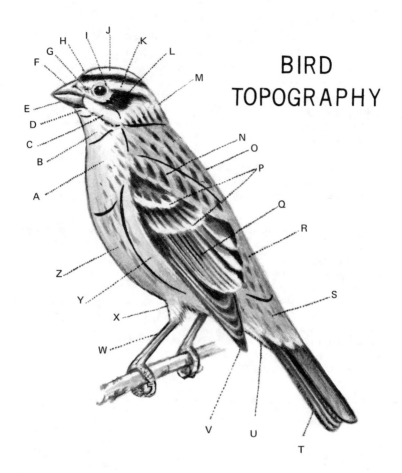

BIRD TOPOGRAPHY

A. Breast	J. Crown	S. Upper tail coverts
B. Throat	K. Eye-stripe	T. Outer tail feathers
C. Cheek	L. Ear patch	U. Under tail coverts
D. Chin	M. Nape	V. Primaries
E. Lower mandible	N. Scapulars	W. Tarsus
F. Upper mandible	O. Back	X. Tibia
G. Lores	P. Wing-bars	Y. Flanks
H. Forehead	Q. Secondaries	Z. Belly
I. Eye-ring	R. Rump	

Many birds may not remain in view long enough for the observer to identify it by casually thumbing through the pages that follow. A basic knowledge of bird topography will help to quickly pinpoint identification marks while a bird remains in view.

When this handbook is not handy, notes should be taken using the proper descriptive terms. A few jottings on a scrap of paper as an identification aid are far superior to trusting one's memory.

THE PLUMAGE CYCLE

One of the more difficult parts of bird study is the gaining of an understanding of the plumage cycle in birds, particularly among those kinds that show seasonal changes in color patterns. Sometimes, a novice bird watcher is positive he is seeing a new species or at least a bird that is out of its normal range when he is actually only watching a familiar bird at a time when it is molting or is in juvenal plumage. The difficulty is sometimes compounded by the fact that some change in the appearance of a bird may come simply from the wearing away of the outer part of the feathers. Thus the Starling appears as heavily white-speckled in winter when the outer parts of its feathers show white specks, but changes to glossy purplish-black and green in summer when these outer feather areas are worn away by the friction of everyday living. In between times, of course, Starlings show areas of gradation between the extremes.

Some understanding of molts and the plumage cycle can be gained by studying the following chart and observing the illustrations of plumage changes on the opposite page and in many of the color plates. For examples of gull plumage changes see pages 118 and 119.

Name Of Plumage	Misc. Observations	Lost By: Name Of Molt
1. NATAL DOWN Plumage (when present) following hatching.	Pelicans hatch naked and develop down later. Woodpeckers hatch naked and generally bypass down stage. Ducks, chicken-like birds, etc., hatch with body down-covered.	1. POSTNATAL MOLT Always a complete molt. Down feathers pushed out by tips of juvenal feathers, the next feathers to appear.
2. JUVENAL PLUMAGE First adult-like feathers but often appear fluffy.	Spotted breast feathers of juvenal robin a familiar example of this plumage.	2. POSTJUVENAL MOLT Many birds lose body feathers but not wing feathers by this molt. In others molt is complete.
3. FIRST WINTER PLUMAGE Feathers adult-type but duller. ♂ often resembles ♀. Retained through first winter and in same species until following summer.	Many birds have just one main complete molt in the late summer of the year. See molts no. 4 and 6.	3. FIRST PRENUPTIAL MOLT In some birds all or part of winter plumage lost here. In other birds this molt does not occur.
4. FIRST NUPTIAL PLUMAGE Possessed during first breeding season.	Males of some species possess bright colored plumage in breeding season.	4. FIRST ANNUAL OR POSTNUPTIAL MOLT Always a complete molt after nesting season usually late summer.
5. ADULT OR SECOND WINTER PLUMAGE Bird loses first year status. Retained through second winter and in some until summer. Like winter plumage of later years.	Male birds of nuptial brilliant plumage may be dull like ♀ in the winter.	5. ADULT OR SECOND PRENUPTIAL MOLT Some males attain bright colors following this molt.
6. ADULT OR SECOND NUPTIAL PLUMAGE Present through second breeding season. Similar to later nuptial plumages.	In most birds the terms Adult Winter and Adult Nuptial Plumages used for second year on.	6. ADULT OR SECOND POSTNUPTIAL MOLT The main molt of the year and following years.

PLUMAGE CYCLE

The ducks and a few other kinds of birds have a somewhat different cycle. Most male ducks have what is called an *"eclipse plumage"* in mid-summer. At this time of wing feather molt they assume a plumage that is dull like the females. The flight feathers are shed and the males are unable to fly for several weeks. In late summer this dull plumage is replaced by a bright plumage to be worn the following fall, winter and spring. This *"eclipse plumage"* is comparable to the winter plumage of other birds. It appears following a postnuptial molt and is lost by an off season prenuptial molt.

TYPES OF BILLS

A. Water and Shorebirds

  1. Edge sieve-like, etc.
    a. Rather wide, flattened
      (swan, duck 12-22 26-32, 38)
    b. High at base (not illus.)
      (goose 36-41)
    c. Gibbous
      (scoter 23-25)
  2. Saw-tooth edges
    (merganser 9-11)
  3. Relatively stout, short to long
    a. Pouch under long bill
      (pelican 42-43)
    b. Strong, of single piece (not illus.)
      (Pied-billed Grebe 3;
        rails 57-61; jaegers and
        gulls 118-130)
    c. Parrot-like
      (Puffin 106)
  4. Relatively long, straight
    (egret 50-51)
  5. Medium long, probing, etc.
    a. Upcurved
      (Avocet 93)
    b. Downcurved
      (Whimbrel 90)
    c. Straight
      (Willit 89)

B. Land Birds

  1. Hooked
    (eagle 141-142)
  2. Chicken-like
    (quail 205-207)
  3. Long, needle-like
    (hummingbird 288-294)
  4. Chisel-like
    (woodpecker 181-190)
  5. Medium straight
    (nuthatch 256-257)
  6. Flattened, etc.
    (kingbird 231-232)
  7. Straight, slight hook
    (thrush 309-313)
  8. Downcurved
    (thrasher 295-300)
  9. Sharp point
    (oriole 323-325)
  10. Convex (not illus.)
    (tanager 326-327)
  11. Conical
    (goldfinch 339-341)
  12. Crossed
    (crossbill 333-334)

EXPLANATORY NOTE: In the above key to bill types only one type is illustrated per category (two in 1a), though many other birds may have similar bills, as for example herons have the same type of bill as egrets. Check color plates for additional help in identification.

WATER BIRDS

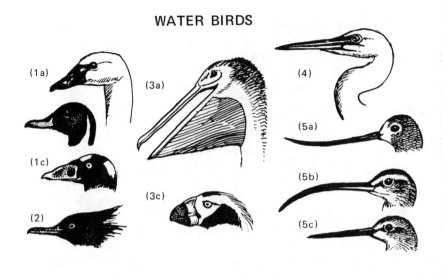

(1a)

(1c)

(2)

(3a)

(3c)

(4)

(5a)

(5b)

(5c)

LAND BIRDS

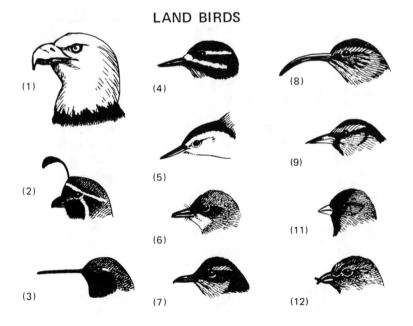

(1)

(2)

(3)

(4)

(5)

(6)

(7)

(8)

(9)

(11)

(12)

A. WATER AND SHOREBIRDS

   1. Swimming feet with front toes lobed or fringed
      a. Nails flattened, rear toe reduced
         (grebes 1-5)
      b. Nails claw-like, rear toe conspicuous
         (Coot 63[illus.]; phalaropes 95-97)
   2. Swimming feet with toes webbed
      a. All four toes joined by web
         (pelicans, cormorants 42-46)
      b. Front three toes only joined by web, hind toe free
         (loons 6-8; geese and ducks 12-32, 34, 36-41 [illus.];
         Avocet 93; jaegers and terns 118-120, 131-139)
      c. Front three toes only joined by web, hind toe absent
         (murres, guillemots, auklets, murrelets and Puffin 98-
         106)
      d. Front three toes only partially webbed, hind toe free
         (Western Sandpiper 79; Willet 89; curlews 90-91
         [illus.])
      e. Front three toes only partially webbed, hind toe absent
         (plovers 64-66 [illus.]; Black Oystercatcher 70; San-
         derling 80)
   3. Front toes typically deeply cleft, narrow, nearly straight, spreading, nails relatively short; for walking, wading in marsh.
      a. Hind toe present
         (herons [illus.], bitterns, ibises 47-56; rails 57-62;
         Black-bellied Plover and relatives 69, 71-78, 81;
         Knot and relatives 83-88; Marbled Godwit 92)
      b. Hind toe absent
         (Mountain Plover 67; Golden Plover 68; Stilt 94)

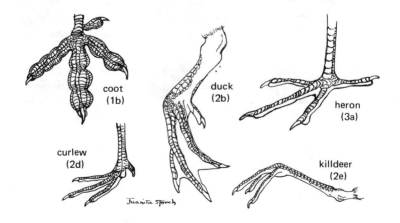

coot
(1b)

duck
(2b)

heron
(3a)

curlew
(2d)

killdeer
(2e)

Juanita Storch

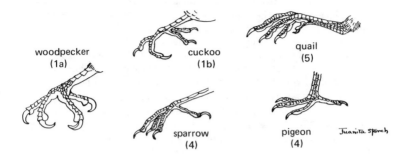

woodpecker (1a) cuckoo (1b) quail (5) sparrow (4) pigeon (4) Juanita Sponch

B. LAND BIRDS

1. Two toes forward, two toes back
   a. For clinging to tree surfaces
      (woodpeckers 181-190 [illus.])
   b. For general perching
      (Yellow-billed Cuckoo 194 [illus.])
   c. For walking, running
      (Roadrunner 175)
2. Feet small, weak, inconspicuous
      (Poorwill 221; swifts 218-220; nighthawks 222-223;
      hummingbirds 288-294)
3. Feet for grasping prey with strong, deeply cleft toes; nails
   sharp and strongly curved
      (vultures, hawks, eagles 140-160; owls 161-173)
4. Perching feet, four toes alike with prominent hind toe and nail,
   toes not conspicuously strong, hind nail usually curved
      (pigeons and doves 210-216 [illus.]; perching birds
      231-369 [illus.])
5. Walking-scratching feet with strong toes, blunt nails, hind toe
   elevated
      (grouse 200-202; Ring-necked Pheasant 203; quail
      205-207 [illus.]; Partridge 208; Chukar 209)
6. Miscellaneous
   a. Three toes forward, one back, outer two front toes part-
      ly fused together
      (Belted Kingfisher 174)
   b. Three toes only, two toes forward, one back
      (Three-toed Woodpecker 189)

BIRD CONSERVATION

Women's hats are no longer adorned with egret plumes and hopefully few blackbirds are baked in pies anymore. These millinery and culinary delights of a former day were ended early in the twentieth century by people who saw birds and other wildlife with more understanding than the prodigal pioneers who settled this country. Passage of the Migratory Bird Treaties with Canada and Mexico and the establishment of many State and Federal refuges through the years have aided many species.

With the advent of popular interest in ecology, the idea of *"good"* and *"bad"* birds has faded with the realization that all life is intricately woven together. Today California's game laws are among the most enlightened in the world. A little more than a decade or two ago such birds as hawks and owls, cormorants, shrikes, and the House Finch were considered undesirable and included on the unprotected list! They are now protected.

But progress in curbing indiscriminate shooting has led to a larger problem, the encroachment of man's civilization on areas vital to the survival of many species. The California Clapper Rail and the Least Tern are but two examples of birds whose habitat needs are delicate enough to be easily destroyed by man in the name of progress.

However, the pessimistic prophecies which shroud so much of this concern need not be so gloomy. Many of the smaller species such as the Mockingbird, Brewer's Blackbird and Hooded Oriole are probably more abundant today than in days when the California Grizzly roamed the state. A saner use of chemical pesticides seems imminent through the work of a generation whose grandparents helped the slaughter of egrets at the turn of the century. There is hope in the increasing sensitivity of more and more people to the absolutely vital role of birds in nature, in their saving and bringing back our spirit in a dangerously artificial and materialistic world.

Perhaps one of the basic questions is why protect endangered species? The economic value of birds is probably not nearly so crucial to man as once was thought and the benefits of an industrial way of life extract unhappy sacrifices from us all. The answer is probably more philosophical than practical and Theodore Roosevelt said it well when he likened the extinction of a species to the perishing of a priceless work of art. Human life would go on if Michelangelo's *David* were shattered to dust or Beethoven's *Pastorale* were irrevocably lost.

Human life would go on, but it would be a little less humane. Perhaps more than all other creatures, birds appear to us as the very embodiment of movement and emotion. Perhaps for no other reason than simply this marvelous sensation and spirit of vibrant life we must guard our bird populations, that our own lives may never lose the vital enrichment of being that birds give us.

PATTERNS OF FLIGHT

Both birds alone and birds in flocks often show distinctive patterns of flight. For example the slow lumbering flight of the Great Blue Heron, with the neck held in an S-shape, is very distinctive, while the twinkling, interweaving, high speed flight of a flock of White-throated Swifts high in the sky helps mark this species. By watching and learning about such flight patterns one can often separate kinds of birds in flight that otherwise might be difficult to tell apart. Thus both the Brewer's Blackbird and the Starling are similar appearing blackbirds but the Brewer's flies with a rapid beat of the wings, followed by a short glide, whereas the Starling has a straight sustained arrow-like flight with extended glides.

Besides the illustrations of some typical kinds of flight patterns shown in this section, several species illustrations in the color plates show flight patterns of special interest. Care should be taken not to accept each category too literally.

The more common patterns of bird flocks in flight are outlined below, while some distinctive patterns of single birds in flight are given on the pages that follow.

PATTERNS OF FLOCKS IN FLIGHT

A. V or Double V-shaped Flocks. *Geese* (illustrated below), *swans 36-41; curlews 91; ibis 48-51; some sandpipers 75-81; and ducks fly in V-shaped flocks 12-35.*

B. Single-file formation. *This is common to the Brown Pelican 43;* (illustrated below), *and most ducks.*

C. Geometric figures (funnels, balls, etc., produced in flight by large flocks, often with sudden swift changes). *Particularly done by the smaller shorebirds 77-82; and the blackbirds 315-319.*

D. Loosely-shaped flocks. *Horned Larks 322; bushtits 252; waxwings 304-305; sparrows 346-369; thrushes 307-313; swallows and martins 224-230.*

E. Flock of birds criss-crossing and swirling at high speed high in the sky. Swifts 218-220.

F. Flock explodes from ground, then planes down to land in new cover. *Quail 206-207.*

G. Flock moves in divisions over ground, the rear division leap-frogging over the ones ahead to feed. *Piñon Jay 196; Redwings 317.*

PATTERNS OF SINGLE BIRDS IN FLIGHT

A. Soaring Flight. Little or no wing-beat as bird circles level or rises on updraft of warm air.

1. Wing-tips down: *White Pelican 42; Magnificent Frigate-bird 107; Black-footed Albatross 108; Wood Ibis 48; jaegers and gulls 118-130; Osprey 140.*
2. Wings straight out: *eagles and buteo hawks 141-149; California Condor 150; Raven 191.*
3. Wings at V-angle: *Zone-tailed Hawk 146* (frequently); *Vulture 151; Crow 192.*

B. Flight Mainly in Straight Line.

1. Slow, methodical wing-beat: *pelicans 42-43; Sandhill Crane, Wood Ibis and herons 47-56; California Condor and Turkey Vulture 150-151* (when traveling); *Snowy Owl 162; Great Gray Owl 164; Great Horned Owl 165.*
2. Deep, powerful wing-beat: *Canada Goose 36; jaegers 118-120.*
3. Short rapid wing-beats followed by quick sail or glide: *accipiter hawks 158-160.*
4. Medium-fast wing-beats, alternating with longer sail or glide: *shearwaters 110-113* (close to water); *Wood Ibis 48; swallows 224-230; Steller's and Scrub Jays 197-198; Robin 307; Brewer's, Redwinged and Tricolored Blackbirds 315-318; goldfinches 339-342.*
5. Rapid wing-beats seldom for extended distance: *hummingbirds 288-294; Mockingbird 297; thrushes 307-313; vireos and warblers 268-287; orioles and tanagers 323-327.*
6. Short flight before dropping into dense vegetation: *Least Bittern 55; rails 57-61; Grasshopper Sparrow 354; Meadowlark 321.*
7. Rapid wing-beat as bird skims close to water (feet often paddle water): *grebes and loons 1-8; diving ducks 9-25;* (illus. page 82); *cormorants 44-46; geese 36-41; sandpipers and relatives 70-97; alcids 98-106; storm petrels 114-117; Whistling Swan 38; Dipper 267; Coot 63.*
8. Straight with an upcurve glide to perch: *Burrowing Owl 170; Pygmy Owl 172; shrikes 301-302;* (see illus. page 187).
9. Undulating, bounding or dipping up and down: *woodpeckers 176-190; Gray and Piñon Jays 195-196; Yellowbilled Magpie 194; Blackbilled Magpie 193; Clark's Nutcracker 199; nuthatches 256-258; warblers 268-282; Gray-crowned Rosy Finch 338; goldfinches 339-342* (see illus. page 199).
10. Jerky with tail often moving up and down: *kinglets, gnatcatchers, parids, (chickadees, nuthatches, wrens) 245-265; Wrentit 266; Dipper 267; Pipit 306.*

A. Bird kept aloft by warm air currents rising from the earth.

Soaring (146)

B. Bird kept aloft by wing-beats.

Deep Wing-beats (42)

Rapid beat and glide (159)

Straight (210)

Irregular rapid beat and glide (315)

C. Flight Direction Varied.

1. Erratic, rising and falling or nose-diving and swooping up: *plovers 64-69; Marsh Hawk 153; Short-eared Owl 166; swifts and swallows 218-230.*

2. Fluttering, similar to erratic but with a light, moth-like effect: *petrels 114-117; Poor-will 221; Bank Swallow 226; flycatchers 231-244; Pipit 306; Horned Lark 322; bluebirds 309-310.*

3. Skimming, wings held still most of time, but occasional swift beats keep bird nearly same height above earth: *pelicans 42-43; tube-nosed fliers 108-117; terns 131-139; White-tailed Kite and Marsh Hawk 152-153; falcons 154-157; Short-eared Owl 166; swifts 218-220; swallows 224-230.*

4. Gliding, wings held still for extended glide slanting downward, usually followed by swift wing-beat: *geese 36-41; ducks 9-35; herons 49-53; Brown Pelican 43; Black-footed Albatross 108; Fulmar 109; shearwaters 110-113; Osprey 140; vultures 150-151; buteos 141-149; falcons and accipiters 154-160; upland gamebirds 200-216; Barn, Snowy, Spotted and Great Gray Owl 161-164; Long-eared Owl 167; Burrowing Owl 170; swallows 224-230; Brown Creeper 249; Mockingbird 297; Robin 307; Roadrunner 175; Meadowlark 321.*

5. Swirling, circling flight at high speed: *terns 131-139; swifts 218-220.*

D. Diving straight down or at steep angle. *Brown Pelican 42* (see illus. page 91); *Wood Ibis 48; terns 131-139;* (see page 126); *falconiformes 140-160; Belted Kingfisher 174; swifts 218-220; nighthawks 222-223; kingbirds 231-233; hummingbirds 288-294.*

E. Vertical, rising at a steep rate.

1. From land: *galliformes 200-209; hummingbirds 288-294; Horned Lark 322.*

2. From water: *dabbling ducks 26-35.*

F. Hovering, staying stationary in air with rapid wing-beats: *petrels 114-117; terns 131-139; Osprey 140; buteo hawks 141-149; White-tailed Kite and Marsh Hawk 152-153; American Kestrel 157; Burrowing Owl 170; kingbirds 231-233; kinglets 245-246; chickadees 253-255; hummingbirds 288-294; Horned Lark 322; bluebirds 309-310.*

G. Flies backward: *hummingbirds 288-294.*

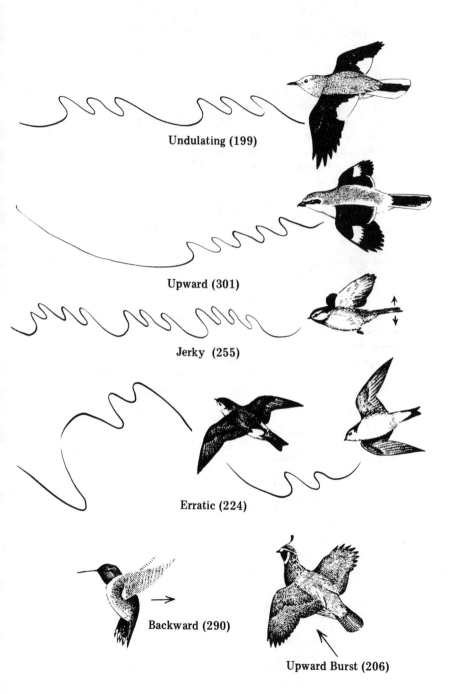

Undulating (199)

Upward (301)

Jerky (255)

Erratic (224)

Backward (290)

Upward Burst (206)

FOOD FORAGING BEHAVIOR

Observation of bird habits generally helps in the characterization of certain birds. Since behavior while foraging for food is one of the aspects of bird activity most frequently encountered in the field, different categories of this behavior have been outlined here for many of the birds included in this book. Use of this section can give the student direction in what to look for and aid in classifying birds who exhibit certain actions in the field. Some of the categories listed here are illustrated in this section, others are shown in color plates elsewhere in the book (illustrations are indicated by page number). Each of the examples listed are given with their species number.

WATER BIRDS
(Birds feeding in, on, or over waters)

A. Birds stand still in water with their long legs holding body above surface.
  1. Suddenly drive bill down to catch prey. *Sandhill Crane 47; herons 49-56* (see opposite page).
  2. Foot stirs bottom mud and then bird seizes food. *Ibis 48; Snowy Egret 51.*
B. Body tilted with tail up and head submerged as bird dabbles for food in shallow water, (see p. 86). *Dabbling ducks 26-36; Common Gallinule 62; American Avocet 93.*
C. Dive to bottom in deep water for food, frequently bringing it to surface, (see p. 82). *Diving ducks 12-25; Common Gallinule 62; American Coot 63.*
D. Birds swim under water to catch free-swimming organisms.
  1. In marine waters.
      a. Use primarily wings to swim.
          1. *Shearwaters 109-113.*
          2. *Common Murre, auklets, murrelets, Pigeon Guillemot, Tufted Puffin 98-106.*
      b. Use feet only.
          1. *Loons and grebes 1-8* (illus. page 27); *cormorants 44-46.*
      c. Flock cooperates to drive fish.
          1. *Double-crested Cormorant 44.*
  2. Freshwaters, use feet only to swim. *Mergansers 9-11; Double-crested Cormorant 44.*
E. Swims or walks under fresh water, aided by wings. *Dipper 267.*
F. Carries clam or other shellfish high in air and drops it to break shell on rocks. *Jaegers 118-120; gulls 121-130,* (see opposite page).
G. Birds feed on organisms on or near water surface and not while wading.
  1. Feed while in flight or dive from flight.
      a. Dive from wing, driving bill just under surface to catch fish. *Brown Pelican 43* (see p. 91); *terns 131-139* (see p. 126); *Belted Kingfisher 174* (see p. 142).
      b. Hovers, stirs water with feet, strikes prey with bill. *Snowy Egret 51,* (see opposite page).

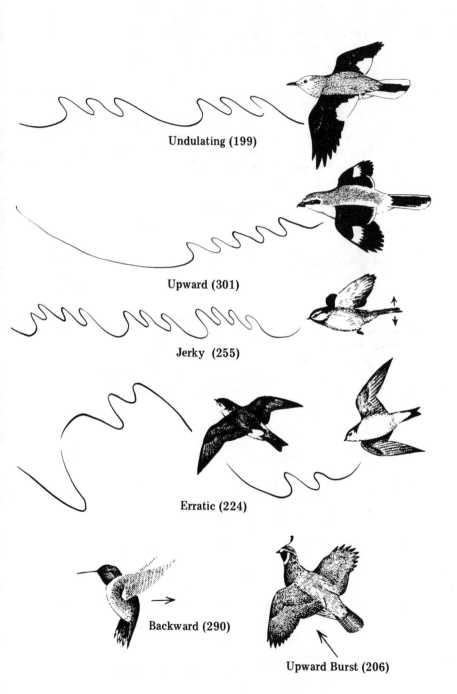

Undulating (199)

Upward (301)

Jerky (255)

Erratic (224)

Backward (290)

Upward Burst (206)

FOOD FORAGING BEHAVIOR

Observation of bird habits generally helps in the characterization of certain birds. Since behavior while foraging for food is one of the aspects of bird activity most frequently encountered in the field, different categories of this behavior have been outlined here for many of the birds included in this book. Use of this section can give the student direction in what to look for and aid in classifying birds who exhibit certain actions in the field. Some of the categories listed here are illustrated in this section, others are shown in color plates elsewhere in the book (illustrations are indicated by page number). Each of the examples listed are given with their species number.

WATER BIRDS
(Birds feeding in, on, or over waters)

A. Birds stand still in water with their long legs holding body above surface.
  1. Suddenly drive bill down to catch prey. *Sandhill Crane 47; herons 49-56* (see opposite page).
  2. Foot stirs bottom mud and then bird seizes food. *Ibis 48; Snowy Egret 51.*

B. Body tilted with tail up and head submerged as bird dabbles for food in shallow water, (see p. 86). *Dabbling ducks 26-36; Common Gallinule 62; American Avocet 93.*

C. Dive to bottom in deep water for food, frequently bringing it to surface, (see p. 82). *Diving ducks 12-25; Common Gallinule 62; American Coot 63.*

D. Birds swim under water to catch free-swimming organisms.
  1. In marine waters.
      a. Use primarily wings to swim.
        1. *Shearwaters 109-113.*
        2. *Common Murre, auklets, murrelets, Pigeon Guillemot, Tufted Puffin 98-106.*
      b. Use feet only.
        1. *Loons and grebes 1-8* (illus. page 27); *cormorants 44-46.*
      c. Flock cooperates to drive fish.
        1. *Double-crested Cormorant 44.*
  2. Freshwaters, use feet only to swim. *Mergansers 9-11; Double-crested Cormorant 44.*

E. Swims or walks under fresh water, aided by wings. *Dipper 267.*

F. Carries clam or other shellfish high in air and drops it to break shell on rocks. *Jaegers 118-120; gulls 121-130,* (see opposite page).

G. Birds feed on organisms on or near water surface and not while wading.
  1. Feed while in flight or dive from flight.
      a. Dive from wing, driving bill just under surface to catch fish. *Brown Pelican 43* (see p. 91); *terns 131-139* (see p. 126); *Belted Kingfisher 174* (see p. 142).
      b. Hovers, stirs water with feet, strikes prey with bill. *Snowy Egret 51,* (see opposite page).

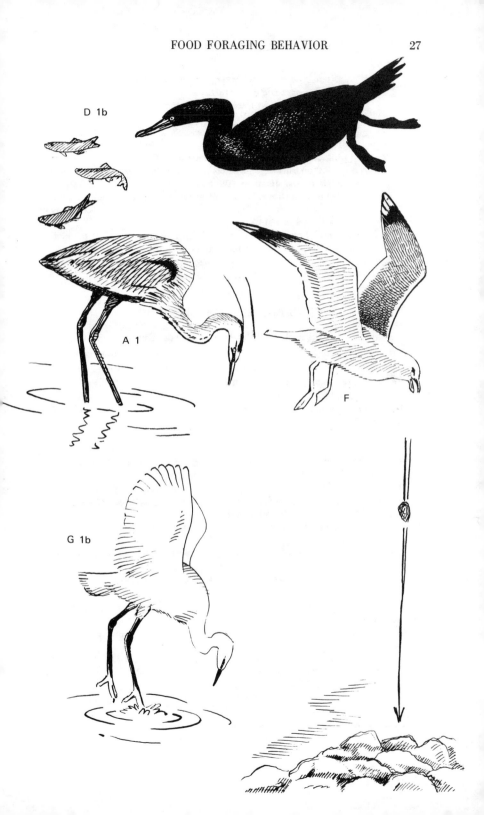

D 1b

A 1

F

G 1b

    c. Often drop down to water in quarreling flocks to scavenge for food. *Jaegers and gulls 118-130.*

    d. Dive from high in tree or air and grab fish with claws. *Osprey 140; Bald Eagle 141.*

    e. Feed while flying close to surface. *Shearwaters 110-131; petrels 114-117.*

  2. Feed while swimming on surface of water or resting there.

    a. Light on surface and catch prey with bill. *White Pelican 42; Black-footed Albatross 108; Fulmar 109.*

    b. Swim on surface of water, often whirling about to pick up small life, or to stir surface of water to make creatures rise. *Phalaropes 95-97,* (see page 110).

H. Feed on shellfish and other organisms on sea bottom near shore. Often dive from surface of water with vigorous forward leaps. *Scoters 23-25.*

I. Rob other birds of their food in the air. *Magnificent Frigate-bird 107; jaegers and gulls 118-130; Bald Eagle 141,* (see p. 130), *larger terns 138-139.*

SHOREBIRDS AND MARSH BIRDS

Many shorebirds and marsh birds are probers of mud, sand or vegetation, searching for food items. Many display distinctive behavior traits as they move about, sometimes while feeding, other times while not. Some may enter shallow water to forage.

A. Turn over rocks and seaweed on shore searching for food. *Turnstones and Surfbirds 71-73.*

B. Often teeter back and forth. *Spotted and Solitary Sandpipers 75-76; Wandering Tattler 84.*

C. Bob up and down. *Spotted and Solitary Sandpipers 75-76; Wandering Tattler 84; Willet 89; yellowlegs 87-88; American Avocet 93.*

D. Run rapidly in and out with waves on beach while feeding. *Semipalmated and Snowy Plovers 64-65; Willet 89; Baird's and Least Sandpipers 77-78; Dunlin 82; Sanderling 80,* (see opposite page).

E. Bill is swept side to side in shallow water like scythe. *American Avocet 93,* (see opposite page).

F. Often stretch wings up before or while feeding. *Willet 89; Marbled Godwit 92.* Godwit frequently spars with bill with other godwits.

G. Frequently jerks head up while feeding. *Killdeer 66; Solitary Sandpiper 75; Willet 89.*

H. Moves about very rapidly and rather erratically over marshy areas probing for food with long bill. *Snipe 74.*

I. Moves about on rocks of seashore, tipping tail and rear of body. *Wandering Tattler 84.*

J. Almost constant shrill twittering while feeding. *Baird's and Least Sandpiper 77-78; Dunlin 82; Western Sandpiper 79.*

K. In feeding moves daintily over mud, leaves of aquatic vegetation or wades in water, quickly jabbing here and there. *Black-necked Stilt 94,* (see opposite page).

L. Secretively stalk prey or seek plant food along edges of marshy streams or in marshes, usually alone. *Rails 57-61,* (see opposite page).

M. Moves over rocks with slow jerky movements prying limpets off substrate and opening shellfish with large powerful bill. *Black Oystercatcher 70.*

N. Move rather slowly over mud-flats or grasslands, probing in ground with long-curved bills. *Whimbrel and Long-billed Curlew 90-91.*

O. Move steadily forward in noisy, compact flocks, often of mixed kinds, over beaches or muddy shores, probing as they go. *Knot 83; Least and Western Sandpipers 78-79; Dunlin 82; Dowitchers 85-86.*

P. Run a few steps, picks at food object, pause, run again, often with head-lowered. *Plovers 65-69.*

Q. "Paddle" (stamp) feet up and down on soft substrate in foraging. Many *gulls (Herring Gull 126).*

BIRDS OF PREY AND SCAVENGERS

Also included here are some birds not normally thought of as birds of prey, but which sometimes capture and kill small animals or feed on carrion. These include birds such as magpies, crows and shrikes.

A. Use powerful, sharp-clawed feet for grasping prey.
    1. Dive from sky on various prey, usually at steep angle. *Soaring hawks, and eagles 141-149; Osprey 140,* (illus. on opposite page).
    2. Hover over field or other terrain, usually in one spot, then drop down on prey. *Kite 152; buteo or soaring hawks 143-149; American Kestrel 157,* (illus. on opposite page); *Marsh Hawk 153; Burrowing Owl 170.*
    3. Harry prey by quartering back and forth low over open country. *Marsh Hawk 153; Short-eared Owl 166,* (illus. on opposite page).
    4. Dives at high speed on bird flocks in flight, striking down individuals. *Peregrine Falcon 155.*
    5. Sneak up (flying) on birds in trees, bushes or on ground, suddenly plunging at them. *Accipiter hawks 158-160; Pigeon Hawk 156.*
    6. Normally dive on prey on ground from perch in tree. *Red-shouldered Hawk 144 and other buteo hawks 141-149; accipiters 158-160 occasionally do this.*
    7. Very quiet gliding, even moth-like flight used in hunting. *Owls 161-173.*
       a. Usually hunt at night or at dusk or early dawn. Most owls *161; 163-165; 167-169; 171-173,* (illus. on opposite page).
       b. Usually hunts at twilight or in daylight low to ground, seeming to bounce when attacking prey. *Burrowing Owl 170.*
       c. Hunt mainly by day. *Short-eared Owl 166; Snowy Owl 162.*
    8. Hunts at night low to ground with rapid flight, almost buzzing. *Elf Owl 171.*

B. With feet not adapted for grasping or tearing prey.
    1. Entirely carrion feeders. Soar high in sky in search of dead creatures then glide down in circles. *Vulture, Condor 150-151,* (illus. p. 134).
    2. Omnivorous, sometimes feeding on carrion, sometimes killing small animals by attacking on ground or in nests, but normally not using thorns or barb wire; eat eggs. *Magpies and crows 191-194,* (illus. p. 33); *jays 195-199.*

A 1

A 3

A 2

A 7a

3. Mainly carnivorous.
   a. Swoop down on prey, then carry it to thorn or barb wire to impale or for tearing flesh to eat. *Shrikes 301-302* (illus. p. 187).
   b. Runs or walks after prey and kills with blow of powerful bill. May capture snakes by circling and tiring them till they can be seized. *Roadrunner 175,*

INSECT EATERS

Insects seek to escape attack by flight, camouflage or by hiding under leaves, debris or bark, etc. Birds in their turn are often specialized in their way of finding and catching these creatures as indicated below.

A. Catch prey mainly in flight.
   1. Fly out, usually from exposed perch to capture flying insect, then fly back, often to same perch. *Acorn and Lewis' Woodpeckers 181 and 190; flycatchers 231-244,* (see p. 166); *bluebirds 309-310; Townsends' Solitaire 313; warblers 268-282* (illus. p. 179).
   2. Often fly high in sky scooping up insects in bills, wings held back at sharp angle and appearing to twinkle in flight. *Swifts 218-220.*
   3. Rarely fly so high; wings held more at right angles in flight; wings do not appear to twinkle. *Swallows 224-230.*
   4. Hunt usually in the evening, flying about high or low, often swerving abruptly after flying insects. *Nighthawks 222-223.*
   5. Hunts mainly in open brushy country at early dawn or dusk by flying up suddenly from ground with fluttering flight to catch insects in flight. *Poor-will 221.*
B. Obtain food (mainly insects) in bushes or trees.
   1. Probe into flowers for nectar and tiny insects and the like while hovering. *Hummingbirds 288-294,* (illus. on page 183).
   2. Chisel and probe bark with chisel-like bill. *Woodpeckers 176-190* (illus. on opposite page).
   3. Spirals up trunk or large branches, probing in crevices for food, then flies down to base of nearby tree to start over. *Brown Creeper 249,* (illus. on opposite page).
   4. Move with jerky motion round or straight up trunk or branches often move down head-first, probing bark for insects, spiders, etc. *Nuthatches 256-258,* (illus. on opposite page).
   5. Robin size birds, foraging in bushes and trees, generally without probing. *Yellow-billed Cuckoo 217; jays and Clark's Nutcracker 195-199; Mockingbird 297; orioles 323-325.*
   6. Sparrow-size or smaller, usually hunting without probing.
      a. Forage upside down and right-side up. *Chickadees 253-255; Plain Titmouse 250; Verdin 251,* (illus. on opposite page).
      b. Rather inconspicuous, moving rather slowly among peripheral twigs and foliage. *Vireos 283-287.*
      c. Tail often tilted up at angle.
         1. Quite secretive, hiding in brushy area. *Wrentit 266.*
         2. Rather bold in movements and often noisy. *Wrens 259-265.*

B 2 page 30

B 6

B 2

B 3

B 4

    d. Very active, flitting, warbler-size birds.
      1. With very long tails. *Gnatcatchers 247-248.*
      2. Nervously and constantly flit wings while foraging and may flutter by vegetation while picking off prey. *Kinglets 245-246.*
      3. Do not regularly flit tails or wings. *Warblers 268-282.*
C. Obtain food items mainly on ground.
    1. Scratch for food in litter and soil, using one foot at a time. *Grouse 200-202; Pheasant 203; Turkey 204; quail 205-207; Gray Partridge 208; Chukar 209.*
    2. Scratch for small life in ground litter, using both feet at same time. *Towhees 365-368; Fox Sparrow 352.*
    3. Thrash leaf-litter with their bills, driving out prey and catching it. May dig in soil with bill. *Thrashers 298-300,* (illus. on opposite page).
    4. Bird pauses, runs quickly and jabs at worm or insect, may bob tail and or head. *Thrushes (including Robins) 307-313,* (illus. on opposite page).
    5. Forage with even walking motion among low grassy vegetation or plowed fields often move head back and forth while walking. *Horned Lark* (walks swiftly) *322; Pipit* (bobs tail up and down) *306; Starling* (often moves in zig-zags) *314; Western Meadowlark 321; blackbirds and Brown-headed Cowbirds 315-320.*
    6. Often runs on ground. May leap into air to catch large insects. *Roadrunner 175.*
    7. Flip over small stones, dead branches, dried mud or cow dung, etc., in search of food. *Flickers 176-178; Cactus Wren 265.*
    8. Forage for insects on the ground near edges of snow banks and on the snow for frozen insects. *Rosy Finches 338.*

SEED, BERRY AND SAP EATERS

    Most of the birds in this category also prey on insects and other small animals, depending on availability. Berries and seeds are eaten depending on seasonal availability. Some even dig in and under snow for seeds and other food. Many of these birds have seed *"cracking"* bills.

A. Larger than sparrow in size.
    1. Most often seen foraging on ground. *Pigeons and doves 210-216; Ring-necked Pheasant 203; Turkey 204; Horned Lark 322; Piñon Jay 196; thrushes 307-312; towhees 365-368; Bobolink 320; quail 205-207.*
    2. Most often seen foraging in trees and bushes. (Illustrated)
      a. Mainly eat nuts, seeds and fruit. *Nutcracker 199; Solitaire 313; waxwings 304-305; Phainopepla 303; Cardinal 328; Black-headed Evening and Blue Grosbeaks 329-331; Pine Grosbeak 333.*
      b. Mainly feed on sap from trees. *Sapsuckers 179-180.*
B. Sparrow-size or smaller.
    1. Most often seen foraging on tops of weed-like plants. *Lazuli Bunting 332; goldfinches 339-341,* (see opposite page).
    2. Most often seen foraging in trees or bushes. *Tanagers 326-327; finches 335-337; Red Crossbill 334.*
    3. Most often seen foraging on ground. *Pipit* (slow-walking) *306; House Sparrow 369; Rosy Finch 338; Lark Bunting 348; juncos 343-345; sparrows 346-364.*

C 3

C 4

A 2a

B 1

Much is still to be learned about bird courtship, but we can give an outline here of some of the more common patterns and some of the birds that demonstrate them. The evolution of courtship in birds is difficult to assess as there is some evidence that a number of birds may have had at one time a more elaborate courtship than they do now. Many small birds of advanced types, such as the sparrows and other fringillids, for example, show little sign of courtship beyond the male singing over his territory, plus some chasing of the female by the male. The following are examples of a few of the more elaborate courtship behaviors, some illustrated, and some only described.

COURTSHIP IN THE AIR

1. **Diving from high altitudes almost to the ground.** Example: Killdeer 66, male and female may both fly high, then plunge earthward with shrill cries. Red-tailed Hawk 143, male and female soar high above ground together, circling, then male may steeply dive at high speed, stopping just before reaching ground, or both sexes may dive together, one sometimes below upside down. Eagles may do this also. Red-shouldered Hawk 144, male dives and side-slips wildly from a great height, squalling loudly, Marsh Hawk 153, male makes a U-shaped dive. White-throated Swifts 219, dive over and over arching their bodies. Male Common Night Hawk 223, dives near ground and female, making a loud boom with his feathers.

2. **Courtship carried out high in air with various gyrations.** Example: Common or Wilson's Snipe 74, flies in great circles, making loud penetrating hum. Long-billed Curlews 91, fly high and low in harmony, uttering long musical whistles. Ospreys 140, chase each other high in the sky, diving, swooping, soaring, sailing, dashing at each other, screaming. Crow 192, male chases female, showing off by gyrations, diving and wheeling, giving rattling sounds and other notes that sound like the gritting of teeth.

3. **Male shows off to female by swooping dives from a low height.** Variations in hummingbird performance are illustrated on opposite page. Anna's Hummingbird 288, makes loud metallic clang or loud chirp just above female. Costa's 289, gives exceedingly shrill cry when chasing female in zigzag flight. Calliope 291, makes flat-sounding *bzzzt* noise like angry bee. Allen's 294, makes buzzing vibratory noise with tail.

4. **A few other examples of courtship in air.** Sage Thrasher 295, male flies with peculiar trembling and fluttering of wings while calling, or may fly in erratic zig-zag flight low to the ground. Loggerhead Shrike 301, male chases female erratically in mock pursuit, both giving peculiar metallic cries; male may hover in air over female. Purple Finch 335, regularly flies up above female, hovers and sings, as also does Horned Lark 322.

COURTSHIP ON GROUND OR ROCKS

1. **Courtship carried out mainly by dances and display.** Example: Sandhill Crane 47 (illus. on opposite page) two or more groups come together on a hill-top and undertake a dance. Brown Pelican 43, with wings slightly

Anna's
288

Allen's
294

47

lifted and neck tilted far back, ponderously and slowly circles squatting female.   Double-crested Cormorant 44, alights near female, bows to her and begins to stalk or dance around her; his neck is outstretched and swollen and he keeps opening and closing his bill. Male Great Blue Herons 49, dance in circles on sandbar, or male jumps about alone, flopping wings. Great Egret 50, exposing raised throat feathers, while erecting white plumes, struts around female. Snowy Egret 51, displays plumes with body bent forward and down, while dancing around female. Green Heron 53, does horn-pipe dance in front of female. Wilson's Snipe 74, with drooping wings and wide-spread tail may strut around female while giving a low sweet and mellow warble. Male Ruffed Grouse 201, (illus. on opposite page) *"drums"* the air with wings and displays tail. Sage Grouse 202, (illus. on opposite page) males stamp ground and display yellow air sacs uttering large plopping noise with deep bubbling notes, while wings are held rigid at sides. Ring-necked Pheasant 203, male runs with short steps around female, inflating feathers and sweeping wing-tip near ground while tail is spread.   Gambel's Quail 207, makes a low cooing note while strutting around female.

2. **Courtship carried out mainly by chase and pursuit over ground.** Birds that do this include sparrows, crows, robins, roadrunners, shrikes, thrashers, etc.

3. **Courtship carried out mainly by posturing and displaying.** This means the male stands or walks back and forth in front of female while spreading wings and tail feathers, swelling throat, and often bowing, strutting, whirling, making loud noises, or singing, etc. Example: Canada Goose 36, with neck stretched low to ground, advances toward female while fleshy tongue is elevated, hissing loudly, quivering and shaking feathers; may bend neck gracefully over female. Green Heron 53, swells throat; American Bittern 54, male crouches low to ground and shows two large white ruffs of feathers; Black Oystercatchers 70, bow awkwardly to each other with necks stretched out, while calling. Male Crow 192, approaches female and bows low, spreading wings and tail, puffing out feathers and sings rattling song. Female Dipper 267, with head lowered spreads and flutters her wings and closely follows singing male. Male Sage Thrasher 295, may bring wings together over back. Male Mockingbird 297, runs across ground in front of female, flitting tail and spreading it, often lifting his head and wings high, showing white undersides while cooing. House Sparrow 369 (see illustration and text page 41).

4. **Courtship carried out mainly by bill touching or picking up nesting material.** In courtship preliminary to nesting either one or both sexes picks up, manipulates or carries nesting material in front of the opposite sex, but usually drops it soon without actually using it for a nest. Grebes, cormorants, mockingbirds, blackbirds, and some sparrows do this. Others touch or caress bills, for example gulls, herons, grebes, cormorants, guillemots, crows, pigeons, cuckoos, roadrunners and sparrows.

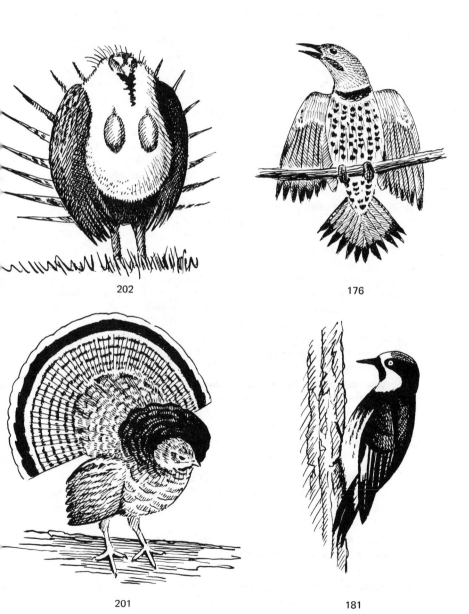

202

176

201

181

COURTSHIP IN BUSHES AND TREES

1. **Courtship carried out mainly by posturing and display.** Example: Most male woodpeckers and sapsuckers 179-190, (illus. page 39), display bright colors by expanding feathers and spreading wings and tails while on branch or trunk. Ruby-crowned Kinglet 245, male sings and displays wings and tail, also raises red patch on head. Male White-breasted Nuthatch 256, may turn back and bow slowly, displaying black and white pattern of spreading tail, while singing; also shows flash of reddish-brown feathers; or may strut toward female. Cedar Waxwing 305, male siddles along limb over to female and rubs his breast against hers. Some vireos and warblers show similar posturing. House Finch 337, (see illustration and text on opposite page).

2. **Courtship carried out mainly by bill hammering on tree.** Example: Woodpecker; light hammering done by smaller woodpeckers (Nuttall's, Downy 184-185; medium by medium-sized woodpeckers (Acorn 181, Hairy 186, Lewis' 190 and sapsuckers 179-180); heavy sound by large woodpeckers (Pileated 187).

3. **Courtship carried out mainly by dances and display.** Example: Flicker 176-178 (illus. page 39) male does dance around tree trunk with body bent from side to side, head tilted back and bill pointed upward with outstretched neck (moved like a baton). Acorn Woodpeckers (illus. page 39) move on and around branches and trunks, dodging and many other antics, male spreading wings and tail in display and bobbing head. Pileated Woodpeckers move back and forth on large limb, pecking at each other's bills, crests elevated. Male Warbling Vireo 287, singing a low mellow warble, struts in short dancing steps around female. Mockingbird 297, male does elaborate dance in front of female. Cedar Waxwing 305, male does delicate little dance on branch by hopping back and forth in front of female and holding and presenting a leaf in his bill, which she may take.

4. **Courtship carried out mainly by chase and pursuit through branches.** Example: Most woodpeckers and sapsuckers do this, also Wrentit 266, and some sparrows 346-364. Loggerhead Shrike 301, male chases female erratically through branches.

COURTSHIP AROUND WATER

1. **Many ducks have aggressive approach of male toward female.** Example: Ruddy Duck 18, which displays two swollen protuberances under neck, and a puffed out chest. Makes noise as tail is pressed forward over back and snapped back.

2. **Males rush about excitedly over water, splashing along on surface, or diving and surfacing near female.** Grebes 1-5. Male coot 63, behavior the same, but elevates tail showing white under tail coverts.

3. **Males swim about regally, while uttering low notes, head low, wings partly upraised and spread into a fan.** Gallinules 62, also displays bright red face and bill.

4. **Wade about in shallow water, bowing and crouching low, or dancing about with widespread wings.** Avocets 93, moving like tight-rope walkers.

Two of the commonest bird species in California—the House Sparrow 369, and House Finch 337—each provide the beginning bird-watcher with examples of courtship which can be readily observed in almost any urban area. In both cases the male displays before the female with drooping of his wings and a raised tail. The courting male House Sparrow puffs out his plumage and hops before the female, repeating his harsh chirrup over and over. The female chatters and responds and will often repel her suitor with rushes at him. Sometimes several males will display before a single female. Except for the drooping wings and raised throat and forehead feathers the male House Finch's plumage looks compressed as he leans toward the female and siddles up to her. The song sounds more intense and is accompanied by an overture squeal not heard in the usual song of this species. House Sparrow courtship will most likely take place on the ground or on a building roof whereas House Finch display is usually observed on a tree branch, telephone wire or fence top.

369

337

One aspect of aggressive behavior in animals is expressed as territoriality. It is probably most highly developed in birds and most birds show some type. Authorities in attempting to define territorial behavior in birds concentrate on one key aspect, the defense against competitors of the same species. Typically a male will defend an area primarily against members of its own species and sex sometime during the year, usually for at least part of the breeding cycle. Many ornithologists accept the brief description of territory in birds as *"any defended area"*. That which is defended varies greatly and includes such things as the nest, the feeding area, the mate, the display area, song post, family and so forth. Means of defense varies including such activities as various types of display, usually aggressive, to song, and occasionally fighting.

The establishment of a territory by a bird performs a number of basic functions during its cycle: The territory restricts the number of birds that can normally occupy an area. The young, sex-partner, nest and eggs are protected. An adequate supply of food and nesting materials is more or less guaranteed. Less interference with the usual breeding cycle activities occurs. Certainly the individual birds familiarity with an area that develops through close attachment over a period of time has its advantages.

Territories have been categorized in a variety of ways. The following breakdown of the basic types is based on Margaret Nice's work "The Role of Territory in Bird Life", *American Midland Naturalist*, Vol. 26, 1941.

1. Mating, nesting and feeding territory.

The most common type and maintained by many California birds, (for example warblers, grosbeaks, and sparrows). Typically the male of a species like the Black-headed Grosbeak 329, arrives first on the breeding grounds in the spring, establishes a territory and defends it. Upon choosing a site the male will advertise his *"ownership"* by singing from conspicuous perches. The female arrives a few days later and the nesting cycle begins.

2. Mating and nesting territory.

Feeding is carried out elsewhere. This is typical of birds such as some of the hawks, some chickadees and the Redwinged Blackbird 317. Every spring newspapers usually carry stories of *"mad blackbirds"* diving at sidewalk strollers from the trees above. This is the Brewer's Blackbird defending its nest site.

3. Mating territory.

A territory used exclusively for courtship and mating such as established by some of the chicken-like birds (example, grouse).

4. Nesting territory.

Only the immediate area around a nest is defended. This is typical of many of the colonial birds including puffins, murres, cormorants, pelicans, gulls, terns, herons and some swallows.

5. **Miscellaneous categories.** Some species defend feeding territories. Others defend roosting territories. There is evidence that the Loggerhead Shrike 301, defends a winter territory.

A few species defend a territory throughout the year as does the Plain Titmouse 250, which apparently remains paired throughout life. The Brown-headed Cowbird 316, establishes no territory of any kind. With few exceptions territories are stationary. However some birds such as Canada Geese 36, may maintain territorial areas that move as the group of geese moves.

Many factors are involved in influencing the size and shape of a bird's territory. The age of a bird, the type of vegetation in an area, the habits of a bird, food requirements, food availability, the function or functions to be performed by the territory, the number of birds present, all may play a role. A Golden Eagle 142, may possess a territory covering 20 square miles; a Great Horned Owl 165 about 120 acres; while Song Sparrows 350, Redwinged Blackbirds 317, and House Wrens 260, generally protect about one acre. Colonial birds like the California Murre 98, defend perhaps no more than a square foot around the nest, while a Cliff Swallow 228, may defend only a few inches around the entrance to its mud nest.

Some birds are communal by instinct and their flocks may or may not establish conspicuous or sizable territories. Herons, for example, often establish large communal nesting areas in trees, especially the Black-crowned Night Heron and the egrets 50-52. These flocks generally do not have special territories from which they drive other flocks away other than in the immediate vicinity of each nest. Crows 192, on the other hand, establish flock territories whose territories fluctuate along their boundaries depending on the power and ability of the individual flock to keep out intruders. It appears that flocks are connected to territories depending on the extent of their internal organization. An organized flock, like those of the Crows and Piñon Jays 196, are more likely to defend the food supply of a special area, while a communal group like the Cliff Swallows 228, who come together primarily just for nesting and because a certain cliff is available for their mud nests are not likely to attempt to dominate the territory near their nests, since each bird individually hunts on his own instead of as an organized flock. It is obvious a large amount of study and observation of the many kinds of bird flocks needs to be made to determine the extent of organization and territorial establishment that is found among each of them.

RANGE AND DISTRIBUTION

Any knowledgeable student of California birds is aware that no species occurs uniformly over the entire state. Instead each species may be found in only certain areas. In using this book it should be clearly understood that the reference to distribution accompanying each species account has to be very general. The distribution pattern of any bird is always subject to possible change depending on its tolerance to the multitude of factors in its environment. Shortage of normal food supply commonly results in distributional changes. Northern species such as the Snowy Owl may be temporarily driven down into parts of California.

A shortage of the pine nut crop in the Sierra may result in many Clark's Nutcrackers appearing in the coast ranges of central California. Invasions and introductions of non-native birds (see page 48) also bring about changes. The Hooded Oriole (see illustration below) has extended its range northward in the last 50 years from southern California to Sacramento. The Condor (see illustration below) has been reduced to just a remnant of its former range, now being found normally just in the mountains inland from Santa Barbara. In an area like the Santa Clara Valley the Brown Towhee and Mockingbird have increased in numbers and range locally with the building up of suburban areas and the planting of accompanying shrubs and trees.

The part of the state where each species occurs is termed its geographic range. The specific environment in which it lives is its ecologic range or habitat. For example, the Gila Woodpecker has a geographic range encompassing S.E. California; its ecologic range consists of streamside woodlands and desert scrub.

In field work, biologists commonly sort birds into descriptive status groups on the basis of seasonal distribution as follows (as indicated in part on the opposite page):

1. Permanent Resident. A species which remains in the same general area year round. For example, the Acorn Woodpecker, whose typical habitat includes open wooded areas containing oaks.

2. Summer Visitor. Species, such as the Northern Oriole, which winter to the south and each spring migrate northward to breed in California.

3. Winter Visitor. One that usually breeds to the north, such as the Ross' Goose, moving south each fall to winter in California. Others may summer in one part of the state and winter in other parts such as does the Red-breasted Sapsucker.

4. Transient. In this book this category refers to a species which typically neither summers nor winters in California but passes through in the spring heading to and/or in the fall returning from the breeding grounds. See map for Arctic Tern on opposite page.

5. Accidental. The occasional occurrence of a species rather infrequently found in California, such as the species listed on page 60 (Check-list of Rare Species).

BASIC SEASONAL DISTRIBUTION PATTERNS

181
Resident
Migrant southward
133
Winter
39
324
Summer
179B
Summer in high mountains. Winter in lowlands.

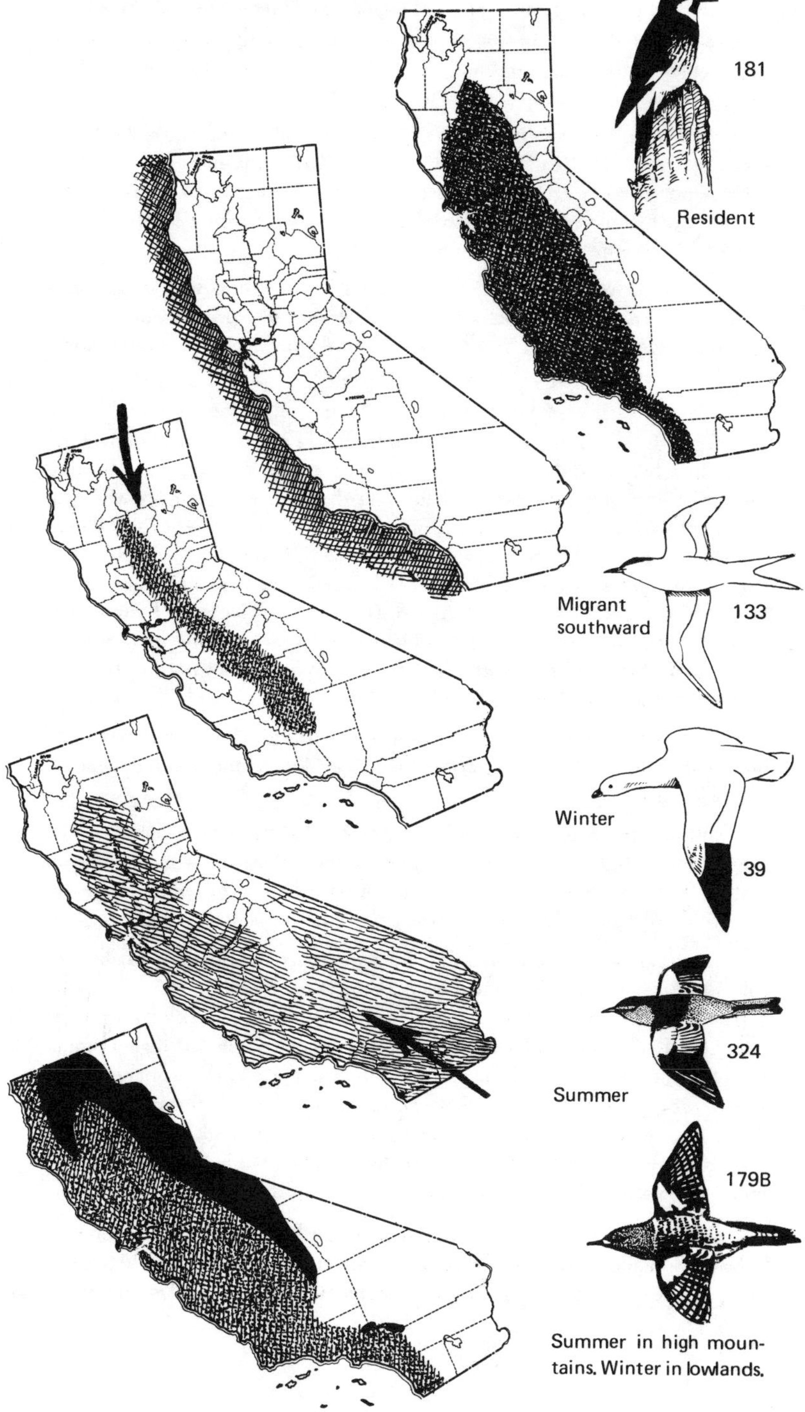

In California the regular seasonal migrations of birds fall into three basic patterns, latitudinal (north-south), altitudinal (up and down mountains) and longitudinal (east-west). A few species do not fall into any of these three categories and can be said to be nomadic to some extent.

Most migratory species of birds occurring in California follow the north-south pattern. The Ross' Goose 39, winters in California and moves north to breed along the central Arctic coast of Canada. The Bullock's Oriole 324, breeds in California and moves south into the tropics to winter. Maps relating to both of these species appear on page 45.

A reverse of the usual north to breed and south to winter pattern is carried out by the Heermann's Gull 125. During the spring-summer adults breed on islands in the Gulf of California after which many then move north to spend the winter along the California coast.

Quite a variety of birds undergo altitudinal migration. Mountain Quail 205, regularly nest in higher elevations of the Sierra and then many individuals move downhill to winter at lower elevations. An unusual feature of the seasonal movement of this species is the fact that individuals apparently walk rather than fly most of the way, spring and fall. Species such as the Williamson's Sapsucker 180, Ruby-crowned Kinglet 245, Mountain Chickadee 255, Robin 307, and Townsend's Solitaire 313 undergo some up and down mountain drifting depending on the severity of the winters. The Sierra Grouse 200, reverses the usual pattern in that individuals move from lower elevations to winter at higher elevations with a return drift to lower elevations to breed in the spring. Like the Mountain Quail, individuals migrate mainly on foot.

The Oregon Junco 344, follows several patterns of movement. It may undertake either altitudinal or latitudinal movements within the state depending on locality.

Species following a longitudinal or east-west pattern are exemplified by the California Gull 127, wintering primarily along the coast while moving inland to breed to the east, and the White-winged Scoter 24, wintering coastwise like the California Gull, and then migrating to central Canada to nest.

An example of individuals and flocks that are essentially nomadic, not following any set pattern of movement, is the Cedar Waxwing 305. The same applies to the frequent rather irregular wanderings of many Clark's Nutcrackers 199. The Red Crossbill 334, is occasionally nomadic within the higher mountains and the Gray-crowned Rosy Finch 338, wanders within the higher Sierra and to the east in the winter. Some species of birds (ex. California Quail 206, Wrentit 266) normally undergo no migration. Others undertake very little migration such as is true of some nuthatches and chickadees 253-258. Some individual Starlings 314, migrate while others are quite sedentary.

Migratory activity is carried out by many birds during the daylight hours. However a majority of the smaller birds that migrate do so by night. A few other species including loons, many shorebirds, geese and ducks, may move either by night or day.

Some reference has been made to the seasonal occurrence of birds in an area (see page 44). The graph below relates specific examples of seasonal occurrence with the time of spring movements.

The dates are recorded graphically for the first-seen records of the fifteen most common summer residents in the Berkeley area, on the east side of San Francisco Bay opposite the Golden Gate. All records shown are based on observations and field notes of various ornithologists. The years 1911 through 1947 are covered.

A complete record for the 37-year period is illustrated for only one species, the Black-headed Grosbeak 329. Nine other species are recorded for 30 or more years; the remaining five for less than 30. These latter five species, the Cliff Swallow 228, Wood Pewee 237, House Wren 260, MacGillivray's Warbler 275, and the Chipping Sparrow 359, have been recorded fewer times for various reasons. The Cliff Swallow, for example, has been erratic at times, failing to appear in Berkeley in certain years. The other four species are either secretive in their habits or appear only in low numbers most years. Consequently, they are not always recorded much earlier than they normally appear in Berkeley; in instances of exceptionally late records, it is assumed that actual first arrivals were overlooked or not sought out.

It is hoped that this information will stimulate others to record data on migration and will call attention to problems which field observers can help to solve.

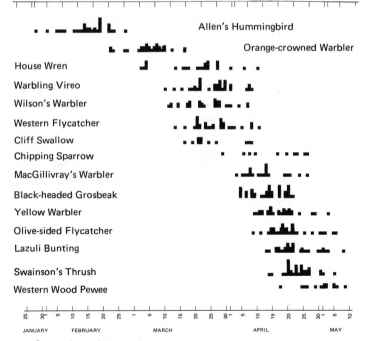

Comparison of dates of spring arrival of summer residents in the Berkeley, California area. Solid black squares indicate first-seen records. (H. Weston, *The Condor*, Vol. 20, 1948.)

INVASIONS AND INTRODUCTIONS OF FOREIGN SPECIES

Any entrance into California of large numbers of birds of a species unknown before can be called an invasion, if made by the birds themselves, or an introduction, if released by man. There have been no major invasions of California by native American birds from the east, but there have been such invasions by two European species, the House Sparrow and the Starling. In recent years the Cattle Egret (see page 94) has extended its southern United States and Mexico range into California.

The first invasion of importance was by the House (or English) Sparrow (see map page 207). Actually this bird is a Weaver Finch, not a true sparrow. This bird has adapted itself so well to the neighborhood of man, his buildings and plantings that it has aggressively spread to all parts of our country where man resides except for a few of the more isolated and wild areas.

The House Sparrow was first introduced into the eastern United States from Europe in 1851. After establishing itself in cities and nearby farms it began spreading westward. Additional releases by man sped up this movement. It first appeared in California at San Francisco about 1872. Some were released there by man. Others may have arrived in the state by accidental travel in railroad grain and stock cars. Some undoubtedly entered California of their own accord. By 1886 House Sparrows were widespread in the San Francisco Bay Area. Nineteen fifteen saw the species in virtually all parts of the state where towns and farms were to be found.

The successful introduction of the Starling into the United States from Europe occurred in New York City in 1890. Sixty birds were released. The species gradually spread by waves of migration over all of the United States, southern Canada and northern Mexico (see page 191). The first Starlings recorded in California, a flock of 40 in Siskiyou County, were observed in January, 1942. The next recorded observation in California was in 1946. By the mid-fifties flocks were wintering in many parts of the state, and by the early 1960's nesting was commonplace and the species was considered resident. Thrity-five pairs of Starlings had been introduced into Portland, Oregon, in 1889 and 1892. However the original pairs disappeared within a few years.

Although the Starling has proved of some value in destroying insect pests, it has also proved to be somewhat of a nuisance around farms, large parks and fairly open areas. Its noisy flocks create many problems for man and frequently tend to intimidate or drive out quieter native species, especially hole nesters.

Over the years a variety of birds not native to California have been released or have escaped into the wild. The releases have been primarily for general aesthetic reasons and as efforts to introduce new game birds. The so-called escaped cage birds have been both accidental and undoubtedly on occasion intentional. None have been as dramatic in their increase in numbers as the House Sparrow and Starling.

Some successful introductions of game birds into California include the:

Ring-necked Pheasant. Earliest introductions were by private individuals about 1885. The state government first released pheasants (140 individuals) in 1889. These first birds were from China. Most released since that time have been game-farm reared.

Turkey. Wild Turkey introductions date back to about 1877. California Department of Fish and Game has released birds in various parts of California since 1908. The first birds were from Mexico and later from Virginia.

Chukar. A game bird introduced into many parts of California (first in 1932). The first birds came from India. Most however have been game-farm bred birds.

Gray Partridge. A game bird that has been planted in many parts of the state. A few were released as far back as 1877. Serious introductions began in 1908.

Over the years a variety of other game birds have been released in many parts of California. A few of these include the Bobwhite, Coturnix, Golden Pheasant and the Guinea Fowl. There is no evidence of breeding populations surviving in the wild today. As late as the fall of 1972 a number of Woodcocks were released in the Sierra foothills southeast of Sacramento.

Successful non-game introductions include birds such as the:

Ringed Turtle Dove. First recorded in the Los Angeles area in 1921. Now well established in parts of southern California as well as some areas in central California. Some authorities consider this and the next listed species game birds.

Chinese Spotted Dove. Probably introduced (or escaped) in the Los Angeles area about 1914. Now well established in parts of southern California, and occasionally seen farther north.

Rock Dove (Domestic Pigeon). Well established in cities and around farms in many parts of the state. Date of original appearance is not known.

Many escaped cage birds have been recorded. Few if any have succeeded in breeding for any period of time. Several parts of the state have reported small parrots and parakeets successfully breeding, and Cardinals have established themselves in an area east of Los Angeles. Other species reported generally lack sufficient data on breeding status.

BIRD SOUNDS

Often birds can be identified in the field as easily through the ear as through the eye. Field situations regularly present bird students with auditory clues as well as visual ones. Learning to identify sounds made by birds is vital as frequently more birds will be heard than seen. On some trips over three-fourths of the birds encountered may be heard rather than seen. Depending on one's sense of hearing is a requirement in work with bird identification.

Sounds produced by birds are usually classified as either songs or calls depending upon their function. Some of the functions performed by these sounds include advertising and defense of territory, courtship, warning, flocking, and species identification. Generally it is very difficult to clearly differentiate between songs and calls.

About 59 percent of living birds in the world today belong to the order Passeriformes. Most of these perching birds are regularly referred to as "*songbirds*" and possess a very well developed voice box called a syrinx. Birds other than these "*songbirds*" possess less specialized voice boxes and as a rule utter many calls but few songs.

Each species has its own recognizable song pattern. These songs are usually given by the males and mainly during the breeding season. The singing ability of females varies greatly from species to species. A few (ex. female Black-headed Grosbeak) utter rather elaborate songs during the nesting season. Sounds other than of vocal origin are usually produced by bill, wings or tail.

There are a number of ways that have proven helpful in identifying and remembering bird sounds in the field. The use of words describing quality (ex. flute-like), kind (ex. trill), time (ex. rapid), pitch (ex. ascending) and loudness (ex. faint) may assist. Recording sounds in field notes using symbols helps (ex. dots, dashes, curves, etc.). Recording sounds phonetically where possible is very useful (ex. "*caw*" of crow, "*coo*" of dove, "*chick-a-dee-dee*" of chickadee). Listen to the sounds in the field, read field guide descriptions and if possible listen to recordings (see references on page 211).

The user of this book must remember that the classification of sounds given here is inescapably arbitrary and artificial and hence possibly subject to misinterpretations. However, it is felt that if this section is used carefully and undogmatically, it will prove useful. The outline that follows is divided first into habitats. After selecting a habitat that fits where you are observing, study the section as a whole to try to find the sound you have heard, then study the description of the species as given by its species number for further aid in identification. This section is not meant to be complete.

BIRD SOUNDS BY MAJOR HABITATS

Sounds of the Open Sea and Rocky Islands Offshore

A. MUSICAL OR SEMI-MUSICAL CALLS OR SONGS
1. Mewing moan: *Black-legged Kittiwake 121.*
2. Nasal calls: *Forster's Tern 'kyarr' 131; Common Tern 'keeyarr' 132.*

3. Squealing: *Parasitic Jaeger* (nasal) *119*.
4. Trills: *Parakeet Auklet 104.*
5. Twittering notes: *Fork-tailed Petrel 114; Ashy Petrel 116.*
6. Whistles:
   a. Hissing whistle: *Pigeon Guillemot 99.*
   b. Low vibrating whistle or trill: *Parakeet Auklet 104.*

B. NON-MUSICAL CALLS
   1. Croaking grunting screams: *Fulmar 109; shearwaters 110-113.*
   2. Deep hoarse moans: *Common Murre 98.*
   3. Growling cries: *Rhinoceros Auklet 105; Tufted Puffin 106.*
   4. Harsh grating or rasping cries: *Cassin's Auklet 103; Pomarine Jaeger 'witch-u' 118; Sabine's Gull 123; Arctic Tern 133; Gull-billed Tern* (throaty rasp) *134.*
   5. Raucous cries: *Black-legged Kittiwake 'ket-wek'* or *'kitti-wek' 121.*
   6. Screeches and groans: *Black-footed Albatross 108.*
   7. Sharp notes: *Marbled Murrelet 'keer' 100.*
   8. Shrill cries (not musical): *Long-tailed Jaeger 'kree' 120.*

Sounds of the Seashore, Bay, Lakeshores, Estuaries, Marshes and Streams

A. MUSICAL OR SEMI-MUSICAL CALLS OR SONGS
   1. Cooing calls: *Whistling Swan 38.*
   2. Liquid songs or notes: *Long-billed Curlew 91.*
   3. Low-pitched *'kaa-ah'*: *Caspian Tern 139.*
   4. Metallic staccato notes: *blackbirds 315-318.*
   5. Plaintive *'chey-way'* or *'twee-ee'*: *Semipalmated Plover 65.*
   6. Short *'twik'* or *'kit'* note: *Sanderling 80.*
   7. Shrill double-notes or triple: *Killdeer 'kee-dee' 66; Spotted Sandpiper 'keet-weet' 76; Greater Yellowlegs 87; Willet 89; Whimbrel 90; Long-billed Curlew 91.*
   8. Staccato or rattling notes: *turnstones 71-72; Willet 'kip-kip-kip' 89.*
   9. Thin mouse-like notes: *sandpipers 77,78,79,81,86.*
   10. Twittering: *White-throated Swift 219; Black Swift 220; swallows 225, 226,229.*
   11. Prolonged wailing, neighing song: *Red-necked Grebe 4.*
   12. Wailing, laughing, yodeling: *Common Loon 6; Arctic Loon 7; Common Scoter 23.*
   13. Whining call: *Herring Gull 126.*
   14. Whistling notes:
       a. Harsh whistle: *American Golden Plover 68; Long-billed Curlew 'Kur-lee' 91.*
       b. Nasal whistle: *Marsh Hawk 153.*
       c. Repeated whistles: *American Widgeon 29; Green-winged Teal 30; Black Oystercatcher 70; Tattler 84; Willet 89; Whimbrel 90; Long-billed Curlew 'kli-li-li-li' 91.*
       d. Single whistle: *Whistling Swan 38; Snowy Plover 64; Golden Plover 'queedle' 68.*
       e. Shrill whistle: *Western Grebe 5.*
       f. Slurred whistle: *Black-bellied Plover 'keee-ur-eeee' 69.*
       g. 2-noted whistle: *Knot 83.*
       h. 3-noted whistle: *yellowlegs 87-88.*

B. LOUD SCREAMING OR VERY UNUSUAL SOUNDS, PARTLY MUSICAL
   1. Abrupt, double notes: *Sandhill Crane 47.*
   2. Cacophonous (loudly mixed calls): *White-fronted Goose 41.*
   3. Cuckoo-like calls, repeated rapidly: *Pied-billed Grebe 3; Least Bittern 55.*

4. Loud cackling or clucking: *Canada Goose 36A; Brown Pelican 43; Gallinule 62; Coot 63.*

5. Loud harsh squealing: *Wood Duck 33; Fulvous Tree Duck 35; gulls 122-130; Least Tern 'zeeeeep' 135; Osprey 140.*

6. Loud quacking: *Most ducks 12-34.*

7. Rapidly repeated screams: *Most gulls 122-130.*

8. Rapidly repeated yelps or yips: *Cackling Goose 360; Snow Goose 40.*

9. Rolling loud shrill sound: *Sandhill Crane 47.*

10. Tooting cries, rapidly repeated: *White-fronted Goose 41; White-faced Ibis 56.*

C. UNMUSICAL SOUNDS
1. Vocal sounds (sounds through the mouth).
   a. Barking: *Arctic Loon 7.*
   b. Clattering *'check-check-chek': Clapper Rail 61.*
   c. Croaking: *Western Grebe 5; Surf Scoter 25; Double-crested Cormorant 44; Pelagic Cormorant 45; Wood Ibis 48; Great Blue Heron 49; egrets 50-51; Coot 63.*
   d. Growling, groaning, snarling: *Red-throated Loon 8; Caspian Tern 139.*
   e. Grunting: *Canvasback Duck 13; cormorants 44-46; White-faced Ibis 56; Virginia Rail 60; Coot 63; Wilson's Phalarope 96.*
   f. Gutteral rasping: *Arctic Loon 7; herons 49,52,53; Coot 63; Caspian Tern 139; Osprey 140.*
   g. Gutteral scolding: *Marbled Godwit 92.*
   h. Hissing: *Least Bittern 55.*
   i. Honking: *Canada Goose 36A; Brant 37; Sandhill Crane 47.*
   j. *'Kuk-kuk-kuk'* call: *Common Egret 50.*
   k. Loud thumping noise *'unk-pah-chunk': American Bittern 54.*.
   l. Rasping *'kik-kik-kik'* call: *Peregrine Falcon 155.*
   m. Rattling call: *Ruddy Duck 18; Ruddy Turnstone 71; Kingfisher 174.*
   n. Snoring: *Double-crested Cormorant 44.*
   o. Tooting: *White-fronted Goose 41.*
2. Mechanical Sounds.
   a. Tail noises.
      1. Bleat sound: *Common Snipe 74.*
   b. Wing noises: Whistling: *Canvasback 13; goldeneyes 19-20; Surf Scoter 25.*

Sounds of the Desert Scrub and Desert Streamside

A. MUSICAL AND SEMI-MUSICAL SONGS
1. Strictly musical songs.
   a. Rising and falling song, a sweet pensive *'peeeer-eeeeee: Summer Tanager 327.*
   b. Trills
      1. Series of buzzing trills: *Brewer's Sparrow 360.*
      2. Song ends in trill: *Black-throated Sparrow 362.*
      3. Insect-like musical trill: *Slate-colored Junco 343.*
   c. Warbling songs.
      1. Warbled notes and trills: *Lark Bunting 348.*
      2. Very sweet warbles: *Bendire's Thrasher 296.*
   d. Whistled songs.
      1. Disjointed whistles: *LeConte's Thrasher 299.*
      2. High clear song of whistled phrases: *Scott's Oriole 325.*

2. Songs with both musical and non-musical phrases.
   a. Monotonous rapid *'chuh-chuh-chuh'*: *Cactus Wren 265.*
   b. Much repetition of phrases and mimicing of other birds: *Mocking bird 297.*
   c. Phrases not repeated or only once: *thrashers 298-300.*
   d. Staccato *'jee-chi-chit'* ending with buzzing *'zzweee'*: *Lucy's Warbler 270.*

B. MUSICAL AND SEMI-MUSICAL CALLS OF LOW OR MEDIUM PITCH
   1. Blustering spluttering notes: *Abert's Towhee 367.*
   2. Churring notes: *Gila Woodpecker 182.*
   3. Cooing calls.
      a. Low *'cooo'*, dropping in pitch: *Roadrunner 175.*
      b. Rather harsh crowing *'coo-uh-kuk-oo'*: *White-winged Dove 213.*
      c. Hollow mournful *'coo-coo-coo'*: *Mourning Dove 214.*
      d. Monotonous soft *'woo-coo'*, *'woo-coo'*: *Ground Dove 216.*
   4. Metallic notes: *Abert's Towhee 367.*
   5. Rolling sound: *Gilded Flicker 177.*
   6. Shrill scolding or peevish notes: *Cactus Wren 265.*
   7. Staccato calls: *Cactus Wren 265.*
   8. Tremulous chattering or chuckling: *Burrowing Owl 170.*

C. LOUD SCREAMING OR VERY UNUSUAL SOUNDS
   1. Cacophonious (unharmonious and varied) calls: *Elf Owl 171.*
   2. Deep booming hollow hooting call: *Great Horned Owl 165.*
   3. Loud cuckoo-like calls, repeated rapidly: *Roadrunner 175; Yellow-billed Cuckoo 217.*
   4. Loud harsh *'krah'* or *'kaaar'*: *Harris' Hawk 149.*
   5. Loud harsh squealing cry or whistle-like scream: *hawks 143,145,147,148.*
   6. Rapidly repeated crowing: *White-winged Dove 'coo-oo-kuk-oo' 213; Yellow-billed Cuckoo,* (explosive *'kak-kak-kak-kow') 217.*
   7. Repeated screams: *Red-tailed Hawk 143; Prairie Falcon 154; American Kestrel 157.*

D. UNMUSICAL SOUNDS
   1. Vocal Sounds.
      a. Buzzing: *Verdin 'tzzeee' 251.*
      b. Gutteral scolding: *Elf Owl 171.*
      c. Hissing: *Vulture 151; Costa's Hummingbird 289.*
      d. Rattling cry: *Ladder-backed Woodpecker 183.*
      e. Squawking: *Gambel's Quail 207.*
   2. Mechanical Sounds.
      a. Click mandibles (beak): *owls 165,168,170,171; Roadrunner 175.*
      b. Drumming with bill: *Gilded Flicker 177; woodpeckers 182-183.*
      c. Wing noises: *Whirring, Gambel's Quail 207; Whistling, Mourning Dove 214.*

Sounds of Sagebrush Desert, Piñon-Juniper and N.E. Grasslands

A. MUSICAL AND SEMI-MUSICAL SONGS
   1. Strictly musical songs.
      a. Bubbling rollicking song: *Bobolink 320.*
      b. Metallic gurgling song: *Brown-headed Cowbird 316.*
      c. Notes, repeated but often with long pauses: *Loggerhead Shrike 301.*
      d. Soft melodious *'sweety-sweety-sweety'*: *Plain Titmouse 250.*
      e. Sweet plaintive notes, rising in *'teee-yee'*, dropping in *'teee-yeer' Lesser Goldfinch 340.*

   f. Thin jerky tinkling song: *Sage Sparrow 363.*
   g. Trills.
      1. Buzzing trill: *Brewer's Sparrow 360.*
      2. Dry rattling trill: *Chipping Sparrow 359.*
      3. Insect-like trill: *Slate-colored Junco 343.*
      4. *'Sweet-sweet-sweet'* song, ending in trill: *Black-throated Sparrow 362.*
   h. Warbling songs.
      1. Very soft warbles: *Scrub Jay 198.*
      2. Many warbles, long drawn-out in even pitch: *Sage Thrasher 295.*
      3. Rich warbling whistles: *Scott's Oriole* (somewhat like *Meadowlark's) 325.*
   i. Whistling songs.
      1. Clear song of many whistled phrases: *Scott's Oriole 325.*
      2. 2 long clear whistled flute-like notes, like *"taps"*: *Vesper Sparrow 346.*
      3. Plaintive whistles followed by long trill: *Black-chinned Sparrow 361.*
      4. Liquid whistles followed by double notes: *Cañon Wren 263.*
  2. Songs with both musical and non-musical phrases.
   a. Harsh chant: *Rock Wren 264.*
   b. *'Zz-zz'* notes.
      1. Churring, burring song: *Green-tailed Towhee 366.*
      2. Buzzing song: *Rufous-sided Towhee 365.*
      3. Sibilant insect-like song: *Grasshopper Sparrow 354.*
      4. Wheezy song: *Brewer's Blackbird 315;* *'tzeedle-tzeedle'* at start.

B. MUSICAL AND SEMI-MUSICAL CALLS
  1. Musical calls.
   a. Cooing calls: *Mourning Dove 214; Burrowing Owl 170; Long-eared Owl 167.*
   b. *'Mew'* or *'meow'* note: *Long-eared Owl 167; Piñon Jay 196; Lesser Nighthawk 222; Rufous-sided Towhee 365; Green-tailed Towhee 366.*
   c. Monotonous low notes: *'poo-woo'* or *'poor-will', Poor-will 221.*
   d. Querying call: *Mountain Quail 205.*
   e. Twittering notes: *swallows 224-229; Western Kingbird 232.*
   f. Whistling notes.
      1. Repeat whistles, over and over: *Mountain Quail 205.*
      2. Tremulous whistle: *Screech Owl 168.*
      3. Whistled *'dee-dee-dee'* notes: *Mountain Chickadee 255; Titmouse 250.*
  2. Semi-musical calls.
   a. Low but sharp notes: *Violet-green Swallow 224; Barn and Cliff Swallows 228-229.*
   b. Low soft sounds.
      1. Chuckling calls: *Burrowing Owl 170.*
      2. Lisping notes: *Bushtit 252.*
      3. Low moaning *'hooooooo'*: *Long-eared Owl 167.*
      4. Sibilant insect-like notes: *Savannah Sparrow 347.*
      5. Soft single notes: *bluebirds 309-310; Meadowlark 321.*
   c. Medium sounds.
      1. Mellow hoot: *Screech Owl 168.*
      2. Metallic notes: *Hairy Woodpecker 186; Brewer's Blackbird 315; Green-tailed Towhee 366.*

3. Nasal call: *Piñon Jay 196; Common Nighthawk 223; White-breasted Nuthatch 256.*
4. Rolling sounds: *flickers 178,179.*
5. Sharp double notes: *Killdeer 'kee-dee' 66.*
6. Sharp single cries: *Red-tailed Hawk 143; Thrasher 295; Grosbeak 329.*
7. Shrill, scolding or peevish notes: *Western Kingbird 232; wrens 261,265.*
8. Shrill notes repeated: *Killdeer 66; Long-billed Curlew 91; Rough-legged Hawk 147; Cooper's Hawk 159; Red-shafted Flicker 176.*
9. Sneeze-like noise: *Short-eared Owl 166.*
10. Squeaky creaking sound: *Brewer's Blackbird 315.*
11. Staccato calls: *Cactus Wren 265; Western Bluebird 309.*
12. Whining sound: *Long-eared Owl 167.*
3. Loud, screaming or very unusual sounds, often partially musical.
    a. Abrupt double notes: *Red and Yellow-shafted Flickers 176-178 .*
    b. Deep hollow hooting calls: *Great-horned Owl 165.*
    c. Loud cackling or clucking: *Sage Grouse 202; Mountain Quail 205.*
    d. Loud mewing whistle: *Rough-legged Hawk 147.*
    e. Loud shrill rapid cries: *hawks 157-158.*
    f. Loud squealing cry or whistle: *hawks 143,145,147.*
    g. Rapidly repeated screams: *hawks 143,158,159; Prairie Falcon154; Peregrine Falcon* (slurred notes) *155.*

C. UNMUSICAL SOUNDS
  1. Vocal sounds (sounds through the mouth).
    a. Croaking: *Raven 191.*
    b. Grunting: *Vulture 151.*
    c. Gutteral rasping: *Crow 192.*
    d. Gutteral scolding: *Piñon Jay 196.*
    e. Hard *'tek'* call: *Slate-colored Junco 343.*
    f. Hissing: *Turkey Vulture 151.*
    g. Hoarse *'kaw-wit, kah-wit':* *Gray Partridge 208.*
    h. Popping, bubbling sound: *Sage Grouse 202.*
    i. Rattling call: *Kingfisher 174; Ladder-backed Woodpecker 183; Hairy Woodpecker 186; Lapland Longspur 349.*
    j. Rasping *'kik-kik-kik':* *Peregrine Falcon 155.*
  2. Mechanical sounds.
    a. Drumming with bill: *Yellow and Red-shafted Flickers 176,178.*
    b. Wing noises.
      1. Whirring: *Grouse 202; Quail 205; Gray Partridge 208.*
      2. Whirring booming noises: *Common Nighthawk 223.*
      3. Whistling: *Mourning Dove 214.*
      4. Wings rattled: *Broad-tailed Hummingbird 292.*
    c. Tail noises, bleat sound: *Common Snipe 74.*

Sounds of Woods, Coniferous Forests, Grasslands, Brushlands, from the Sierra to the Seas and outside of Deserts

A. MUSICAL AND SEMI-MUSICAL SONGS
  1. Strictly musical songs.
    a. Brisk, variable song of *'tweek-twees-ah'* at start: *Hermit Warbler 277.*
    b. Differently-pitched long musical breezy: *Varied Thrush 308.*
    c. Distinctive *'wit-chee-chee'* song: *Yellowthroat 271.*

d. Flute-like, very beautiful song, with up and down notes: *Hermit Thrush 311.*
e. Light *'see-see-weetee-see'* song: *Yellow Warbler 274.*
f. Liquid and semi-liquid songs.
   1. Liquid rising and falling songs: *Bobolink* (rollicking) *320; Black-headed Grosbeak* (powerful) *329; Blue Grosbeak 331; Lincoln Sparrow 351.*
   2. Metallic gurgling songs: *Redwing and Tricolored Blackbirds 317-318.*
g. Long drawn-out quavering rapidly-repeated melodious song: *Winter Wren 259.*
h. Plaintive 3-noted song: *Golden-crowned Sparrow 357; Harris' Sparrow 364.*
i. Repeated *'saay-see-say'* song: *White-crowned Sparrow 356.*
j. Rising and falling songs other than liquid.
   1. Cheerful set of 4 rising and falling notes (a clear carol): *Robin 307.*
   2. Rocking chant: *Rock Wren 264; MacGillivray's Warbler 275.*
   3. Similar to Robin's, but with short *'peer-weee'* phrases: *Western Tanager 326.*
k. Soft melodious *'sweety-sweety-sweety'*, from oaks: *Plain Titmouse 250.*
l. Shrill notes.
   1. Shrill *'see-lit'*, *'see-lit'*, *'see-lit'*, followed by varied notes: *Nashville Warbler 269.*
   2. Shrill *'ti-dee-dee'* notes surround a soft phrase: *Ruby-crowned Kinglet 245.*
   3. Thin shrill song starts with 2 notes *'weet-weet'* or *'hew-hew'*: *Lazuli Bunting 332.*
m. Sunny loose musical song ending in nasal *'cheee-wheer'*: *House Finch 337.*
n. Thin, jerky tinkling song: *Sage Sparrow 363.*
o. Trills.
   1. Buzzing trills: *Oregon Junco 344; Brewer's Sparrow 360.*
   2. Chattering or quivering trill: *Oregon Junco 344; Gray-headed Junco 345.*
   3. Even monotonous notes, ending with low-pitched trill: *Audubon's Warbler 282.*
   4. Dry rattling trill: *Rock Wren 264; Chipping Sparrow 359.*
   5. Dry weak trill: *Orange-crowned Warbler 268.*
   6. Insect-like trill with buzz: *Oregon Junco 344.*
   7. Mixture of warbled notes and trills: *Pine Siskin 342.*
   8. Rapidly repeated *'tink-tink-tink'*; ending in trill: *Brown Towhee 367.*
   9. Series of slow notes and trills: *Loggerhead Shrike 301.*
   10. Soft delicate trills follow 2-3 high notes: *Bewick's Wren 261.*
   11. Soft liquid notes, followed by rough trill: *sparrow 361.*
p. Two different alternated songs, starting *'see-see-see'*: *Redstart 273.*
q. Twittering canary-like song: *American Goldfinch 339; Lawrence's Goldfinch* (more broken) *341.*
r. Flute-like spiralling upward song: *Swainson's Thrush 312.*
s. Warbling songs.
   1. Loud long warbling song: *Solitaire 313.*
   2. Lifting and falling short-noted warble: *Blue Grosbeak 331.*

3. Many evenly-pitched warbles: *Sage Thrasher 295.*
4. Sweet warbles: *Warbling Vireo 287.*
5. Swift warbling song with notes rolling over and over: *Purple Finch 335.*
6. Very soft warbles: *Steller's Jay 197; Scrub Jay 198.*
7. Vibrant warble, ending in *'churrrrr': Cassin's Finch 336.*
8. Warbled notes and trills: *Lark Bunting 348.*
9. Warbled *'tu-tee-tu-tee', 'tay-tay'* song: *Red Crossbill 334.*
t. Whistles.
  1. Bell-like whistles: *Cañon Wren 263.*
  2. Deep notes turn into clear whistles: *Hooded Oriole 324.*
  3. Clear, whistled single and double notes: *Bullock's Oriole 323.*
  4. Many clear whistled phrases: *Scott's Oriole 325.*
  5. Rich melodious whistling song: *Pine Grosbeak 333.*
  6. Whistled notes, followed by trill: *Black-chinned Sparrow 361.*
  7. Series of slow whistles and trills: *Loggerhead Shrike 301.*
2. Songs with both musical and non-musical phrases.
  a. Harsh chant: *Rock Wren 264.*
  b. Many *'zz-zz'* notes.
    1. Churring, burring song: *Green-tailed Towhee 366.*
    2. Buzzing song: *warblers 278-279; Sparrow 354; Towhee 365.*
    3. Sibilant insect-like song: *Townsend's Warbler 278; Sparrows 347,354.*
    4. Staccato *'hee-she-chi-zzwee': Lucy's Warbler 270.*
    5. Wheezy song: *Black-throated Gray Warbler 279; Phainopepla 303; Brewer's Blackbird 315.*
  c. Rough *'tseer-eep', 'grrreea'* song: *Evening Grosbeak 330.*
  d. Variable songs of *'churrs',* harsh notes, whistles, buzzes, trills, mixed together: *Yellow-breasted Chat 276; Mockingbird 297; California Thrasher 298; Northern Shrike 302; Lark Sparrow 353.*
B. MUSICAL OR SEMI-MUSICAL CALLS
  1. Musical calls.
    a. Cooing calls. *Owl 170; Roadrunner 175; Pigeon, doves 210-214.*
    b. *'Fee-fee'* call: *Say's Phoebe 'phee-eee' 235; Black Phoebe 236.*
    c. *'Mew'* or *'meow'* notes: *Long-eared Owl 167; Lesser Nighthawk 222; Black-tailed Gnatcatcher 248;* towhees *365-366.*
    d. Monotonous low notes: *Poor-will 221.*
    e. Musical *'dreer'* note: *Rufous-crowned Sparrow 358.*
    f. Nasal but musical *'pee-weeee'!: Western Wood Pewee 237.*
    g. Querying call: *California and Mountain Quail 205-206.*
    h. Reedy *'tseee-dee-ree': Horned Lark 322.*
    i. Sweet *'seep-eh-dee-rr': Traill's Flycatcher 240.*
    j. Sweet plaintive *'tee-yeer'* note: *Lesser Goldfinch 340.*
    k. Sweet *'whoo-yee'* call: *Lark Bunting 348.*
    l. Twittering notes: *swifts 218-220; Violet-green Swallow 224; Barn Swallow 229.*
    m. Whistled notes.
      1. Harsh whistle: *Long-billed Curlew 91; White-tailed Kite 152.*
      2. Nasal whistles: *Marsh Hawk 153.*
      3. Repeated whistles: *Pygmy Owl 172; Saw-whet Owl 173.*
      4. Single plain whistle: *Pygmy Owl 172; Sage Thrasher 295; Cedar Waxwing 305.*

5. Tremulous whistle: *Screech Owl 168.*
2. Semi-musical calls.
  a. Low but sharp notes: *swallows 224-230; phoebes 235-236; Olive-sided Flycatcher 238; Hermit Thrush 311.*
  b. Soft or low sounds, not sharp.
    1. Chuckling calls: *Burrowing Owl 170.*
    2. Lisping notes: *Golden-crowned Kinglet 246; Creeper 249; Bushtit 252.*
    3. Purring sounds: *Lesser Nighthawk 222.*
    4. Sibilant insect-like notes: *Blue-gray Gnatcatcher 247; Savannah Sparrow 347.*
    5. Soft clucking notes: *California Quail 206.*
    6. Soft single notes: *Varied Thrush 308; bluebirds 309-310; Western Meadowlark 321.*
    7. Low *'chuck-chuck'* notes: *Lesser Nighthawk 222.*
  c. Medium sounds, neither very loud nor very soft.
    1. Buzzing notes: *Allen's Hummingbird 294; Pine Siskin 342.*
    2. Churring notes: *Lewis' Woodpecker 190.*
    3. Mellow hoots: *Screech Owl 168; Flammulated Owl 169.*
    4. Harsh *'chay-chay-chay': Steller's Jay* (faster) *197; Scrub Jay* (slower) *198.*
    5. Metallic notes: *Downy Woodpecker 185; Hairy Woodpecker 186; Brewer's Blackbird 315; Redwinged and Tricolored Blackbirds 317-318; Green-tailed Towhee 366; Brown Towhee 367; Abert's Towhee 368.*
    6. Nasal calls: *Common Snipe 74; Common Nighthawk 223; White-breasted Nuthatch 'kyeer-kyeer' 256; Red-breasted Nuthatch 'yhank-yhank' 257.*
    7. Rolling sounds: *flickers 176-178; Acorn Woodpecker 181.*
    8. Shrill, scolding or peevish notes: *White-throated Swift 219; Western Kingbird 232; wrens 260,261,262,265; Yellowthroat 271, juncos 343-345.*
    9. Sharp single cries: *Red-tailed Hawk 143; Steller's Jay 197; Dipper 267; Sage Thrasher 295; Black-headed Grosbeak 329; House Sparrow 369.*
    10. Shrill notes repeated: *Long-billed Curlew 91; hawks 157-159; flickers 176,178; Black Swift 220.*
    11. Squeaky creaking sound: *Steller's Jay 197; blackbirds 315-319.*
    12. Staccato calls: *Cactus Wren 265; Western Bluebird 309.*
    13. Wheezy notes: *Warbling Vireo 287; Pine Siskin 342.*
    14. Whining sound: *Sharp-shinned Hawk 160; Long-eared Owl 167.*
    15. Whinny or Whicker: *Lesser Nighthawk 222.*
    16. 3-syllabled *'ker-ka-go': California Quail 206.*
3. Loud screaming or very unusual sounds, but usually partially musical.
  a. Abrupt startling double notes: *Killdeer 66; flickers 176-178; woodpeckers 181,187,188.*
  b. Cacophonous calls: *Nutcracker 199.*
  c. Cuckoo-like calls, repeated rapidly: *Yellow-billed Cuckoo 217.*

    d. Hollow hooting call: *Great Gray Owl 164; Great-horned Owl* (booming) *165; Blue Grouse* (muffled sound) *200; Band-tailed Pigeon 210.*

    e. Loud harsh *'krah'* or *'kaar'* call: *Ferruginous Hawk 148; Harris' Hawk 149.*

    f. Loud squealing cry or whistle: *Wood Duck 33; gulls 124,126-130; hawks 143,144,147.*

    g. Rapidly-repeated loud crowing: *Ring-necked Pheasant 203; White-winged Dove 213; Yellow-billed Cuckoo 217.*

    h. Rapidly-repeated screams: *gulls 124-130; hawks 153-160.*

    i. Shrill high *'kik-kik-kik': hawks 159-160.*

    j. Shrill hooting call: *Spotted Owl 163.*

    k. Tooting cries rapidly repeated: *Saw-whet Owl 173.*

C. UNMUSICAL SOUNDS
   1. Vocal sounds.
     a. Barking.
       1. Like a dog: *Spotted Owl 163.*
       2. Sneezy bark: *Saw-whet Owl 173.*
     b. Cawing: *American Crow 192.*
     c. Croaking: *Raven 191.*
     d. Filing noises: *Saw-whet Owl 173.*
     e. Gutteral rasping: *Crow 192.*
     f. Gutteral scolding: *Gray Jay 195; Steller's Jay 197; Scrub Jay 198.*
     g. Hissing: *Vulture 151; Barn Owl 161; Ruffed Grouse 201; Costa's Hummingbird 289.*
     h. Rattling: *Kingfisher 174; Roadrunner 175; Hairy Woodpecker 186.*
     i. Squeaking: *Red-shafted Flicker 166; Starling 314.*
     j. Wheezing: *Brown-headed Cowbird 316.*
   2. Mechanical sounds.
     1. Click mandibles: *owls 161-173; Roadrunner 175.*
     b. Drumming with bill: *woodpeckers 176-190* (small woodpeckers give light taps).
     c. Wing noises.
       1. Buzzing: *hummingbirds 288-294.*
       2. Clapping: *Ring-necked Pheasant 203.*
       3. Drumming: *Ruffed Grouse 201.*
       4. Fluttering noise high in air: *Short-eared Owl 166.*
       5. Rattling noise: *hummingbirds 292-293.*
       6. Whirring: *grouse 200-201; quail 205-206; Chukar 209.*
       7. Whirring boom: *Common Nighthawk 223.*
       8. Whistling: *falcons 154-157; Mourning Dove 214.*
     d. Tail noises.
       1. Bleat sound: *Common Snipe 74.*
       2. Peep or popping sound: *Anna's Hummingbird 288.*

CHECK-LIST OF RARE SPECIES

The following birds are not otherwise described in this book. Most of those listed are of rather infrequent occurrence in California. Several diagnostic field characters are indicated for each. This list has been modified after McCaskie G., et. al. 1970. "A Check-list of the Birds of California." *California Birds* 1:4-28.

WATER AND SHOREBIRDS	DISTINGUISHING FEATURES

Yellow-billed Loon, *Gavia adamsii*—25"; largest loon, bill yellowish, lower half curved up.

Least Grebe, *Podiceps dominicus*—6½"; with slender dark bill.

Wandering Albatross, *Diomedea exulans*—White with black wing-tips; largest ocean bird.

Short-tailed Albatross, *Diomedea albatrus*—35"; white with black wings and tip of tail.

Laysan Albatross, *Diomedea immutabilis*—28"; body white with dark back and upper wings.

Cape Petrel, *Daption capense*—13"; checkered upper parts; two white patches on each wing.

Galapagos Petrel, *Oceanodroma tethys*—16"; dark body; white rump; forked tail.

Least Petrel, *Halocyptena microsoma*—5½"; overall dark.

Wilson's Petrel, *Oceanites oceanicus*—6½"; dark with white wing patch and rump; feet yellow.

Pale-footed Shearwater, *Puffinus carneipes*—18"; very large, with black-tipped yellowish bill.

New Zealand Shearwater, *Puffinus bulleri*—16"; light gray above; wings, tail, cap dark.

Red-billed Tropicbird, *Phaethon aethereus*—35"; black-streaked on white wings; long tail.

White-tailed Tropicbird, *Phaethon lepturus*—26"; black band on white wings; long tail.

Blue-footed Booby, *Sula nebouxii*—32"; blue feet, bill; white back patch; brown wing.

Brown Booby, *Sula leucogaster*—28"; yellow feet, bill; all dark brown upper parts.

Little Blue Heron, *Florida caerulea*—22"; slaty-blue body; reddish-brown head, neck.

Cattle Egret, *Bubulcus ibis*—19"; white, with brown crest and breast; immature all white, (illus. on page 94).

Reddish Egret, *Dichromanassa rufescens*—25"; shaggy reddish-brown head and neck.

Louisiana Heron, *Hydranassa tricolor*—24"; very slender neck; blue above, white below.

Yellow-crowned Night Heron, *Nyctanassa violacea*—22"; distinctive black and white face.

White Ibis, *Eudocimus albus*—23"; white with pinkish face, bill and legs.

Roseate Spoonbill, *Ajaia ajaja*—30"; greenish spoonbill and head; reddish wings and belly.

Trumpeter Swan, *Olor buccinator*—50"; long slender neck; white except for dark bill.

Emperor Goose, *Philacte canagica*—18"; white head and hind neck; black throat; dark body.

Black-bellied Whistling Duck, *Dendrocygna autumnalis*—Black below, white area on wing.

Black Duck, *Anas rubripes*—16"; white wing-linings contrast with dark body; yellow bill.

European Wigeon, *Anas penelope*—13½"; gray sides and rusty head in ♂; dark tail.

Tufted Duck, *Aythya fuligula*—12"; white sides; head with thin crest.

King Eider, *Somateria spectabilis*—16"; large white wing patch on dark wing; dark belly.

Purple Gallinule, *Porphyrula martinica*—11"; red-white face; purple body, greenish back.

American Oystercatcher, *Haematopus palliatus*—16"; white below, black above; red bill.

Wilson's Plover, *Charadrius wilsonia*—6"; wide dark band below white neck; black bill.

European Jacksnipe, *Lymnocryptes minimus*—7½"; slow direct flight.

Upland Plover, *Bartramia longicauda*—10"; small head, short bill, thin neck, long tail.

Rock Sandpiper, *Calidris ptilocnemis*—8"; short neck; plump body; greenish legs.

Sharp-tailed Sandpiper, *Calidris acuminata*—7"; buffy breast; white band above eye.

White-rumped Sandpiper, *Calidris fuscicollis*—6"; white rump, lightly spotted breast.

Curlew Sandpiper, *Calidris ferruginea*—7"; prominent down-curved bill; white rump.

Stilt Sandpiper, *Micropalama himantopus*—7½"; long greenish legs; dark edged wings; white rump.

Semipalmated Sandpiper, *Calidris pusillus*—5"; like Western Sandpiper but bill shorter.

Buff-breasted Sandpiper, *Tryngites subruficollis*—6½"; buff color; back feathers buff-edged.

Bar-tailed Godwit, *Limosa lapponica*—15"; black and white barred tail; up-curved beak.

Ruff, *Philomachus pugnax*—10"; ♂ brown with ruff; white patches at base of tail.

Skua, *Catharacta skua*—18"; dark brownish gray; large white patches near wing ends.

Glaucous Gull, *Larus hyperboreus*—25"; heavy bill; long white tail; pale gray wings.

Black-headed Gull, *Larus ridibundus*—15"; resembles a large Bonaparte's Gull.

Laughing Gull, *Larus atricilla*—15"; black head; white neck; all gray wings; white tail.

Franklin's Gull, *Larus pipixcan*—14"; similar to above, but with black and white wing-tips.

Little Gull, *Larus minutus*—10"; smallest gull; black head; white body; white-tipped wings.

Black Skimmer, *Rhynchops niger*—17"; large red bill; lower mandible longer; black wings.

Thick-billed Murre, *Uria lomvia*—15"; narrow white streak by thick short bill.

Craveri's Murrelet, *Endomychura craveri*—9"; black above, white below; dark under-wing coverts.

Horned Puffin, *Fratercula corniculata*—14"; red-tipped yellow bill; white head; no tufts.

LAND BIRDS	DISTINGUISHING FEATURES

Broad-winged Hawk, *Buteo platypterus*—14"; broad-barred black and white tail; reddish below.

Gyrfalcon, *Falco rusticolus*—20"; brownish-black, marked with white, especially on face.

Sharp-tailed Grouse, *Pedioecetes phasianellus*—15"; narrow-pointed, white-edged tail.

Inca Dove, *Scardafella inca*—7"; gray, white-bordered tail; red and black-tipped wings.

Black-billed Cuckoo, *Coccyzus erythrophthalmus*—11"; long, white-spotted, grayish tail; black bill.

Whip-poor-will, *Caprimulgus vociferus*—9"; ♂ has gray, white-bordered tail; name is song.

Chimney Swift, *Chaetura pelagica*—5"; looks like Vaux's Swift, but throat grayish.

Broad-billed Hummingbird, *Cynanthus latirostris*—3½"; ♂ dark green; blue throat; orange bill.

Thick-billed Kingbird, *Tyrannus crassirostris*—8¼"; thick bill, white and yellowish underparts.

Tropical Kingbird, *Tyrannus melancholicus*—8"; underparts bright yellow; orange crown.

Scissor-tailed Flycatcher, *Muscivora forficata*—13"; extremely long divided black tail.

Great Crested Flycatcher, *Myiarchus crinitus*—8"; rusty wings and tail; yellow belly.

Wied's Crested Flycatcher, *Myiarchus tyrannulus*—7½"; like Ash-throated, but yellower.

Eastern Phoebe, *Sayornis phoebe*—6"; whitish underparts; dark gray above; head black.

Least Flycatcher, *Empidonax minimus*—5"; told by song, a repeated dry *shee-beck*.

Coues' Flycatcher, *Contopus pertinax*—7"; like Olive-sided, but no white streak on center of breast.

Blue Jay, *Cyanocitta cristata*—11"; only jay with white on blue wings and tail.

Pine Nuthatch, *Sitta pusilla*—3½"; like Pygmy (257), but more white on rear of neck.

Gray Catbird, *Dumetella carolinensis*—8"; only dark gray bird with rusty under tail coverts.

Brown Thrasher, *Toxostoma rufum*—10"; rusty-brown above, heavily streaked below.

Curve-billed Thrasher, *Toxostoma curvirostre*—10"; red-orange eye; dark tail; streaked front.

Wood Thrush, *Hylocichla mustelina*—7"; large brown spots on white breast.

Red-throated Pipit, *Anthus cervinus*—5½"; bold black streaking of body.

White-eyed Vireo, *Vireo griseus*—6"; white wing-bars and bright yellowish sides.

Yellow-throated Vireo, *Vireo flavifrons*—5"; yellow breast and throat; yellow spectacles.

Yellow-green Vireo, *Vireo flavoviridis*—6"; bright yellow sides and under tail coverts.

Red-eyed Vireo, *Vireo olivaceus*—5½"; prominent white eye-stripe; bluish-gray cap; red eye.

Philadelphia Vireo, *Vireo philadelphicus*—4¾"; yellowish breast and plain green-gray wings.

Prothonotary Warbler, *Protonotaria citrea*—4¾"; plain blue-gray wings; golden head.

Worm-eating Warbler, *Helmitheros vermivorus*—4½"; black-streaked head; brownish colors.

Golden-winged Warbler, *Vermivora chrysoptera*—4¼"; golden wing patch and crown.

Blue-winged Warbler, *Vermivora pinus*—4¼"; white wing-bars; narrow black eye line; yellow body.

Tennessee Warbler, *Vermivora peregrina*—4½"; white or greenish underparts, green back.

Virginia's Warbler, *Vermivora virginiae*—4¼"; like Lucy's (270), except for yellow rump.

Parula Warbler, *Parula americana*—3¾"; yellow patch on blue back; blue head; yellow throat.

Magnolia Warbler, *Dendroica magnolia*—4½"; yellow throat and broad white tail band.

Cape May Warbler, *Dendroica tigrina*—4¾"; yellow rump, rusty cheeks, white wing patch.

Black-throated Blue Warbler, *Dendroica caerulescens*—4½"; ♂ black cheeks, throat; blue back.

Black-throated Green Warbler, *Dendroica virens*—4½"; golden cheek; black throat in ♂.

Cerulean Warbler, *Dendroica cerulea*—4"; only white throated, blue backed warbler.

Blackburnian Warbler, *Dendroica fusca*—4½"; ♂ with bright orange throat.

Yellow-throated Warbler, *Dendroica dominica*—4½"; white belly, yellow throat; black and white upper parts, including white stripe over eye.

Grace's Warbler, *Dendroica graciae*—4½"; yellow eye stripe and throat contrast with white belly.

Chestnut-sided Warbler, *Dendroica pensylvanica*—4½"; narrow chestnut side-markings.

Bay-breasted Warbler, *Dendroica castanea*—5"; ♂ with rusty sides, throat and head.

Blackpoll Warbler, *Dendroica striata*—5"; black crown and "whiskers", white cheeks on ♀.

Pine Warbler, *Dendroica pinus*—5"; white wing-bars, white belly, yellow-green body.

Prairie Warbler, *Dendroica discolor*—4"; olive back, yellow below, wags tail.

Palm Warbler, *Dendroica palmarum*—4½"; wags tail; olive rump; yellow under-tail coverts.

Ovenbird, *Seiurus aurocapillus*—5"; black stripe on orange crown; olive upper parts; streaked breast.

Northern Waterthrush, *Seiurus noveboracensis*—5½"; walks with bobbing motion; light eye streak below dark brown crown; brown back, heavily streaked breast.

Louisiana Waterthrush, *Seiurus motacilla*—5½"; like above but throat unstreaked.

Kentucky Warbler, *Oporornis formosus*—4½"; black mustache, yellow throat and eye-ring.

Connecticut Warbler, *Oporornis agilis*—5"; similar to MacGillivray's Warbler (275), with gray hood, but white eye-ring complete and no mottled black and white on throat.

Mourning Warbler, *Oporornis philadelphia*—5"; similar to 276, but usually lacks eye-ring.

Hooded Warbler, *Wilsonia citrina*—4½"; ♂ has black hood and yellow face.

Canada Warbler, *Wilsonia canadensis*—5"; necklace of black spots; yellow spectacles and grayish-olive back.

Painted Redstart, *Setophaga picta*—5"; black head; red breast; white patches on wings and tail.

Orchard Oriole, *Icterus spurius*—6"; brick-red body, black hood and back.

Scarlet-headed Oriole, *Icterus pustulatus*—7½"; black stripings on back; orange head.

Rusty Blackbird, *Euphagus carolinus*—8"; like Brewer's Blackbird (315), but more black, less glossy purple and green in ♂; ♀ darker, fall ♂ has much white in front.

Boat-tailed Grackle, *Cassidix mexicanus*—16"; ♀ 12"; long v-shaped tail wider at end.

Bronzed Cowbird, *Tangavius aeneus*—7"; like Brewer's Blackbird (315), but bill shorter and thicker; wings of ♂ bronzed-green; rest of body bronzed black; red eye.

Scarlet Tanager, *Piranga olivacea*—6½"; ♂ only bird with red body and black tail and wings.

Hepatic Tanager, *Piranga flava*—7"; like Summer Tanager (326), but has dark cheek and bill.

Rose-breasted Grosbeak, *Pheucticus ludovicianus*—7½"; ♂ with rose bib and black hood.

Indigo Bunting, *Passerina cyanea*—5"; ♂ is brilliant iridescent blue with brown wings.

Varied Bunting, *Passerina versicolor*—4½"; ♂ with purple body, red-capped head.

Painted Bunting, *Passerina ciris*—4½"; ♂ with blue head, red underparts; yellow on back.

Dickcissel, *Spiza americana*—6"; ♂ with black bib, chestnut wing patch; yellow breast.

Black Rosy Finch, *Leucosticte atrata*—6"; similar to Gray-crowned (338), but blacker.

Common Redpoll, *Acanthis flammea*—5"; red cap; black chin, rose breast of ♂; wingbars.

Baird's Sparrow, *Ammodramus bairdii*—5"; orange-brown stripe through crown.

Sharp-tailed Sparrow, *Ammospiza caudacuta*—5"; broad orange triangle on face, solid crown.

Cassin's Sparrow, *Aimophila cassinii*—5½"; plain breast; dark gray tail; faintly streaked crown.

Tree Sparrow, *Spizella arborea*—5½"; bright rusty cap; central breast spot; dark legs.

Clay-colored Sparrow, *Spizella pallida*—5"; brown cheek patch; light streak through the crown; white streak over eye; brown rump, plain white undersides in adult.

Field Sparrow, *Spizella pusilla*—5"; unstreaked rusty crown; pink bill and legs; no dark eye line.

Swamp Sparrow, *Melospiza georgiana*—5"; adult with red cap, gray eye-stripe, white throat with thin dark streak, dark bill and gray face; wings reddish.

McCown's Longspur, *Calcarius mccownii*—5½"; tail mostly white; rusty blotch at bend of wing; dark streaks on gray hind neck.

Chestnut-collared Longspur, *Calcarius ornatus*—5½"; dark triangle on white tail.

Snow Bunting, *Plectrophenax nivalis*—6"; large white wing-patches; much other white.

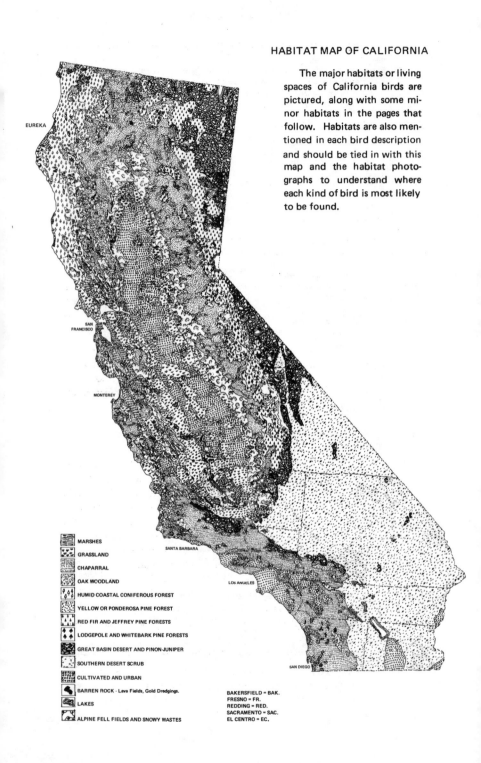

HABITAT MAP OF CALIFORNIA

The major habitats or living spaces of California birds are pictured, along with some minor habitats in the pages that follow. Habitats are also mentioned in each bird description and should be tied in with this map and the habitat photographs to understand where each kind of bird is most likely to be found.

EUREKA

SAN FRANCISCO

MONTEREY

SANTA BARBARA

LOS ANGELES

SAN DIEGO

MARSHES
GRASSLAND
CHAPARRAL
OAK WOODLAND
HUMID COASTAL CONIFEROUS FOREST
YELLOW OR PONDEROSA PINE FOREST
RED FIR AND JEFFREY PINE FORESTS
LODGEPOLE AND WHITEBARK PINE FORESTS
GREAT BASIN DESERT AND PINON-JUNIPER
SOUTHERN DESERT SCRUB
CULTIVATED AND URBAN
BARREN ROCK - Lava Fields, Gold Dredgings.
LAKES
ALPINE FELL FIELDS AND SNOWY WASTES

BAKERSFIELD = BAK.
FRESNO = FR.
REDDING = RED.
SACRAMENTO = SAC.
EL CENTRO = EC.

DISTRIBUTION OF BIRDS BY HABITAT

A habitat, as listed here, indicates where a bird finds suitable environmental conditions for its way of life, such as a grassland or oak woodland. Each bird is usually adapted to fit into certain habitats. Some birds are somewhat characteristically restricted to a single habitat, as is the case with the Wrentit, whose usual home is among the brushy areas called chaparral. One of the delights of bird study is to investigate and note how a particular bird adapts itself to the habitat in which you find it. Thus the dark colors of the Steller's Jay and the Varied Thrush help them to merge into and become a part of the shadows found in deep woods, while the light colors of the Western Meadowlark and the Horned Lark are well-suited to open prairies and grasslands. One of the most amazing cases of adaptation is that of the Dipper. It is a chunky-bodied, short-tailed land bird that has become a living part of mountain streams, walking under water, using its wings in its search for food.

The following categories of habitats and the pictures and lists of species of birds on the following pages should help you better understand the nature of habitats in California and the birds that frequent each. When you are out-of-doors, refer to this section as an aid in determining which birds you are most likely to see in each habitat you enter.

SCRUB GROUP—any area where bushes are the most numerous plants.
   Desert Scrub—many thorny bushes; mainly in southeastern California.
   Sagebrush—mainly gray aromatic shrubs; found in east and northeast.
   Chaparral—stiff-twigged, small-leaved bushes; dry foothill country; related softer-leaved Scrub is on coast.
GRASSLAND GROUP—grasses and wild flowers dominate here.
   Savannah—widely spread oak trees are scattered over grasslands.
   Grassland—large grassy areas of foothills and valleys.
   Alpine Meadows—grassy wildflower areas of summer, high in mountains.
WOODLAND GROUP—woods that have smaller trees than main forests.
   Piñon-Juniper Woodland—scrubby trees often mixed with sagebrush in E.
   Oak Woodland—close groups of oaks in central or western foothill areas.
   Streamside Woodland—groups of willows, cottonwoods, alders, by water.
CONIFEROUS FOREST GROUP—mainly coniferous trees in large woods.
   Coastal Forest—mainly Douglas Fir and Redwood forests near coast.
   Mountain Forest—Yellow Pine and Red Fir forests of middle elevations.
   Subalpine Forest—often stunted and scattered trees of high elevations.
GEOLOGIC GROUP—inland cliffs; sea cliffs; seashore, bayshore and mud flats.
MARSH GROUP— freshwater marsh; salt marsh.
WATER GROUP—lakes and ponds; rivers and streams;shallow sea, bay waters and estuaries; deep sea waters (far offshore).
CIVILIZATION GROUP—eucalyptus groves; cultivated lands; parks; buildings.

The above habitat categories and the following lists of birds have been modified after Miller, 1951; Ruth, 1960; and Sans and Stoff, 1959.

Characteristic birds of Desert Scrub. Photo by Donald Myrick: Courtesy, Jepson Herbarium, University of California.

168 Screech Owl	251 Verdin
171 Elf Owl	265 Cactus Wren
175 Roadrunner	270 Lucy's Warbler
177 Gilded Flicker	289 Costa's Hum-
207 Gambel's Quail	mingbird
213 White-winged	296 Bendire's
Dove	Thrasher
221 Poor-will	299 Le Conte's
222 Lesser Night-	Thrasher
hawk	300 Crissal Thrasher
239 Vermilion Fly-	301 Loggerhead
catcher	Shrike
248 Black-tailed	362 Black-throated
Gnatcatcher	Sparrow

Characteristic birds of Sagebrush. Photo by SBBG—6: Courtesy, Jepson Herbarium, Univ. of California.

202 Sage Grouse	360 Brewer's
221 Poor-will	Sparrow
243 Gray Fly-	363 Sage Sparrow
catcher	365 Rufous-sided
295 Sage Thrasher	Towhee
346 Vesper Sparrow	

Characteristic birds of Chaparral. Photo by W.S. Head.

205 Mountain	285 Gray Vireo
Quail	288 Anna's Hum-
206 California	mingbird
Quail	294 Allen's Hum-
221 Poor-will	mingbird
243 Gray Fly-	298 California
catcher	Thrasher
248 Black-tailed	332 Lazuli Bunting
Gnatcatcher	352 Fox Sparrow
261 Bewick's Wren	356 White-crowned
266 Wrentit	Sparrow
268 Orange-crown-	358 Rufous-crowned
ed Warbler	Sparrow
275 MacGillivray's	366 Green-tailed
Warbler	Towhee

361 Black-chinned	365 Rufous-sided
Sparrow	Towhee
363 Sage Sparrow	367 Brown Towhee

Characteristic birds of Piñon-Juniper Woodland. Photo by G. Van Horn: Courtesy, Jepson Herbarium, Univ. of California.

168 Screech Owl	250 Plain Titmouse
183 Ladder-backed	252 Bushtit
Woodpecker	261 Bewick's Wren
196 Piñon Jay	301 Loggerhead
198 Scrub Jay	Shrike
234 Ash-throated	323 Scott's
Flycatcher	Oriole

Characteristic birds of Oak Woodland. Photo by Vinson Brown.

165 Great Horned	214 Mourning
Owl	Dove
168 Screech Owl	247 Blue-gray
181 Acorn Wood	Gnatcatcher
pecker	250 Plain Titmouse
184 Nuttall's	252 Bushtit
Woodpecker	260 House Wren
190 Lewis' Wood	279 Black-throated
pecker	Gray Warbler
198 Scrub Jay	283 Hutton's Vireo
210 Band-tailed	309 Western Blue-
Pigeon	bird

Characteristic birds of Streamside Woodland. Photo by David Lehning.

144 Red-shouldered	254 Black-capped
Hawk	Chickadee
149 Harris' Hawk	272 Wilson's Warbler
152 White-tailed	274 Yellow Warbler
Kite	276 Yellow-breasted
159 Cooper's Hawk	Chat
167 Long-eared Owl	284 Bell's Vireo
176 Red-shafted	287 Warbling Vireo
Flicker	290 Black-chinned
182 Gila Wood-	Hummingbird
pecker	312 Swainson's
185 Downy Wood-	Thrush
pecker	316 Brown-headed
192 Common Crow	Cowbird
193 Black-billed	327 Summer
Magpie	Tanager
201 Ruffed Grouse	329 Black-headed
216 Ground Dove	Grosbeak
217 Yellow-billed	339 American Gold-
Cuckoo	finch

225 Tree Swallow	350 Song Sparrow
240A-B Alder & Wil-	368 Abert's
low Flycatchers	Towhee

Characteristic birds of the Sea Cliffs.
Photo by James Roberts.

44-46	Cormorants	103-105	Auklets
70	Black Oyster-	106	Tufted Puffin
	catcher	114-117	Storm-petrels
98	Common Murre	129	Western Gull
99	Pigeon	141	Bald Eagle
	Guillemot	191	Common Raven
100-102	Murrelets	220	Black Swift

Characteristic birds of Sea and Bay
Shores and Mud Flats. Photo by
James Roberts.

64	Snowy Plover	77	Baird's Sandpiper
65	Semipalmated	78	Least Sandpiper
	Plover	79	Western
68	American Golden		Sandpiper
	Plover	82	Dunlin
69	Black-bellied	83	Wandering
	Plover		Tattler
70	Black Oyster	84	Knot
	catcher	85	Short-billed
71-72	Turnstones		Dowitcher
73	Surfbird	91	Curlews
76	Spotted	306	Water Pipit
	Sandpiper		

Characteristic birds of the Freshwater Marsh. Photo by G. Van Horn:
Courtesy, Jepson Herbarium, University of California.

26	Mallard	54	American Bittern
27	Gadwall	55	Least Bittern
28	Pintail	56	White-faced Ibis
29	American	59	Sora
	Wigeon	60	Virginia Rail
30	Green-winged	62	Common
	Teal		Gallinule
31	Blue-winged Teal	74	Common Snipe
32	Cinnamon Teal	89	Willet
34	Northern	93	American Avocet
	Shoveler	94	Black-necked
35	Fulvous Whist-		Stilt
	ling Duck	96	Wilson's
36	Canada Goose		Phalarope
49	Great Blue	136	Black Tern
	Heron	153	Marsh Hawk
50	Great Egret	166	Short-eared
51	Snowy Egret		Owl

262	Long-billed	318	Tricolored
	Marsh Wren		Blackbird
271	Common Yel-	319	Yellow-headed
	lowthroat		Blackbird
317	Redwinged	350	Song Sparrow
	Blackbird		

Characteristic birds of the Saltwater Marsh. Photo by H.G. Weston, Jr.

49 Great Blue Heron	78 Least Sandpiper
57 Black Rail	79 Western Sandpiper
58 Yellow Rail	82 Dunlin
60 Virginia Rail	85 Short-billed Dowitcher
61 Clapper Rail	166 Short-eared Owl
65 Semipalmated Plover	347 Savannah Sparrow
66 Killdeer	350 Song Sparrow
69 Black-bellied Plover	

Characteristic birds of Lakes and Ponds. Photo by H.G. Weston, Jr.

1 Eared Grebe	63 American Coot
3 Pied-billed Grebe	66 Killdeer
5 Western Grebe	127 California Gull
6 Common Loon	128 Ring-billed Gull
9 Common Merganser	134 Gull-billed Tern
	139 Caspian Tern
12 Redhead	140 Osprey
13 Canvasback	141 Bald Eagle
17 Bufflehead	

Characteristic birds of Running Fresh water. Photo by Michael Abel.

9 Common Merganser	76 Spotted Sandpiper
22 Harlequin Duck	174 Belted Kingfisher
33 Wood Duck	267 Dipper
53 Green Heron	

Characteristic birds of the Deep Sea. (No photo shown.)

98 Common Murre	109 Northern Fulmar
99 Pigeon Guillemot	110-113 Shearwaters
100-102 Murrelets	114-117 Storm-petrels
103-105 Auklets	118-120 Jaegers
106 Tufted Puffin	121 Black-legged Kittiwake
108 Black-footed Albatross	123 Sabine's Gull
	133 Arctic Tern

Characteristic birds of Grassland. Photo 25, Courtesy of Jepson Herbarium, University of California.

91 Long-billed Curlew	321 W. Meadowlark
154 Prairie Falcon	322 Horned Lark
157 American Kestrel	347 Savannah Sparrow
170 Burrowing Owl	351 Lincoln's Sparrow
222 Lesser Nighthawk	354 Grasshopper Sparrow
320 Bobolink	

Characteristic birds of Savannah Photo by Vinson Brown.

142 Golden Eagle	233 Cassin's Kingbird
143 Red-tailed Hawk	297 Mockingbird
145 Swainson's Hawk	301 Loggerhead Shrike
151 Turkey Vulture	315 Brewer's Blackbird
157 American Kestrel	337 House Finch
194 Yellow-billed Magpie	340 Lesser Goldfinch
214 Mourning Dove	353 Lark Sparrow
231 E. Kingbird	
232 W. Kingbird	

Characteristic birds of Alpine Meadow. Photo by H. G. Weston, Jr.

199 Clark's Nutcracker	338 Gray-crowned Rosy Finch
310 Mt. Bluebird	344 Dark-eyed Junco
322 Horned Lark	356 White-crowned Sparrow

Characteristic birds of Coastal Forest. Photo by James A. Roberts.

163 Spotted Owl	230 Purple Martin
168 Screech Owl	244 W. Flycatcher
172 Pygmy Owl	246 Golden-crowned Kinglet
176 Red-shafted Flicker	249 Brown Creeper
186 Hairy Woodpecker	258 Pygmy Nuthatch
195 Gray Jay	259 Winter Wren
197 Steller's Jay	305 Cedar Waxwing
200 Blue Grouse	308 Varied Thrush
218 Vaux's Swift	311 Hermit Thrush
	335 Purple Finch

Characteristic birds of Mountain
Forest. Photo by H.G. Weston, Jr.

160 Sharp-shinned Hawk	237 Olive-sided Flycatcher
163 Spotted Owl	238 Western Wood Pewee
169 Flammulated Owl	256 White-breasted Nuthatch
172 Pygmy Owl	
173 Saw-whet Owl	258 Pygmy Nut-hatch
179A Yellow-bellied Sapsucker	269 Nashville Warbler
186 Hairy Wood-pecker	277 Hermit Warbler
188 White-headed Woodpecker	286 Solitary Vireo
	307 American Robin
197 Steller's Jay	326 Western Tanager
200 Blue Grouse	
223 Common Nighthawk	245 Gray-headed Junco
224 Violet-green Swallow	359 Chipping Sparrow

Characteristic birds of Inland
Cliffs and Rocky Areas. Photo by:
© B. P. Tatum.

150 California Condor	227 Rough-winged Swallow
154 Prairie Falcon	228 Cliff Swallow
155 Peregrine Falcon	229 Barn Swallow
	235 Say's Phoebe
161 Barn Owl	236 Black Phoebe
219 White-throated Swift	263 Cañon Wren
	264 Rock Wren
220 Black Swift	338 Gray-crowned Rosy Finch

158 Goshawk	255 Mountain Chickadee
164 Great Gray Owl	
179A Yellow-bellied Sapsucker	257 Red-breasted Nuthatch
180 Williamson's Sapsucker	282 Yellow-rumped Warbler
187 Pileated Wood-pecker	310 Mt. Bluebird
	311 Hermit Thrush
189 3-Toed Wood-pecker	313 Townsend's Solitaire
195 Gray Jay	330 Evening Grosbeak
199 Clark's Nut-cracker	333 Pine Grosbeak
	334 Red Crossbill
241 Hammond's Flycatcher	336 Cassin's Finch
	342 Pine Siskin
245 Ruby-crowned Kinglet	344 Dark-eyed Junco

Characteristic birds of Subalpine
Forest. Photo by H. G. Weston,
Jr.

Characteristic birds of Shallow Sea, Estuaries and Bays. Photo by James Robert.

1-5 Grebes	44-46 Cormorants
6-8 Loons	95-97 Phalaropes
10 Red-breasted	99 Pigeon Guillemot
Merganser	107 Magnificent
15-16 Scaup Ducks	Frigatebird
19-20 Goldeneyes	122-130 Gulls
21 Oldsquaw	131-139 Terns
23-25 Scoters	140 Osprey
43 Brown Pelican	141 Bald Eagle

Characteristic birds of Eucalyptus Groves. Photo by A. Kono, Save the Redwoods League.

176 Red-shafted	294 Allen's
Flicker	Hummingbird
237 Olive-sided	344 Dark-eyed Junco
Flycatcher	367 Brown Towhee
288 Anna's Hummingbird	

Characteristic birds of Cultivated Land. Photo by Greg Twain.

192 Common Crow	317 Redwinged
211 Rock Dove	Blackbird
212 Spotted Dove	320 Bobolink
215 Ringed Turtle	321 Western
Dove	Meadowlark
228 Cliff Swallow	324 Northern Oriole
229 Barn Swallow	328 Cardinal
236 Black Phoebe	337 House Finch
260 House Wren	344 Dark-eyed Junco
297 Mockingbird	350 Song Sparrow
307 American	352 Fox Sparrow
Robin	354 Grasshopper
309 Western	Sparrow
Bluebird	356 White-crowned
314 Starling	Sparrow
315 Brewer's	357 Golden-crowned
Blackbird	Sparrow

Characteristic birds of Buildings. (No photo.)

211 Rock Dove	236 Black Phoebe
228 Cliff Swallow	337 House Finch
229 Barn Swallow	369 House Sparrow

Most California birds are monogamous during the period of nesting and raising young. Birds pair off at this time and then separate following the breeding season. A few species, for example the Condor, Canada Goose, and Wrentit, remain paired for longer periods of time, perhaps for life. Others are regularly polygamous, the male mating with several females, (ex. Pheasant and Turkey). A few (ex. Redwinged Blackbird) occasionally practice polygamy.

Most monogamous birds share the task of nest building with many variations occurring in the role each sex plays. With some such as the woodpeckers, Kingfisher and Wrentit, male and female share equally. The males of most passerine birds help but the female does most of the work. Males of most wrens build a *"dummy"* nest while the female constructs the final nest by herself. Female hummingbirds generally complete a nest without the male being involved while the reverse is true of the Phainopepla.

The type of nest is characteristic of each species of bird. Most species follow a fairly consistent pattern in nest-building in terms of use of materials, shape and size, and location. A great variety of materials is used depending on the species of bird, including such varied items as grass, twigs, lichens, spider webs, hair, feathers, mud and various objects of man such as string.

The open cup is perhaps the commonest type of nest and is usually found associated with some type of vegetation. In structure nests vary from a slight depression in the ground as demonstrated by gulls and terns, to the finely sculptured mud nests of Cliff Swallows (see page 163), the pendulous nests of orioles (see above illus.), and the Bushtit (see page 170). Other variations include the nighthawk which prepares no nest, laying eggs on the ground, the Burrowing Owl which nests underground, the Belted Kingfisher which digs holes in earthen banks and the woodpeckers which excavate holes in trees. Unique is the female Brown-headed Cowbird which builds no nest, instead laying her eggs in the nests of other species of birds.

Within California a wide range may be found in egg size, shape and color, although each species lays a characteristic egg. Egg size varies from ½ inch average length (Calliope Hummingbird) to 4¼ inches (California Condor). Species that produce precocial young usually lay larger eggs (ex. California Quail) than similar sized species producing altricial young (ex. Robin).

Egg shape varies from round (most owls) to elongate (some cormorants), to very pointed at one end (murre). Eggs of most species are typically ovoid.

Coloration of eggs also exhibits great variation. Some are white but most are pigmented, either uniformly colored or variously marked. More prominent pigmentation is generally associated with eggs in exposed nests, white or light-colored eggs usually with species laying eggs in hidden places.

Numbers of eggs laid in a clutch by California birds vary from one egg by some sea birds, to two, typical of hummingbirds, to ten to fifteen or more by quail and waterfowl. Most species produce but one clutch of eggs each year. Some songbirds lay two. Condors may lay but one every other year.

1.

3.

2.

4.

(1) TOP ROW: *American Bittern 54, Great Blue Heron 49, Coot 63.* BOTTOM ROW: *Avocet 93, Snipe 74, Green Heron 53, Least Bittern 55.*

(2) TOP ROW: *White-faced Ibis 56, Pelagic Cormorant 45, Pintail Duck 28.* BOTTOM ROW: *Forster's Tern 131, Fork-tailed Petrel 114, Snowy Plover 64, Killdeer 66.*

(3) TOP ROW: *Red-shouldered Hawk 144, Turkey Vulture 151, Cooper's Hawk 159.* BOTTOM ROW: *American Kestrel 157, Pigeon Hawk 156, Ruffed Grouse 201, Roadrunner 175.*

(4) TOP ROW: *Barn Owl 161, Horned Owl 165, Saw-whet Owl 173, Burrowing Owl 170.* BOTTOM ROW: *Acorn Woodpecker 181, Steller's Jay 197, Red-shafted Flicker 176, Gilded Flicker 177, Black-billed Magpie 193.*

(5) TOP ROW: *California Quail 206, Scrub Jay 198, Brown Towhee 367, Mourning Dove 214.* BOTTOM ROW: *Dark-eyed Junco 344, Barn Swallow 226, Marsh Wren 262, Common Yellowthroat 271, English Sparrow 269.*

(6) TOP ROW: *Lark Sparrow 353, Song Sparrow 350, Summer Tanager 327, Ash-throated Flycatcher 234.* BOTTOM ROW: *Costa's Hummingbird 289, Anna's Hummingbird 288, Wilson's Warbler 272, Bushtit 252, Bell's Vireo 284.*

5.

8.

6.

9.

7.

(7) TOP ROW: *Bohemian Waxwing 304, Mockingbird 297, Shrike 301, American Robin 307.* BOTTOM ROW: *Yellowheaded Blackbird 319, Tricolored Blackbird 318, Brewer's Blackbird 315, Meadowlark 321.*

(8) TOP ROW: *Grosbeak 329, Bluebird 309, Cardinal 328, Western Kingbird 232.* BOTTOM ROW: *House Finch 337, House Wren 260, Ruby-crowned Kinglet 245, Plain Titmouse 250, Gnatcatcher 247.*

(9) TOP ROW: *Black Phoebe 236, Phainopepla 303, Swainson's Thrush 312, Northern Oriole 324.* BOTTOM ROW: *Chipping Sparrow 359, Bewick's Wren 261, Lazuli Bunting 332, Tree Swallow 225.*

YOUNG
BIRDS

Young birds that remain in the nest, dependent on parental care are nestlings. When these leave the nest they are then referred to as fledglings and remain so until they become independent of the parents. Young birds with feathers are called juveniles until they become sexually mature. Immature refers to any bird which has not acquired its fully adult plumage.

When hatched, young birds appear as one of two general types, either altricial or precocial (as shown in above illustrations). Birds are altricial (ex. sparrow) whose young at hatching usually have their eyes closed, are naked or nearly so and are unable to support themselves on their legs or feed themselves. Precocial young (ex. quail) hatch out with eyes open, legs well developed and covered with down feathers. They leave the nest soon after hatching and are generally able to feed themselves. Examples of birds having altricial young include the tube-nosed swimmers, pelicans and cormorants, herons, hawks, pigeons and doves, cuckoos, owls, hummingbirds, kingfishers, woodpeckers and the perching birds.

Precocial birds include the loons, grebes, waterfowl, galliformes, rails and coots, many of the shorebirds, the nighthawks and poorwills. The precocial forms usually include ground-nesting birds that regularly feed on the ground or in water and are typically runners, divers or swimmers. Margaret Nice (1962. Vol. 8, Trans. Linnean Soc. New York) found four basic patterns of behavior for precocial young. Gulls, terns, murres and a few others stay at or near the nest, even though able to walk. Others, including loons, grebes, and coots, follow the parents away from the nest and receive food from them. Most gallinaceous chicks follow parents from the nest and are shown food which they then pick up while the young of waterfowl follow the parents but find their own food.

A few ornithologists further sub-divide to include the categories semi-altricial, such as the tube-nosed swimmers, herons and hawks that are covered with down but are unable to leave the nest, and semi-precocial, such as the murres, gulls and terns, where the downy young stay at the nest for some time even though they are able to walk.

Some generalities can be made about the length of time altricial young stay in the nest. It ranges from about 8-10 days (some sparrows) to many months (Condor). There appears to be some correlation with respect to the following; the larger species and those with longer egg incubation periods have longer nestling periods, while species nesting in exposed places (ex. grosbeaks) have shorter nestling periods than those nesting in cavities (ex. woodpecker).

WATER AND SHOREBIRDS

GREBES: ORDER PODICIPEDIFORMES. Grebes: Family Podicipedidae. Distinguished from most ducks by weak flight, swift diving, narrow head and erect neck; legs far back on body and tailless look.

1. EARED GREBE, *Podiceps nigricollis.* **Range and habitat:** Resident in most of state, breeding primarily on inland waters, on marshy edges of freshwater lakes, mostly east of Sierra. Winters mainly in salt or estuarine waters along the coast. **Distinguished by:** Winter plumage similar to Horned Grebe, but cheeks not as white; *whitish patch more back of ear.* Slim bill appears slightly upturned. In spring and summer upper parts, neck and chest are black; *goldish fan-shaped tuft behind eye; white patch in wing visible in flight.* **Voice:** A peeping *wheelk-wheelk*, and a drawn-out *whoo-ik* call.

2. HORNED GREBE, *Podiceps auritus.* **Range and habitat:** Winter visitor (Oct.-Apr.) along entire coast, rarely inland, usually in lakes, shallow seas and bays near shore. **Distinguished by:** In winter, *clear white cheeks, foreneck and abdomen, which contrast sharply with black on top of head and back.* In spring, head black with buff-colored horn-like tufts back of eyes; foreneck, chest and sides chestnut; back blackish, belly white. *A large white patch at rear of inner wing shows in flight.* **Behavior:** Like most grebes, swims rapidly under water to catch small fish. **Voice:** A rare harsh *krrah*, often repeated.

3. PIED-BILLED GREBE, *Podilymbus podiceps.* **Range and habitat:** Widely resident in state, both inland and along coast, in shallow waters of lakes, bays and ocean. **Distinguished by:** Generally an overall brownish-black in color; *conspicuous black throat patch in breeding season. The only grebe not showing a white patch in wing in flight.* Distinctive thick blunt bill, with black ring near tip in spring and summer. **Behavior:** Expert forward diver, or simply sinks quietly out of sight; seldom seen flying; seldom seen in sizable groups, often alone. **Voice:** A loud *cuk-cuk-cuk-kow-kow* cry in spring-summer. Also has a stuttering *kik-kik-kik!*

4. RED-NECKED GREBE, *Podiceps grisegena.* **Range and habitat:** Winter visitor, primarily along central sea coast (Oct.-Apr.), in shallow sea and lake waters. **Distinguished by:** Larger than all grebes but Western, with prominent *yellowish bill; white patch shows in each wing in flight; dark neck contrasts with white throat;* brownish neck becomes reddish in spring. **Voice:** Rather rare trilling calls.

5. WESTERN GREBE, *Aechmophorus occidentalis.* **Range and habitat:** Resident in state (Sept.-Apr.) on waters of sea; or just inland from coast; breeds on inland lakes, mainly at higher elevations in N.E. part of state. **Distinguished by:** *Largest grebe in California, with long slender neck;* bill long, slender and yellowish. **Behavior:** Flies with very rapid wing-beat, with head and neck outstretched in front. Like all grebes, takes off from water by running over surface first. **Voice:** A rough or shrill, file-like *krr-kree*, or rolling croak.

GREBES

1 Summer

Winter

2

Summer

Winter

3

Winter

Summer

Immature

Floating nest of mud and grass moored to reeds.

Extreme rearward position of grebe and loon legs makes walking difficult and infrequent.

4

Summer

Winter

5

Grebes and loons can regulate their buoyancy. By compressing trapped air bubbles out of their plumage, they can submerge until only their heads break the surface like a periscope.

COLOR PLATE 1

1. Eared Grebe   12-14"
2. Horned Grebe   12-15"
3. Pied-billed Grebe 12-15"
4. Red-necked Grebe   18-20"
5. Western Grebe   24-29"

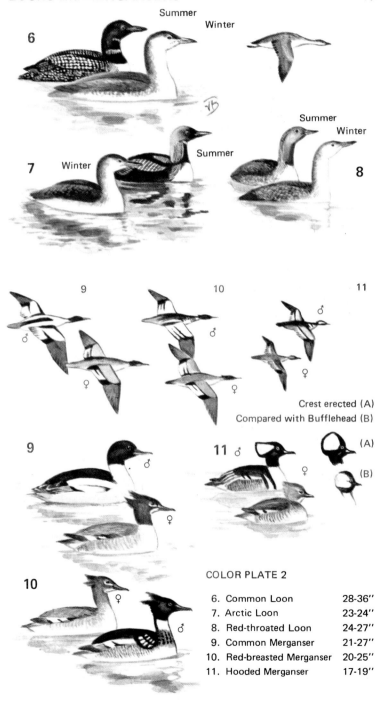

Summer
Winter

6

7 Winter

Summer

Summer
Winter

8

9

10

11

Crest erected (A)
Compared with Bufflehead (B)

9 ♂

11 ♂   (A)

♀   (B)

♀

COLOR PLATE 2

6. Common Loon   28-36"
7. Arctic Loon   23-24"
8. Red-throated Loon   24-27"
9. Common Merganser   21-27"
10. Red-breasted Merganser 20-25"
11. Hooded Merganser   17-19"

LOONS: ORDER GAVIIFORMES. Loons: Family Gaviidae. Extraordinarily expert swimmers, catching fish under water; larger than ducks, but with shorter necks than geese; legs appear far in rear of body; expert divers; fly with rapid steady wing-beats; take to air from water, paddling feet. In flight the head is held lower than the body. Large feet webbed.

6. COMMON LOON, *Gavia immer.* **Range and habitat:** Common winter visitor on ocean along coast (Oct.-May), less often on bays and lakes. **Distinguished by:** Up to goose size; *head appears thicker and longer, and bill thicker* than in other loons; in winter, blackish-gray general color, with cheek, throat, and underparts white; in spring, head black, *back checkered with black and white.* **Behavior:** Fly in loose flocks, the individuals dispersing widely in pairs or singly. Excellent diver and rapid swimmer using paddle feet.Catches water life, mostly large fish. **Voice:** Long, wailing *oooo-ah-eeee* call, like wild laughter or yodeling.

7. ARCTIC LOON, *Gavia arctica.* **Range and habitat:** Common winter visitor along coast (Sept.-May) on ocean and coastal lakes. **Distinguished by:** Resembles Common Loon at a distance, but smaller, with thinner bill. White below and blackish-gray above. *In spring black bars appear on back* (not speckled as in Red-throated Loon); throat black and hind neck gray. Bill straight. **Voice:** Gutteral *oook* or wailing *aaaa-eek* cries.

8. RED-THROATED LOON, *Gavia stellata.* **Range and habitat:** Common along coast (Sept.-May), in shallow sea and bays; unusual on lakes. **Distinguished by:** All our loons are similar in appearance in the water in the winter, but this loon has a *back speckled with white.* In spring and summer the brownish gray head and rufous throat patch are unmistakable. *Slender bill slightly upturned at tip.* **Voice:** Duck-like but usually quiet.

DUCKS, GEESE AND SWANS: ORDER ANSERIFORMES. Family Anatidae.

Mergansers. Bills narrow and saw-toothed-edged for catching fish underwater. Body, neck and head in flight held distinctively horizontal; flight swift.

9. COMMON MERGANSER, *Mergus merganser.* **Range and habitat:** Common winter visitor, primarily in coastal fresh waters; scattered inland. Summer resident along streams and lakes in northern forested areas and Sierra. **Distinguished by:** Slender bill; ♂ with bill and feet reddish-orange, *black back and green head and neck;* ♀ *with reddish-brown head and neck;* head often with crest (usually in ♂). **Behavior:** Dives and catches prey underwater; rests and nests on ground or in trees. **Voice:** Hoarse *cruck* (Hoffman).

10. RED-BREASTED MERGANSER, *Mergus serrator.* **Range and habitat:** Common winter visitor on coastal waters; less frequent on inland bodies of water. **Distinguished by:** ♂ with *conspicuous rugged-appearing crest.* ♀ much like female Common Merganser, but lacks sharp color break between neck and breast; crest conspicuous. **Behavior:** · Often swims on surface with head and neck underwater in search of food; feet held far apart. **Voice:** Faint *quack.*

11. HOODED MERGANSER, *Lophodytes cucullatus.* **Range and habitat:** Uncommon but regular winter visitor in salt and freshwater sloughs, marshes, ponds and slow-moving streams. **Distinguished by:** ♂ *with white blotch on head bordered with black* (resembles the smaller Bufflehead 17); *fan-shaped crest.* ♀ lacks crest of ♂; head brown. **Behavior:** Usually nests in trees often high off ground; very wary. **Voice:** Broken *quack.*

DIVING DUCKS: Dive deeply for food (both animal and plant); in rising from water, they first patter along surface with feet, as shown in color plate.

12. REDHEAD, *Aythya americana.* **Range and habitat:** Resident, throughout the year, usually in freshwater marshes, associated with open ponds; breeds mainly in Central Valley and to the N.E. **Distinguished by:** ♂ graying back and sides; *prominent forehead on reddish-brown head completely different from sloping profile of otherwise similar Canvasback;* tail grayish-black, abdomen white; ♀ generally brownish, with white underparts. **Behavior:** Mixes with other ducks on water; nests in marsh vegetation.

13. CANVASBACK, *Aythya valisineria.* **Range and habitat:** Winter visitor, primarily in shallow coastal waters, bays and nearby marshes along entire coast. **Distinguished by:** *Sloping profile of reddish-brown head; rather long neck, reddish-brown in ♂. Both sexes have grayish-white backs,* and long sloping dark bills. ♀ has brownish head, neck and breast. **Behavior:** Spends much time sleeping on water, head under wing; in flight V-shaped flocks give whistling sound. Seldom mixing with other ducks on water.

14. RING-NECKED DUCK, *Aythya collaris.* **Range and habitat:** Uncommon migrant and winter visitor over much of state, some breeding in N.E. corner of state; prefers deeper bodies of fresh water. **Distinguished by:** ♂ *with black back; vertical white stripe on side and purplish-black head and neck,* set off by inconspicuous reddish-brown ring on neck. ♀ generally brownish, with white underneath, eye-ring and lower face white. Grayish bill of both sexes black-tipped. **Behavior:** Flies fast and low over water; nests usually in grassy places. **Voice:** Inconspicuous low *quack,* and a low whistle.

15. GREATER SCAUP, *Aythya marila.* **Range and habitat:** Winter visitor mainly to coastal areas of state, in coastal bays, marshes and estuaries; most common to the north. **Distinguished by:** ♂ *dark head, neck and breast, may show greenish iridescence; dark back mottled with white; bill bluish.* Both sexes show prominent white stripe along hind border of wing. ♀ brownish with white on face at base of bill. **Behavior:** Flies swiftly in compact flock with loud rustling noise.

16. LESSER SCAUP, *Aythya affinis.* **Range and habitat:** Widespread migrant and winter visitor to coastal areas. **Distinguished by:** *Much like 15, but slightly smaller; dark head of ♂ with purplish iridescence;* wings when spread show shorter white strip than 15. **Behavior:** Grubs for food on bottom, stays under water long time. **Voice:** A loud *scaup* and purring sound.

17. BUFFLEHEAD, *Bucephala albeola.* **Range and habitat:** Common winter visitor to coastal bays and sloughs, occasionally inland; few breed in N.E. **Distinguished by:** ♂ *has fluffy dark head with large white patch; back blackish; rest white.* ♀ grayish-brown above, white blotch on side of head. **Behavior:** Unusual diving duck because it rises straight up from water when taking flight; generally rides high in water. **Voice:** A hoarse rolling sound.

18. RUDDY DUCK, *Oxyura jamaicensis.* **Range and habitat:** Common resident in ponds, lakes, bays with marsh vegetation nearby. **Distinguished by:** *Stubby appearance, thick short neck; ♂ in breeding season has rusty sides and upper parts. Both sexes have large white areas on face and stiff upturned tails.* **Behavior:** Small duck, but lays very large eggs in a basket-like nest made of and concealed in emergent vegetation; tail often held erect, fan-shaped; in flight considerable noise made by rapid beating of wings. **Voice:** Usually quiet.

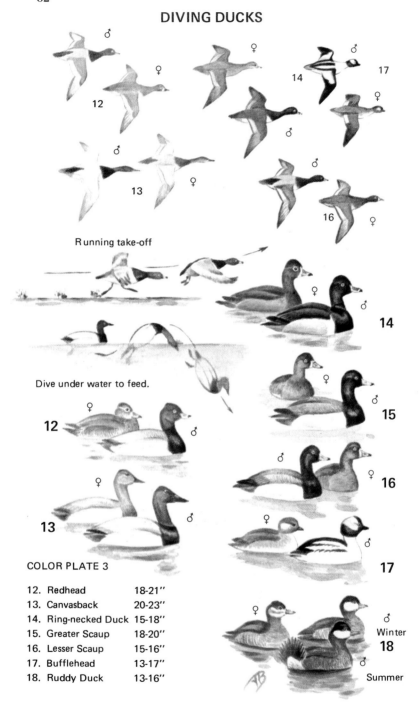

DIVING DUCKS

Running take-off

Dive under water to feed.

COLOR PLATE 3

12.	Redhead	18-21"
13.	Canvasback	20-23"
14.	Ring-necked Duck	15-18"
15.	Greater Scaup	18-20"
16.	Lesser Scaup	15-16"
17.	Bufflehead	13-17"
18.	Ruddy Duck	13-16"

Winter

Summer

DIVING DUCKS

COLOR PLATE 4

19. Common Goldeneye	16-20"
20. Barrow's Goldeneye	16-20"
21. Oldsquaw	15-23"
22. Harlequin Duck	15-17"
23. Black Scoter	17-21"
24. White-winged Scoter	20-23"
25. Surf Scoter	18-22"

19. COMMON GOLDENEYE, *Bucephala clangula.* **Range and habitat:** Common winter visitor, mainly coastal in northern half of state, favoring rather open saltwater bays and estuaries. **Distinguished by:** ♂ *has puffy-looking round black head with white spot between base of bill and yellow eye; head shiny appearing greenish at times*; dark-tipped wings showing much white in flight. ♀ has brownish head with whitish collar. **Behavior:** Wings whistle in flight; vocally are quiet birds.

20. BARROW'S GOLDENEYE, *Bucephala islandica.* **Range and habitat:** Not very abundant resident, usually coastal in winter on waters associated with salt marshes; in summer usually on higher mountain lakes of northern Sierra. **Distinguished by:** *Unlike 19, ♂ possesses a distinct white crescent between eye and bill; dark head may appear purplish and back is darker.* ♀ similar to above ♀. **Behavior:** Feed by diving and probing bill under rocks; bathes by rising in water and swishing it over themselves with wings. **Voice:** Hoarse *croak*, and mewing call.

21. OLDSQUAW, *Clangula hyemalis.* **Range and habitat:** Irregular and not very abundant winter visitor to open sea as well as coastal estuaries and bays. **Distinguished by:** ♂ *has long narrow, dark central tail feathers* (only other duck in our area with such feathers is the Pintail); *head and neck mostly white in winter, but in breeding season they become black except for white blotch on face.* ♀ more brownish, but much white on head and neck in winter. **Voice:** Very vocal, with constant *henk-a-lik* musical call.

22. HARLEQUIN DUCK, *Histrionicus histrionicus.* **Range and habitat:** Winters along coast south to central area, often in rough ocean waters near rocky islands and cliffs; breeds on western slope of Sierra from central portion northward in lakes and swift mountain streams. **Distinguished by:** ♂ *a distinctive blue-gray with reddish-brown on sides and irregular white markings on head and body.* ♀ dark brown above, with 3 white spots on side face. **Behavior:** Likes to dive for food in turbulent waters where it is very agile; rather shy; often rests on rocks. **Voice:** Squeaks.

23. BLACK SCOTER, *Melanitta nigra.* **Range and habitat:** Irregular winter visitor along coast in ocean waters from surf out. **Distinguished by:** *Only all black ♂ duck, except for orange-yellow swelling at upper base of bill.* ♀ dark brown but with whitish sides of head. **Behavior:** All three scoters dive mainly for mussels and clams, swimming with great agility with both wings and feet. **Voice:** Wailing *cooley* call.

24. WHITE-WINGED SCOTER, *Melanitta deglandi.* **Range and habitat:** Common winter visitor along entire coast in ocean waters and bays; a few nonbreeders present through summer. **Distinguished by:** ♂ *similar to 23, but has white patch on wing and white spot below eye;* ♀ brownish with 2 dull white spots on side of head. **Behavior:** Occasionally forages on beaches; likes flocks.

25. SURF SCOTER, *Melanitta perspicillata.* **Range and habitat:** Abundant winter visitor along coast in ocean surf and bays; a few seen in summer. **Distinguished by:** ♂ *black with white on back of head, forehead and around base of bill;* ♀ grayish-brown with 2 white spots on side of head. Whistling sound regularly made by wings as birds rise from water. **Voice:** Usually silent; grunting sounds.

DABBLING DUCKS. Do little diving, but feeding instead in shallow water, tipping body forward so tail is in air; take flight from water surface by bounding nearly straight up. Most show distinctive colorful rectangle on back edge of each wing (called *speculum*). Sexes differ in plumage colors.

26. MALLARD, *Anas platyrhynchos*. **Range and habitat:** Resident in most of state in marshes, ponds and rivers, at lower elevations in the winter. **Distinguished by:** ♂ *with green head and neck, separated by a white ring from the reddish-brown breast.* ♀ mottled brown. Both sexes have conspicuous white borders on both sides of metallic blue wing patch. **Behavior:** Often associates with Pintails; fly into cold areas in spring much sooner than most ducks. **Voice:** ♀ has loud *quack*; ♂ softer; a very vocal duck.

27. GADWALL, *Anas strepera*. **Range and habitat:** Common resident in many parts of the state, particularly inner valleys, in marshes, ponds and streams; most abundant in winter. **Distinguished by:** ♂ with grayish-brown head and neck; breast, back and sides grayish to grayish-brown; undersides of wings and abdomen white; black under tail; *patch on hind edge of wing black with some brown and white.* ♀ plain mottled brown, but differs from ♀ Mallard by showing white in wings. Both have yellow-orange legs. **Behavior:** Occasionally dives for food as well as dabbling; often wanders far from water into fields. **Voice:** A rather reedy *quack*.

28. PINTAIL, *Anas acuta*. **Range and habitat:** Abundant winter visitor in much of state, mainly in freshwater marshes and ponds, but may occur in saltwater bays; some remain to breed mostly in Central Valley. **Distinguished by:** ♂ *with very long pointed dark tail, wavy white lines on grayish back and sides; long slim neck, white in front, dark brown behind; black under tail.* ♀ is slender and streaked brown in color. In flight both sexes show whitish border to wing patch at center rear of wing. **Behavior:** Early migrants in fall and spring, and early spring breeders; nest on ground often some distance from water. **Voice:** *quack* and *cua-cua*, and a mellow whistle.

29. AMERICAN WIGEON, *Anas americana*. **Range and habitat:** Common widespread winter visitor, primarily in lakes, ponds and freshwater marsh-marshes near grasslands; occasionally in bays; a few remain to breed in the north. **Distinguished by:** ♂ *has brownish head with white crown and green patch behind the eye; pinkish-brown sides and breast.* ♀ also pinkish-brown on sides, but head and neck light gray, spotted with brown; back and breast brown. **Behavior:** Rather restless and nervous, quick to take flight; flocks turn and twist in fast flight; runs on land; nests on ground usually away from water. **Voice:** *Quack, quack*, or a rather musical *whew*.

30. GREEN-WINGED TEAL, *Anas crecca carolinensis*. **Range and habitat:** Widespread common winter visitor in most freshwater areas and coastal bays; a few remain to nest primarily in north. **Distinguished by:** ♂ *has reddish-brown head with metallic green patch behind eye; slender white crescent appears on gray side.* ♀ generally brown, but feathers on back edged with buff. In both sexes metallic green patch on wing edged with white. **Behavior:** Flocks fly rapidly in close formation, turning as one; agile on land. **Voice:** ♂ whistles; ♀ has *quack*.

86

DABBLING DUCKS

♂

♀

27

29

26 ♀

♂

♀

♀ 28 ♂

♂ 30

♀

26 ♂ ♂ (eclipse) ♀

♀ ♂ 27

♀ ♀ ♂ 29

28 ♂

♀ ♂ 30

COLOR PLATE 5

26. Mallard 20-25''
27. Gadwall 19-22''
28. Pintail 26-30''
29. American Wigeon 18-22''
30. Green-winged Teal 12-15''

Dabbling ducks spring
almost vertically out of the water;
feed by tipping to reach food at
the bottom of shallow water.

COLOR PLATE 6

31.	Blue-winged Teal	15-16″
32.	Cinnamon Teal	15-17″
33.	Wood Duck	18-20″
34.	Northern Shoveler	17-21″
35.	Fulvous Whistling Duck	20-21″

31. BLUE-WINGED TEAL, *Anas discors.* **Range and habitat:** Uncommon winter visitor and migrant in many parts of the state, in ponds and reservoirs and occasionally rivers; some breed in northeast part of state. **Distinguished by:** ♂ *has gray head with white crescent in front of eye; large blue patch on forward part of wing and a green speculum behind it; underparts, except for white by tail, a unique pinkish buff with many small black spots;* bill blackish. ♀ dark brown above with feathers edged with buff; light gray and spotted brown below; throat and chin whitish. **Behavior:** rather timid duck; fast flyer in close flocks with much turning and twisting; a late migrant in spring, early in the fall. **Voice:** A *peep* or *quack.*

32. CINNAMON TEAL, *Anas cyanoptera.* **Range and habitat:** Fairly common widespread summer visitor and migrant in areas of fresh water such as ponds, and slow-moving water with marsh vegetation or grasses nearby; uncommon winter visitor, mainly in San Joaquin Valley and southern coastal slope of the state. **Distinguished by:** ♂ *darkish cinnamon-red duck with prominent blue patch on forepart of each wing, green speculum behind*; bill blackish; feet orange-yellow with grayish webs. ♀ is similar to ♀ 31. **Behavior:** Similar in mannerisms to 31, but seldom seen in large flocks; often forages on land and by dabbling around edges of water. **Voice:** Usually quiet, but ♀ gives low *quack*; ♂ a rattling chatter.

33. WOOD DUCK, *Aix sponsa.* **Range and habitat:** Resident mainly in Central Valley and in coast ranges of central California; commoner in winter; migrants occasionally move south; found in areas of fresh water, especially near slow-moving streams bordered by cottonwoods, willows, etc. **Distinguished by:** ♂ *beautifully colored in winter and spring, with metallic green head crested with violet and lined with white; breast reddish-brown, sides buffy.* ♀ generally brown and white; eye ring white; slicked back crest apparent. ♂ like ♀ in summer and fall, but more white under chin. **Behavior:** Nests in cavities in larger trees. **Voice:** A noisy bird with a variety of calls.

34. NORTHERN SHOVELER, *Anas clypeata.* **Range and habitat:** Abundant widespread winter visitor and migrant in shallow freshwater bodies, such as ponds and nearby marshy areas; a few remain to breed. **Distinguished by:** ♂ *conspicuous with iridescent green head, white chest, reddish-buff sides, and white flanks at base of greenish-black tail; prominent blue patch on front half of wing, green patch behind.* ♀ mottled brown. Both sexes have large spoon-shaped bills. **Behavior:** Regularly sit low on water with bill held in a downward slant; may forage by swimming along with large bill partially submerged, straining out small food items. **Voice:** Normally quiet, but have a variety of calls such as *took-took* and a *quack.*

35. FULVOUS WHISTLING DUCK, *Dendrocygna bicolor.* **Range and habitat:** Common summer visitor, mainly to San Joaquin Valley and Pacific slope of southern California over to Imperial Valley, in freshwater marshes; a few appear in winter. **Distinguished by:** *Relatively long neck and legs; body blackish-brown on back, rest tawny except white under tail and on throat; wings in flight appear blackish.* **Behavior:** Nocturnal; has been known to but seldom nests in trees; builds nest of grass in marshes. **Voice:** Whistling cry.

Geese: Unlike most ducks, they regularly feed on the ground away from water. Large, heavy-bodied birds with broad, rounded tails, short legs and long necks; sexes alike in color.

36. CANADA GOOSE, *Branta canadensis*. **Range and habitat:** Widespread common migrant and winter visitor, on or near most bodies of fresh water, occasionally on salt water. Feed ("graze") on a variety of grasslands, fields and croplands. Summer visitor primarily in northeast part of state. **Distinguished by:** Several varieties, separated mainly by size and voice; all generally grayish-brown birds, with *black head and long neck contrasting with lighter-colored body and wings; white patches on cheeks join on throat;* tail feathers black, white toward bases; bill and feet black. **Behavior:** Typically fly in V-shaped line; very watchful when feeding in fields. **Subspecies:** *Common Canada Goose,* about 36" long, with deep honking cry. *Hutchin's Goose,* 34" long, similar call, but slightly higher-pitched. *Lesser Canada Goose,* 27-32", call still more high-pitched. *Cackling Goose,* 23-26"; very shrill, rapid *yuk-yuk-yuk-yuk* call.

37. BRANT, *Branta bernicla.* **Range and habitat:** Common winter visitor and migrant along entire coast, particularly on bays where eel grass is available for food. **Distinguished by:** A small goose with black head, neck and breast; a white patch appears on sides of neck below head (white missing on immatures). *Black cheeks* distinguish this species from the varieties of white-cheeked Canada Geese. White underneath tail often conspicuous. **Behavior:** Rapid flight, usually low over water. **Voice:** Low *cronk* call.

38. WHISTLING SWAN, *Olor columbianus.* **Range and habitat:** Common winter visitor, mainly in Central Valley; a few on coastal slope to the south, normally on or near freshwater lakes and ponds, some rivers and occasionally in brackish or saltwater along coast. **Distinguished by:** *Large, all white birds with very long necks;* feet and bill black; yellow spot usually found between base of bill and eye. **Behavior:** Neck held out straight when flying; fly V-shaped or diagonal lines. Flight graceful. **Voice:** Soft *woo-woo* and whistle-like notes.

39. ROSS' GOOSE, *Chen rossii.* **Range and habitat:** Not very abundant winter visitor and migrant, mainly in Central Valley; in freshwater marshes and lakes; regularly forages in cultivated fields and grasslands. **Distinguished by:** Looks like Snow Goose but smaller; small bill is reddish. **Behavior:** Habits much like Snow Goose. **Voice:** Soft grunting call or *key-ek-key-ek.*

40. SNOW GOOSE, *Chen caerulescens.* **Range and habitat:** Common winter visitor, mainly in Central Valley; habitat as Ross' Goose. **Distinguished by:** White; feet reddish; bill reddish with *black edges; wing tips black;* head and *upper neck occasionally stained rust color;* immature grayish white. **Behavior:** Quite noisy in flight; flies in V-formation. **Voice:** A nasal *kaar* and soft *cuk-cuk.*

41. WHITE-FRONTED GOOSE, *Anser albifrons.* **Range and habitat:** Common winter visitor to Central Valley in freshwater marshes and open bodies of water; feeds in open fields. **Distinguished by:** Body grayish-brown with *irregular black bands on belly; tail dark brown above, white at base;* bill pinkish with *white patch of feathers around base;* feet yellowish-orange. **Behavior:** Gregarious; very vocal in flight; flies in V-shaped flocks. **Voice:** High pitched *tooting* cry of 2-8 notes.

90

SWANS and GEESE

A

B

D

36

38

Mute Swan
(domesticated)

37

Immature

Adult

39

40

Adult

41

Immature

COLOR PLATE 7

36. Canada Goose A   25-43"
36. Hutchin's B   34"
36. Lesser (not shown) C 27-32"
36. Cackling D   23-26"
37. Brant   22-29"
38. Whistling Swan   50-55"
      Wingspread 6-7'

39. Ross' Goose   20-26"
40. Snow Goose   23-28"
41. White-fronted Goose 27-30"

Adult

PELICANS and CORMORANTS

43

Brown pelican diving for fish.

Immature

42

Immature

44

45

Immature

46

COLOR PLATE 8

42.	White Pelican	55-70''
	Wingspread 8-9'	
43.	Brown Pelican	50-54''
	Wingspread 6½'	
44.	Double-crested Cormorant	30-36''
45.	Pelagic Cormorant	24-25''
46.	Brandt's Cormorant	32-33''

PELICANS, CORMORANTS: ORDER PELECANIFORMES. Have special pouch in throat area; all four toes of foot joined by webbing; fish-eating.

Pelicans: Family Pelecanidae. Very large pouch below bill for holding fish.

42. WHITE PELICAN, *Pelecanus erythrorhynchos.* **Range and habitat:** During spring and summer found mainly on inland lakes; winters in west central and southern parts of California; widespread in migration. **Distinguished by:** *A large heavy-bodied white bird with a prominent head and bill; bill and large throat patch yellowish-orange; outer parts of wings black.* Immature with grayish-brown and black on back of head. **Behavior:** Flocks fly in line, flapping and then sailing, appearing to follow the leader; occasionally fly in V-formation. Does not dive from on the wing, but normally captures fish by quick thrust of bill while sitting on the water.

43. BROWN PELICAN, *Pelecanus occidentalis.* **Range and habitat:** Resident along entire coast, breeding south of Monterey Bay, characteristically in coastal ocean waters, seldom on fresh water; nests on offshore islands. **Distinguished by:** *Grayish-brown body and whitish head and neck in winter; back of neck brown in summer. Immature brownish above, whitish below. Large dark bill and pouch usually held close to neck.* **Behavior:** Often seen low over the ocean, close to shore, alternating slow methodical wing-beats with sailing. May "follow the leader" in flock, often changing elevation as he does. When feeding, usually capture fish by diving into water while in flight.

Cormorants: Family Phalacrocoracidae. Snake-like necks; dive from surface and swim fast to catch fish underwater; on perch often open wings to dry.

44. DOUBLE-CRESTED CORMORANT, *Phalacrocorax auritus.* **Range and habitat:** Resident along entire coast of California and on inland lakes, in fresh, salt and estuarine waters. Breeds regularly in trees around lakes. **Distinguished by:** *A large black water bird with an orange-yellow throat pouch. Breeding plumage has tufts of white feathers above and behind eyes.* **Behavior:** Necks of cormorants curve slightly upward as they fly low over the water with rapid wing-beats, while similar-appearing loons appear to fly with neck curved slightly downward. Beat of wings much faster than that of gulls. When courting ♂ and ♀ both stretch their necks and heads high with the orange pouch strongly displayed. **Voice:** Snoring grunt, especially when courting.

45. PELAGIC CORMORANT, *Phalacrocorax pelagicus.* **Range and habitat:** Resident along entire length of California coast in salt waters; nests primarily on sea-cliffs on offshore islands. **Distinguished by:** *Smaller than 44 and 46, with thinner bill, more slender neck and smaller head. Entire plumage is shiny black; in spring develops a double crest and contrasting white patches appear (most conspicuous in flight).* **Voice:** A deep droning note.

46. BRANDT'S CORMORANT, *Phalacrocorax penicillatus.* **Range and habitat:** Abundant resident along entire California coast in saltwater areas, nesting on offshore islands; not found in interior. **Distinguished by:** *Similar to 44, but throat is dark with brownish feathers bordering pouch; in breeding season pouch is blue and slender white feathers appear on sides of head and on back.* **Voice:** Soft pig-like grunt, mainly in breeding season.

CRANES: ORDER GRUIFORMES (in part, see Rails on page 97).
   Cranes: Family Gruidae. Told from similar-looking large herons by
crane having neck extended instead of S-shaped in flight. Tail feathers down-
curved.
   47. SANDHILL CRANE, *Grus canadensis.* **Range and habitat:** Both resident and migrant in interior valleys, in marshes, lake borders and grasslands.
Distinguished by: Looks like large light-gray heron tinged with brown, *with
long feathers on lower back drooping over wings and tail.* Top of head area
over eye to bill, bald and red. **Voice:** A rumbling, rolling, deep, honking
ker-rr-rr-roooo, with call repeated.
   HERONS, BITTERNS, IBISES: ORDER CICONIIFORMES. Long-
necked, long-legged, long-billed wading birds. Area between base of bill and
eye bare of feathers. Unlike most birds, portion of leg above ankle joint de-
void of feathers. **Wood Ibises: Family Ciconiidae.** Tail rather short; Wings wide
and rounded. Feed on animal life near water.
   48. WOOD IBIS, *Mycteria americana.* **Range and habitat:** Sporadic visitor along south coast and Colorado River, mainly summer, in shallow bay,
salt marsh, lake waters and rivers. **Distinguished by:** *Looks like large white
heron with dark, naked head and tail and back half of wings black. Bill stout-
er than heron's and down-curved at tip.* **Behavior:** In flight, it stretches neck
straight out instead of in S-curve, as in herons, and flies by alternate sailing
and flapping. Immature birds dark gray in color. **Voice:** A hoarse croak.
   Herons and Bitterns: Family Ardeidae. Bills long, straight, pointed in
flight; head and long neck drawn back against body in S-shape; legs held
straight out behind; slow wing beat in flight.
   49. GREAT BLUE HERON, *Ardea herodias.* **Range and habitat:** Resident near fresh and salt water, including lakes, streams, marshes, tidal areas
and occasionally offshore on floating rafts of kelp. Found mainly west of the
Sierra Nevada. **Distinguished by:** One of the largest wading birds in California,
standing to 4' high; neck, body and wings bluish-gray; head whitish. **Behavior:**
May stand with head and neck extended or drawn back against body while
waiting to strike at prey. Slow movements and patient waiting when feeding.
Voice: Hoarse croaks, sounding like *krakk, krahnkk!*
   50. GREAT EGRET, *Casmerodius albus.* **Range and habitat:** Widespread resident except for high mountains and dry parts of deserts, mainly in
marshy areas, tidal flats, irrigated land, rivers and lake edges. **Distinguished
by:** *All white plumage, yellowish bill and black legs and feet.* **Behavior:** Slow
movements and patient waiting when feeding. **Voice:** Harsh low *caaaw.*
   51. SNOWY EGRET, *Egretta thula.* **Range and habitat:** Widespread
resident at low elevations primarily in Central Valley and coastal areas in tidal
flats and marshes. **Distinguished by:** Much as No. 50, but smaller in size; bill
black, *with yellow toes contrasting with black legs and feet; often shows distinctive plumes of feathers on head and back.* **Behavior:** May stir water with
feet when foraging, then strikes with bill. **Voice:** Hoarse *cawk.*

LARGE WADERS
and EGRETS

Immature **47**

Adult

necks outstretched

47

48

Adult

48

Adult

49

50

51

Winter

Summer

Cattle Egret ↑
(Bubulcus ibis)

This species is a recent arrival in Calif. (McCaskie, *Condor,* 67, 1964) spreading either westward from southeastern U.S. (first seen 1952) or pushing northward from Mexican coast. At present, most likely to be seen in southern part of state. Distinguished from similar-sized snowy egret by chunkier appearance and yellow bill. White plumage in winter. Breeding adults buff-colored on crown, nape, lower breast and back. Immatures have blackish legs. Associates with livestock.

COLOR PLATE 9

47. Sandhill Crane   33-48"
48. Wood Ibis   36-46"
49. Great Blue Heron   42-54"
50. Great Egret   37-41"
51. Snowy Egret   23-24"

HERONS, BITTERNS and IBIS

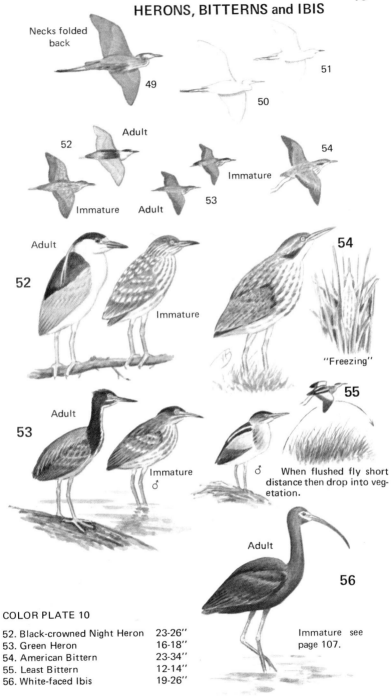

Necks folded back

49

50

51

52   Adult

54

Immature

Immature   Adult   53

Adult

52

Immature

54

"Freezing"

53   Adult

55

Immature
♂

♂   When flushed fly short distance then drop into vegetation.

Adult

56

Adult

Immature see page 107.

COLOR PLATE 10

52. Black-crowned Night Heron   23-26"
53. Green Heron   16-18"
54. American Bittern   23-34"
55. Least Bittern   12-14"
56. White-faced Ibis   19-26"

52. BLACK-CROWNED NIGHT HERON, *Nycticorax nycticorax*. **Range and habitat:** Breeds widely in state from seacoast to middle Sierra elevations along margins of marine and fresh bodies of water. Frequently roosts in trees some distance from water; nesting colonies usually associated with clumps of trees. Winters in greatest numbers in southern part of state. **Distinguished by:** A thick body; *the only heron with a black back and top of head;* in breeding, several white plumes extend back from head; eyes red. Immature have plumage mottled grayish-brown. **Behavior:** Normally roost in trees during the day and forage at night; patient stalking of food in water is done by slow movements or long patient waits. **Voice:** Short hoarse *cwa-cwa*.

53. GREEN HERON, *Butorides virescens*. **Range and habitat:** Widespread in migration; a few winter to south; breeds primarily from west central California south in tree thickets near water. **Distinguished by:** A small dark heron, *with shorter than usual greenish-yellow legs; face, sides and back of neck and upper breast reddish-brown;* back bluish-green. **Behavior:** When disturbed, often jerks tail up and down and raises crest of feathers; generally solitary in habits; usually utters loud squawk when startled into sudden flight. **Voice:** A sharp scolding *kuk-kuk* or a *keeyow* call.

54. AMERICAN BITTERN, *Botaurus lentiginosus*. **Range and habitat:** Widely distributed in thick vegetation in freshwater marshes, primarily west of Sierra Nevada. **Distinguished by:** Characteristic stocky body; *mottled and streaked brownish plumage is good camouflage in vegetation; black wing-tips conspicuous in flight.* **Behavior:** Seldom seen before it flies because of habit of remaining motionless in vegetation with bill pointed upward; when taking flight utilizes a slow beat of wings; seldom seen in the open. **Voice:** A thumping *oonk-ka-choonk*, like a stake being driven in with a wooden mallet. Also gives a *kuk-kuk-kuk* cry when flushed.

55. LEAST BITTERN, *Ixobrychus exilis*. **Range and habitat:** Common summer visitor, chiefly in Central Valley and southern coastal area of state, especially in marshy borders of lakes and ponds; nests low in marsh vegetation. **Distinguished by:** A very small heron with *conspicuous reddish-brown wing patches and black back and top of head;* adult ♀ has brownish back. **Behavior:** Extremely secretive in habits, rarely leaving marsh vegetation; hides by blending into background; takes flight slowly with rather awkward appearing wingbeats. **Voice:** A soft *cooing* call.

Ibises: Family Threskiornithidae. Ibises are long-legged marsh birds. They have large down-curving bills which they use to feed upon crayfish, snakes, cutworms and grasshoppers. They fly by alternating flapping and sailing, sometimes in large loose flocks and sometimes in a long straggling line.

56. WHITE-FACED IBIS, *Plegadis chihi*. **Range and habitat:** Uncommon summer visitor in southern California and interior valleys to north; widespread in migration; scattered winter visitor in south; frequents marshy areas. **Distinguished by:** A very large bird. *Head, neck and body purplish-red-brown; tail and wings greenish-bronze; white band rimming eye and base of bill.* **Behavior:** Erratic flight of wing-beats alternate with gliding, with head and neck outstretched. **Voice:** Soft *cruk*, but generally very silent.

CRANES, RAILS, GALLINULES, COOTS: ORDER GRUIFORMES (in part).
Rails, Gallinules and Coots: Family Rallidae. General marsh birds.

57. BLACK RAIL, *Laterallus jamaicensis.* **Range and habitat:** Fall and winter visitor north to Tomales Bay, resident in southern California, primarily in pickleweed of coastal salt marshes; some in moist marshy vegetation in or near fresh water. **Distinguished by:** *Small, sparrow-size; chestnut area on back of neck;* otherwise mainly black marked with white. **Behavior:** Extremely secretive; very seldom seen. **Voice:** Soft *klee-kle, klae-ee* call.

58. YELLOW RAIL, *Coturnicops noveboracensis.* **Range and habitat:** Rare, mostly a winter visitor in coastal freshwater marshes; occasional in salt marsh and grassy fields. **Distinguished by:** *Yellowish-brown with black and white markings* on the back and sides. Shows white wing patch in flight; short yellow bill. **Behavior:** Extremely secretive. **Voice:** *Tick-tick* notes.

59. SORA, *Porzana carolina.* **Range and habitat:** Resident; in summer found widespread in state mainly in freshwater marshes and other wetlands; some in saltwater marshes; may move south in winter. **Distinguished by:** *Gray-brown color with black around face and throat;* short yellow bill; white under tail. **Behavior:** Seldom seen, moving mainly in marsh vegetation; when disturbed, may fly short distances with feet dangling before dropping out-of-sight. **Voice:** A whistling note and regularly a whinnying call.

60. VIRGINIA RAIL, *Rallus limicola.* **Range and habitat:** Resident; widespread in summer, moving to lowlands and south in winter, mainly in freshwater marshes and along coast in salt marshes. **Distinguished by:** Like 61, *but smaller and less grayish;* generally rusty colored with gray on side of head; bill long and slender; like most rails has body appearing flattened from side to side. **Behavior:** Very quiet bird, seldom seen in flight or out in the open. **Voice:** Variety of *kuet-ta, kuke-ta* calls, monotonous *wack.*

61. CLAPPER RAIL, *Rallus longirostris.* **Range and habitat:** Resident of salt marshes and marshy edges of lakes, primarily from San Francisco south. **Distinguished by:** Long legs, long bill, dark gray-brown above; *reddish-brown breast;* black and white bands on sides and belly; white patch visible under short tail cocked upwards. **Voice:** Slow *kek-kek-kek,* then speeds up.

62. COMMON GALLINULE, *Gallinula chloropus.* **Range and habitat:** Mainly summer visitor in marshlands of Central Valley and south through state in vegetation bordering freshwater areas. **Distinguished by:** Blackish body and white under tail like Coot, but with *yellow-tipped red bill and red forehead plate* plus white side stripe on body; feet yellowish-green with long toes. **Behavior:** Like coot pumps head and neck when swimming; flicks tail when walking; wades through marsh vegetation or swims near it. **Voice:** Primarily a chicken-like clucking call.

63. AMERICAN COOT, *Fulica americana.* **Range and habitat:** Widespread abundant resident on or near various freshwater bodies. In winter large flocks regularly occur on saltwater bays and estuaries. **Distinguished by:** *Grayish-black color with whitish-blue bill and white under tail.* Long lobed toes. **Behavior:** Pumps head and neck when swimming, dabs bill at plants, dives; forages in open fields; paddles for distance to get started on flight.

RAILS

Immature

60

Adult

57

58

61

59

Adult **62**

Immature

Adult

COLOR PLATE 11

63 Immature

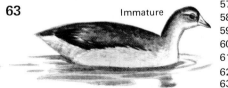

57. Black Rail	5-6''
58. Yellow Rail	6-7½''
59. Sora	8-9''
60. Virginia Rail	9-10''
61. Clapper Rail	16-18''
62. Common Gallinule	12-14''
63. American Coot	13-16''

PLOVERS

64

65

66
67

68
Winter

69
Winter

64

Summer

Winter

Summer

68

65

Summer

Summer

Winter

66

Summer

69

nest and
eggs

67

Winter

COLOR PLATE 12

64. Snowy Plover   6"
65. Semipalmated Plover   6-8"
66. Killdeer   10-11"
67. Mountain Plover   8-10"
68. American Golden Plover   10-11"
69. Black-bellied Plover   11-13"

SHOREBIRDS, GULLS AND TERNS: ORDER CHARADRIIFORMES.

Plovers, Turnstones: Family Charadriidae. Small to medium-sized plump-bodied shorebirds with comparatively short bills, swollen near tips; tail and neck short; flight rapid and direct. Plovers are quite active when foraging.

64. SNOWY PLOVER, *Charadrius alexandrinus.* **Range and habitat:** Common resident along most of coast on sandy ocean beaches; occasionally along shores of inland waters; in winter most abundant to south. **Distinguished by:** Small *whitish bird with incomplete black collar;* black bar separates white forehead and yellowish-brown top of head; white stripe on wing shows in flight. **Behavior:** Vigorous, fast flying; regularly forages at high tide-line on beaches; new-hatched active babies covered with down. **Voice:** *Twee-twee* cry common.

65. SEMIPALMATED PLOVER, *Charadrius semipalmatus.* **Range and habitat:** Common migrant in fall and spring along entire coast, infrequent inland, on sandy open beaches or more often mudflats of inland marshes and tidal flats of larger bays; sporadic winter visitor in southern California; a few remain along coast in summer. **Distinguished by:** *Black stripe on head and another on neck and upper breast;* white collar; back, wings and tail grayish-brown; *legs orange-yellow.* **Behavior:** When feeding flies more than runs from place to place; mixes with other shorebirds. **Voice:** Gurgling *chi-wee.*

66. KILLDEER, *Charadrius vociferus.* **Range and habitat:** Widespread resident throughout much of state in summer, generally avoiding the most northern parts in winter; most frequently near fresh water, less often near salt water; seen also in short grassy fields and grassy parks in towns. **Distinguished by:** *Two black bands on white chest;* white ring around neck; white marks on dark wings; reddish-brown on rump and upper base of tail, best seen in flight; blackish tail white-tipped. **Behavior:** Regularly feigns injury when nest or young threatened; nests on open gravelly soils, eggs blending into background; often runs instead of flying when disturbed; repeatedly jerks body upward when standing. **Voice:** *Kee-kil-de-dee* cry; often calls in flight.

67. MOUNTAIN PLOVER, *Charadrius montanus.* **Range and habitat:** Relatively uncommon winter visitor, mainly in interior valleys and southern California coastal valleys among sparse vegetation usually away from water. **Distinguished by:** Brown above; tail pale brownish with dark band near tip with white edge; whitish belly; *in flight white lining of wings a good field character.* **Behavior:** Like killdeer; runs more often than flies. **Voice:** Whistles and croaks.

68. AMERICAN GOLDEN PLOVER, *Pluvialis dominica.* **Range and habitat:** Scarce migrant along entire coast, mainly in autumn, primarily on beaches and mudflats. **Distinguished by:** In fall plain mottled dark brown above, brownish-white below; *in spring gold-brown above, black below.* **Behavior:** Feeds on open ground. **Voice:** Hoarse whistled *kweedle-ee* or *kwee.*

69. BLACK-BELLIED PLOVER, *Pluvialis squatarola.* **Range and habitat:** Common coastal migrant, on seashore, mudflats and open fields near water, occasional in San Joaquin Valley. **Distinguished by:** Like 68, but has *whitish rump patch and tail, and underwing axillar feathers are black.* **Behavior:** Flies fast in small flocks; often stand on one leg. **Voice:** Whispered whistles.

SHOREBIRDS

Oystercatchers: Family Haematopodidae.

70. BLACK OYSTERCATCHER, *Haematopus bachmani.* **Range and habitat:** Resident along entire coast on rocky shores. **Distinguished by:** *Large black shorebird with long laterally flattened red bill, reddish eyelids, pinkish legs and feet.* **Behavior:** Moves with slow jerky motions, nodding its head as it goes; feeds mainly on shellfish by prying them off rocks and breaking them open with its bill. **Voice:** Sharp *whick-wick;* also loud whistling note.

Turnstones, Surfbirds, etc.: Family Charadriidae (in part).

71. RUDDY TURNSTONE, *Arenaria interpres.* **Range and habitat:** Occasional migrant along seacoast. **Distinguished by:** Reddish-brown back and black chest band; in *flight much white on the back, rump, tail and wings* contrasts with black and reddish-brown of upper parts; legs orange. In winter grayish above with black markings, white below. **Behavior:** Turns over kelp and beach stones in search for food. **Voice:** Single *kwet* and *kuk a kuk.*

72. BLACK TURNSTONE, *Arenaria melanocephala.* **Range and habitat:** Common migrant and winter visitor along rocky seacoast. **Distinguished by:** *Plump bird,* with black upper parts, laced and streaked with white; *underparts white except for dark breast.* In winter grayish-brown above. In flight broad white and black areas appear above. **Behavior:** As in 71; both turnstones often stand in groups on rocks bursting into flight when waves strike.

73. SURFBIRD, *Aphriza virgata.* **Range and habitat:** Migrant and winter visitor on rocky shores of entire coast. **Distinguished by:** *Tail with white base and black tip plus white band down middle of outstretched wing* in flight; feet yellow; *streaked and spotted* appearance in late spring and summer, in winter grayish overall above with white on throat and above eye. **Behavior:** Runs in and out with waves on exposed rocky shore. **Voice:** Shrill *kee-week!*

Snipes, Sandpipers, Curlews, etc.: Family Scolopacidae.

74. COMMON SNIPE, *Capella gallinago.* **Range and habitat:** Primarily a winter visitor in west-central and southern California, widespread in migration, *in freshwater marshes,* wet grasslands and streamside vegetation. **Distinguished by:** Light-striped and spotted brown body and wings (outer wing darker), *white and black striped head; long straight bill;* in flight brown rump and orange band visible on tail. **Behavior:** Flies zig-zag. **Voice:** Raspy call.

75. SOLITARY SANDPIPER, *Tringa solitaria.* **Range and habitat:** Widespread but uncommon migrant, on shores of lakes and rivers and in streamside vegetation. **Distinguished by:** Generally grayish-brown color with light spots above, *but no white bars on wings or above eye* as in 76; tail dark and white banded. **Behavior:** Swift light flight; uses abandoned nests of birds like robins for nesting and may teeter body like 76. **Voice:** Shrill *weet-weet-weet.*

76. SPOTTED SANDPIPER, *Actitis macularia.* **Range and habitat:** Widespread migrant with some breeding north and some wintering in south, on seashores, sea rocks, shores of lakes and rivers. **Distinguished by:** *White bar on inner wing* and streak over eye; large spots below in summer. **Behavior:** vibrating fluttering flight; bobs body, also tips rear up and down. **Voice:** *Peet.*

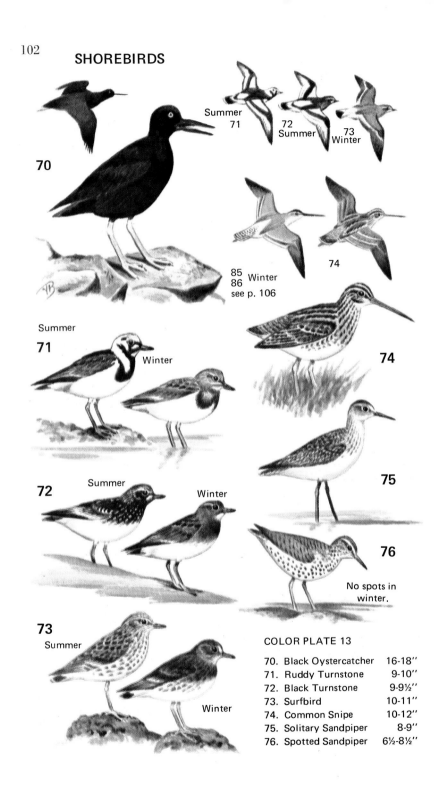

SHOREBIRDS

Summer
71

72
Summer

73
Winter

70

85
86 Winter
see p. 106

see p. 106

74

Summer
71

Winter

74

72 Summer

Winter

75

76

No spots in
winter.

73

Summer

Winter

COLOR PLATE 13

SMALLER SHOREBIRDS

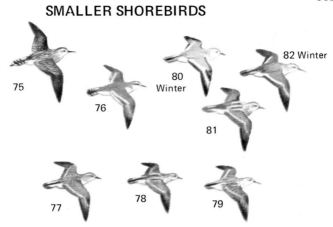

"Peeps" — small sparrow-sized Sandpipers

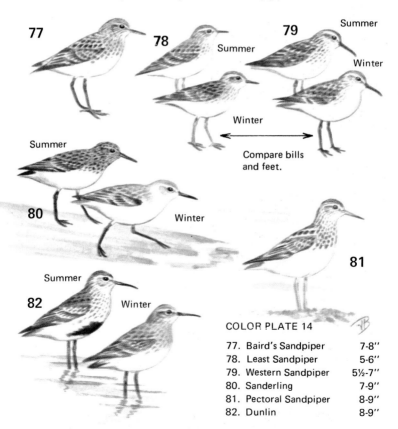

COLOR PLATE 14

77.	Baird's Sandpiper	7-8''
78.	Least Sandpiper	5-6''
79.	Western Sandpiper	5½-7''
80.	Sanderling	7-9''
81.	Pectoral Sandpiper	8-9''
82.	Dunlin	8-9''

77. BAIRD'S SANDPIPER, *Calidris bairdii*. **Range and habitat:** Uncommon fall migrant along coastal beaches; rarer in spring, usually inland in low vegetation near bodies of water. **Distinguished by:** Long wings extend somewhat beyond tail; brownish above, with pale edgings to dark feathers giving *scaly appearance; whitish line over eye;* brown breast marked with dark spots; outer wings appear dark; throat and belly white; legs black. Immature paler above. **Behavior:** In feeding, makes deliberate quick dashes picking at food rather than probing for it; often seems tame. **Voice:** Harsh single *kereee* call.

78. LEAST SANDPIPER, *Calidris minutilla*. **Range and habitat:** Abundant widespread migrant, some coastal in winter; occur at edges of a great variety of bodies of water. **Distinguished by:** *Sparrow size* and shorter wings than 79, also *somewhat darker brown above;* otherwise very similar, except for browner breast, yellowish legs and thinner shorter bill. In spring darkens to blackish-brown above. **Behavior:** Diligently pick at surface food and regularly probe in mud; habitually occur in flocks, alone or with other shorebirds; when startled have zig-zag flight. **Voice:** A variety of *peep* like call notes.

79. WESTERN SANDPIPER, *Calidris mauri*. **Range and habitat:** Abundant migrant, chiefly coastal; associated with marshes and mudflats and other water edges; winter visitor north to S.F. Bay. **Distinguished by:** Legs and bill black, the latter tapered toward the *slightly down-curved tip;* generally brownish gray above in winter, more reddish in spring; plain white below; *white stripe above eye and dark streak through the eye.* **Behavior:** In feeding it follows waves in and out as do many shorebirds; probes in soft mud or sand for food as well as regularly picking on surface. **Voice:** Short *chreep* note.

80. SANDERLING, *Calidris alba*. **Range and habitat:** Common migrant and winter visitor along seacoast. **Distinguished by:** *Plump small grayish-white bird* in winter, with conspicuous white stripe and *black triangle* visible in wing in flight; legs black; in spring reddish-brown on upper parts. **Behavior:** On sandy beaches runs in and out with the coming and going of the wave line, picking at food uncovered by the sea; also probes with bill in wet sand; straight low direct flight. **Voice:** Soft *tet-tet* or *tweet;* twitters softly.

81. PECTORAL SANDPIPER, *Calidris melanotos*. **Range and habitat:** Uncommon but regular fall coastal migrant, associated with ground near tidal mark. **Distinguished by:** Back and top of head dark brown, richly streaked with reddish-brown or reddish-brown and pale gray; inner tail feathers dark blackish-brown, outer ones pale brown; *dark breast color ends abruptly against white belly.* **Behavior:** Often crouches in grass, flushing with loud cry; zig-zag flight. **Voice:** Loud *creeek-creeek.*

82. DUNLIN, *Calidris alpina*. **Range and habitat:** Common coastal migrant, associated with beaches, mudflats and marshlands; some remain through the winter. **Distinguished by:** The *bill with slightly down-curved tip is longer than head;* in winter generally ashy-gray above with black-trimmed wings and black tail, white above eye; in spring black on belly and reddish-brown on back. **Behavior:** Commonly mixes with flocks of other sandpipers. **Voice:** Low stacatto rasping trill.

83. KNOT, *Calidris canutus.* **Range and habitat:** Uncommon coastal migrant, mainly on sandy beaches and mudflats; a few wintering in south. **Distinguished by:** *A plump sandpiper,* generally gray-streaked and white in fall and winter, noted by *showing white rump-in-flight;* outer wings blackish. In spring and summer shows reddish-brown face and underparts. **Behavior:** Probes in sand and among rocks for small organisms; also may feed by wading breast deep in shallow water; *fly swiftly in compact flocks, turning and twisting as one;* on ground usually move in deliberate groups. **Voice:** A low buzzing whistle *tzu-tsu,* or a low gutteral croak.

84. WANDERING TATTLER, *Heteroscelus incanus.* **Range and habitat:** Mainly a migrant along outer seashore with a few coming at other times of the year. **Distinguished by:** Dark grayish or brownish-gray above; belly *heavily barred with dark-gray in spring-summer,* gray-brown to white below in winter-fall; white bar over eye; legs yellow. **Behavior:** Generally solitary, working in rocky intertidal zone in search of food among rocks and vegetation; often bobs and teeters body; when disturbed may crouch among rocks. **Voice:** Shrill *wee-wee-wee* call.

85. SHORT-BILLED DOWITCHER, *Limnodromus griseus.* **Range and habitat:** Migrant west of Sierra along beaches and on mudflats, lakeshores and marshes, some winter to the south. *Mainly saltwater.* **Distinguished by:** *Long straight bill, with white rump and lower back, white tail with black bands;* sides of breast and belly usually spotted. Color more grayish fall-winter, brownish in spring-summer. **Behavior:** Quite tame; feed by rapid and deep probing of long bill in mud, with head sometimes completely underwater; may swim with bobbing head motion; compact flocks in flight, but may scatter on landing. **Voice:** Metallic *two-two-two.*

86. LONG-BILLED DOWITCHER, *Limnodromus scolopaceus.* **Range and habitat:** Common migrant, particularly in Central Valley; found in habitats like 85; *mainly freshwater;* about ¾ of wintering dowitchers in California are Long-bills. **Distinguished by:** Very similar to 85, but *bill usually longer* and sides of breast and belly heavily barred; more reddish-brown on underparts in spring; back dark-mottled. **Behavior:** As in 85. **Voice:** Single *keek* call.

87. GREATER YELLOWLEGS, *Tringa melanoleuca.* **Range and habitat:** Widespread common migrant primarily along edges of ponds and marshes; some winter in southern half of state. **Distinguished by:** *Whitish tail with black bars,* white rump and *long yellow legs;* ashy brown above in winter, turning to blackish, marked with light gray in spring; head light with dark streaks. **Behavior:** Often wades body-deep in shallow water reaching for prey with quick darts of bill, often bobbing and weaving body; sometimes runs through water striking right and left; jerky movement when walking; swift strong high flight. **Voice:** 3-4 whistled sharp *whew* notes.

88. LESSER YELLOWLEGS, *Tringa flavipes.* **Range and habitat:** Uncommon migrant along marshes and mudflats. **Distinguished by:** Looks like above bird, but *smaller, 9-11" as opposed to 12-14";* tail bands paler. **Behavior:** Much as with 87. **Voice:** Soft *tu-tu* notes.

SHOREBIRDS

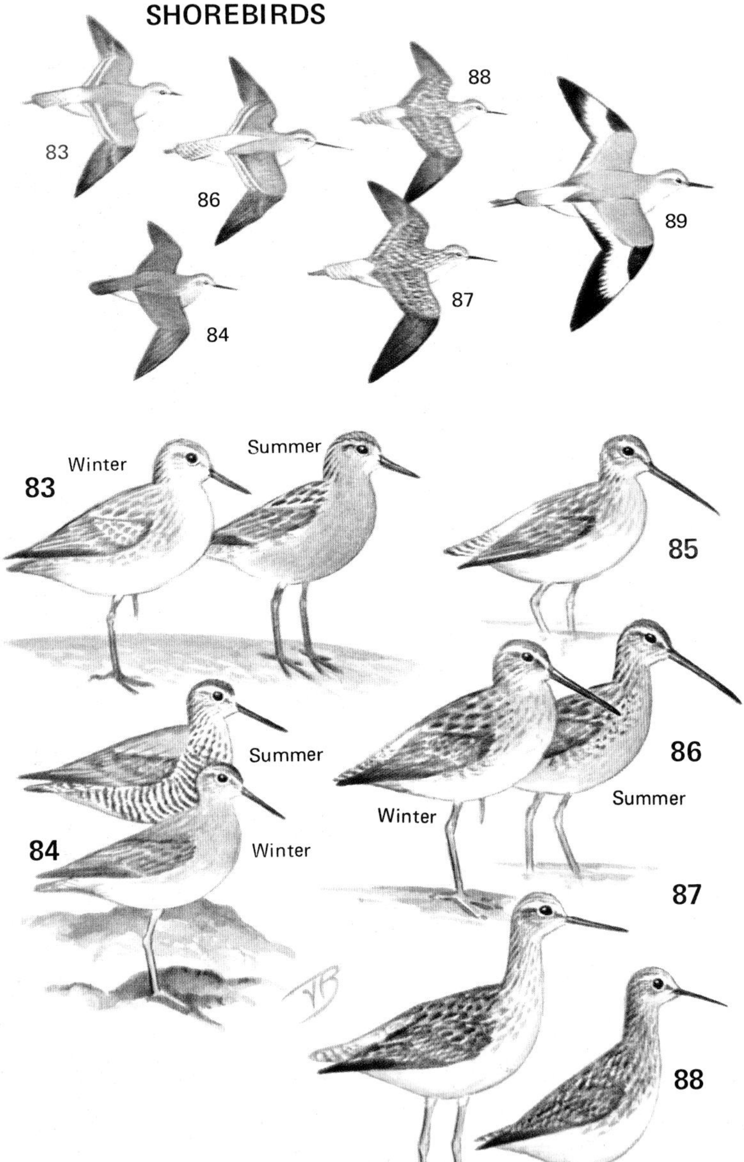

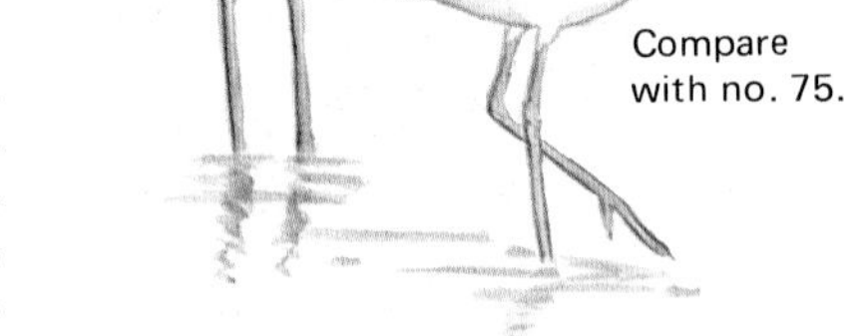

83
86
88
89
84
87
83
Winter
Summer
85
Summer
84
Winter
86
Winter
Summer
87
88

Compare
with no. 75.

COLOR PLATE 15

83. Knot	10-11"
84. Wandering Tattler	10-11"
85. Short-billed Dowitcher	10-11"
86. Long-billed Dowitcher	11-13"
87. Greater Yellowlegs	13-15"
88. Lesser Yellowlegs	10-11"

SHOREBIRDS

90

92

93

91

94

89 Winter

Summer

Winter

Summer

93

Immature White-faced Ibis
56

90

94

91

92

COLOR PLATE 16

89. Willet   15-16"
90. Whimbrel   15-18"
91. Long-billed Curlew 20-26"
92. Marbled Godwit   16-20"
93. American Avocet   16-20"
94. Black-necked Stilt 13-17"

89. WILLET, *Catoptrophorus semipalmatus*. **Range and habitat:** Abundant coastal migrant associated with beaches and salt marshes; fewer numbers in winter, some nesting to the N.E. in wetlands. **Distinguished by:** *Thicker bill than similar Yellowlegs;* distinct *black, white and gray wing pattern seen in flight;* underparts whitish in winter, barred in spring-summer. **Behavior:** Head often jerked about; strong direct flight but appears slow; on ground often stands still with head drawn down; when head bobs back tail is lowered; very noisy. **Voice:** Loud shrill *whee-teee* call, or *phee-will-willet;* loud *key-yee.*

90. WHIMBREL, *Numenius phaeopus*. **Range and habitat:** Mainly common migrant, coastwise and in Central Valley; associated with beaches, marshes and areas near shallow water; some winter to the south. **Distinguished by:** *Black and white striped head,* long down-curved bill; grayish-brown mottled above, whitish below. **Behavior:** Walks with rapid jerky strides usually in a straight line; flock often flies in long straight or curved line. **Voice:** Shrill *whii-whii-whii* whistling cry; also a *cur-lee-u* call.

91. LONG-BILLED CURLEW, *Numenius americanus*. **Range and habitat:** Summers in N.E. of state; winter visitor and migrant along coast and in interior valley west of Sierra; in summer breeding to the N.E. Habitats chiefly beaches and salt marshes in winter, grasslands near water in summer. **Distinguished by:** *Very long down-curved bill;* large size with long legs; *head with only one white stripe;* brownish mottled above with black-tipped wings, grayish or grayish-brown to reddish-brown below. Reddish-brown shows under wings in flight. **Behavior:** Flocks both surface feed and deep feed with long probing bills; when alighting it swoops upward for an instant before landing showing reddish-brown under the wing; rapid flyer. **Voice:** Harsh *cur-leeee!* but many shrill and squealing notes.

92. MARBLED GODWIT, *Limosa fedoa*. **Range and habitat:** Common migrant chiefly coastwise associated with beaches, mudflats and freshwater shorelines; some wintering to the south. **Distinguished by:** Long bill *slightly curved upward; a large mottled brown or reddish-brown shorebird,* showing reddish-brown under wings in flight. **Behavior:** Wings often stretched high. **Voice:** Querulous *kee-kerker* cry; also harsh *querk;* says name godwit.

Avocets and Stilts: Family Recurvirostridae. Bills straight or upcurved.

93. AMERICAN AVOCET, *Recurvirostra americana*. **Range and habitat:** Common summer resident to open wetlands of western and N.E. sections of state; winter S.F. south. **Distinguished by:** A long-legged *black and white wading bird, with rufous neck and head in spring* and summer, grayish in fall-winter; legs blue. **Behavior:** Upturned bill swept scythe-like, side to side in shallow water, when feeding. **Voice:** Loud shrill *wheeei* call.

94. BLACK-NECKED STILT, *Himantopus mexicanus*. **Range and habitat:** Chiefly summer resident in wet areas of valleys, and along coast; some winter south of San Francisco. **Distinguished by:** *Very long-legged wading bird;* body basically black above, white below; *legs reddish.* **Behavior:** Sometimes hover over their nests on rapidly-beating wings; often feigns injury to draw enemy away from young or nest. **Voice:** Loud *yip-yip-yip* call.

Phalaropes: Family Phalaropodidae. Resemble sandpipers, but swim much more frequently and have lobed toes. ♀ more colorful and larger than ♂. Whirl on surface of water when foraging for food.

95. RED PHALAROPE, *Phalaropus fulicarius.* **Range and habitat:** Chiefly migrant in coastal ocean and bays, occasionally on seashore. **Distinguished by:** *The larger ♀ in spring has a white face, black top of head and chin, reddish-brown underparts,* mottled gray and brown back; black and white on outer parts of wings; bill yellow. ♂ in spring similar, but hind neck and top of head brown. Both sexes in fall and winter appear grayish above and white below. **Behavior:** Gregarious; most truly pelagic of all phalaropes; regularly spins and dabbles while foraging on surface of ocean. **Voice:** *Zwit.*

96. WILSON'S PHALAROPE, *Steganopus tricolor.* **Range and habitat:** Summer visitor in N. E. of state and Central Valley; migrant southward in marsh areas and in shallow bay and lake waters. **Distinguished by:** Spring and summer has grayish-black band through eye and down neck; upper parts grayish and blackish, but ♀ *with more reddish-brown areas and tannish streaks on side.* Winter and fall gray above, white below; bill long and black. **Behavior:** Feed more by wading than do 95 and 97, sweeping bill from side to side while walking; may forage in wet grassland; also whirl around while feeding on water. **Voice:** Low grunting, also *wa-hoo!*

97. NORTHERN PHALAROPE, *Lobipes lobatus.* **Range and habitat:** Migrant in coastal areas and some to interior, in shallow sea, bay and lake waters. **Distinguished by:** *Reddish-brown collar on breast in spring, brighter on ♀;* yellowish-brown streaked on back; upper part of head dark, the *throat white.* In fall and winter darker gray above than 95 and 96. **Behavior:** Swift erratic flight of flock in concert; swims buoyantly with head held high and nodding. **Voice:** Sharp shrill *keet* call; also a soft low *kitt.*

Murres and Puffins: Family Alcidae. Birds of open ocean and rocky shores; distinctive short necks and very fast wing-beats; use wings in swimming.

98. COMMON MURRE, *Uria aalge.* **Range and habitat:** Resident in open sea and on rocky islands south to southern California. **Distinguished by:** *Black and white pattern; head, upper neck and back black* in spring and summer; side of head, chin and throat white in fall and winter. **Behavior:** Lay eggs on rock on cliff shelves, etc., nesting in large colonies. **Voice:** Hoarse *aarha-a* cry plus a whistle.

99. PIGEON GUILLEMOT, *Cepphus columba.* **Range and habitat:** Resident in open ocean, islands and rocky coastal cliffs, mainly south to Channel Islands. **Distinguished by:** In spring and summer *all black except for white wing patch;* in fall and winter mottled gray-white, wings black and white, feet red. **Behavior:** Alcids patter along surface with feet in taking flight. **Voice:** A whistle.

100. MARBLED MURRELET, *Brachyramphus marmoratus.* **Range and habitat:** Resident chiefly offshore usually south to Monterey Bay; nests inland in tunnels in coastal coniferous forest. **Distinguished by:** The *only Alcid with dark brown upper parts* and brownish-black barred underparts in spring and summer. In fall and winter told by *white band between dark back and wing.* **Behavior:** Alcids have rapid flight close to water. **Voice:** Shrill *keeyer-keer.*

PHALAROPES and LARGE ALCIDS

95 Summer ♀

Foraging by spinning around to churn up tiny crustaceans

Winter

96 ♀ Summer

Winter

♀ Summer

97

Winter

98 Winter

98

99

99

Summer

Winter

Summer

FB

COLOR PLATE 17

95. Red Phalarope   7½-9"
96. Wilson's Phalarope   8-10"
97. Northern Phalarope   7-8"
98. Common Murre   16-18"
99. Pigeon Guillemot   13-14"

SMALLER ALCIDS

111

COLOR PLATE 18

100.	Marbled Murrelet	9-10''
101.	Xantus' Murrelet	9½-11''
102.	Ancient Murrelet	9½-11''
103.	Cassin's Auklet	8-9½''
104.	Parakeet Auklet	9-10''
105.	Rhinoceros Auklet	14-16''
106.	Tufted Puffin	14½-16''

101. XANTUS' MURRELET, *Endomychura hypoleuca*. **Range and habitat:** Resident on islands off southern California coast; winter visitor north to central California off coast. **Distinguished by:** All dark grayish-black above and all white below, white under wings except gray-brown tips of flight feathers; *looks like small murre except bill much shorter and body thicker.* **Behavior :** Nests hidden in cavities under boulders or in cliffs; feed on small forms of sea life, which they get from rocky tide pools or by diving. Flight is made by rapid wing-beats, almost buzzing; active at night. **Voice:** Twittering whistle.

102. ANCIENT MURRELET, *Synthliboramphus antiquus*. **Range and habitat:** Common winter visitor on deep ocean waters along coast. **Distinguished by:** In winter similar to Marbled Murrelet, *being dark grayish-black above and with white neck band, but no white stripes on back;* in summer white plume appears on head and ladder-like white and black markings appear at base of neck; bill light color. **Behavior:** Straight swift flight very close to water surface; often swim in small groups of 4-6 birds. It usually leaps a bit out of water and curves over neatly in dive. **Voice:** A faint but shrill whistle.

103. CASSIN'S AUKLET, *Ptychoramphus aleuticus*. **Range and habitat:** Common resident offshore. **Distinguished by:** Small Alcid; differs from Murrelets and 104 by dark gray coloration to waterline except *for white spot over eye and light spot at base of lower bill,* and from 105 by much smaller size. Some white on belly. In winter other small Alcids are marked with white. **Behavior:** For nesting, it tunnels into soil on islands or sometimes uses niches on cliffs. Flight swift and direct, but may clumsily bang into some obstruction. **Voice:** Rasping *reek-a-reek* chorus at night.

104. PARAKEET AUKLET, *Cyclorrhynchus psittacula*. **Range and habitat:** Occasional winter visitor offshore in deep sea and on rocky islets. **Distinguished by:** *Small size, black above and white below, but mottled gray on breast;* sometimes shows short thick upturned red bill. **Behavior:** Flies higher above water than most other Alcids; bouyant rapid swimmer and excellent diver. **Voice:** Low whistle.

105. RHINOCEROS AUKLET, *Cerorhinca monocerata*. **Range and habitat:** Common winter visitor offshore in deep sea and on rocky islets. **Distinguished by:** *Larger size and thicker yellow bill than most auklets,* dark grayish-brown above and grayish on throat, sides and upper breast; white below. **Behavior:** Swims low in water with head drawn in close to chunky body; swift diver, swimming underwater for long distances, seeming to prefer to dive and swim rather than fly when attacked or alarmed. **Voice:** Piercing crys.

106. TUFTED PUFFIN, *Lunda cirrhata*. **Range and habitat:** Resident offshore south to southern California Islands.   **Distinguished by:** *Large reddish triangular bill;* in winter blackish above and grayish below; in spring and summer blackish all over except for white on side of head and *long yellowish-brown ear-tufts; feet red.* Immature dark above but often whitish on belly. **Behavior:** Nests hidden in deep crevices in rocks or in burrows in ground of islands. The heavy body and small wings makes rising from water appear difficult. Flight strong with rapid wing-beats; legs held far apart when taking flight from cliffs. **Voice:** A quiet bird; some low calls.

FRIGATE-BIRD: ORDER PELECANIFORMES (in part): Family **Fregatidae.** Magnificent gliders, soarers and high-speed fliers; sharply hooked bill.

107. MAGNIFICENT FRIGATE-BIRD, *Fregata magnificens*. **Range and habitat:** Occasional visitor off southern coast, especially when driven north by storms. **Distinguished by:** Black color; *long, slender, forked tail; long narrow wings with sharp angles at wrists;* ♂ *red throat* ♀ *white breast.* **Behavior:** Extraordinary speed and agility in flight; skims water without lighting to pick up dead or living food; bullies other birds into dropping food and seizes it on wing. Does not swim, but perches on rocky islands.

TUBE-NOSED SWIMMERS: ORDER PROCELLARIIFORMES. Webfooted ocean birds, nesting on ocean islands. Bill has "jigsaw" appearance, with prominent hook at tip; external nostrils on top of bill, tubular in appearance. Feed mainly on fish taken from ocean surface.

Albatrosses: Family Diomedeidae. Very long narrow wings, heavy bill. 108. BLACK-FOOTED ALBATROSS, *Diomedea nigripes*. **Range and habitat:** Resident on ocean, usually far from shore, occasionally near coast. **Distinguished by:** *Extraordinarily long narrow wings;* general over-all color blackish-brown; some *white around base of bill* with some grayish toward end of wings and above and below base of tail. **Behavior:** Seems to scarcely move a muscle as it skims, glides and soars above waves, especially in windy weather; plops down suddenly in water to seize fish, squid or other live food. **Voice:** Groans and screeches loudly when fighting with other birds over food.

Shearwaters, Fulmars: Family Procellariidae. Primarily gull-like in appearance; regularly fly near surface of ocean with extreme skill; flight alternates wing-beating and gliding. Shearwaters have narrower wings, tails and bills than Fulmars. Catch small fish and crustaceans on surface of the sea.

109. NORTHERN FULMAR, *Fulmarus glacialis*. **Range and habitat:** In winter numbers vary on offshore ocean waters, mainly Point Reyes south. Scattered individuals appear in summer. **Distinguished by:** Stocky head, neck and body; stout *hooked bill* aids in distinguishing this bird from gulls; *greenish-orange bill with black near base* is distinctive. Two-color phases as shown. **Voice:** Grunting hoarse cry of *ik-ik-ik* or *arg-og-og-arrrr.*

110. PINK-FOOTED SHEARWATER, *Puffinus creatopus*. **Range and habitat:** Common on offshore waters, mainly south of the Farallon Islands, in open ocean; least frequent in winter. **Distinguished by:** Mainly white below, grayish-brown above, except for grayish-white areas in outstretched wings. *Feet pinkish; bill pinkish with dark tip.* Large size and slower wing-beats distinguish it from other shearwaters.

111. SOOTY SHEARWATER, *Puffinus griseus*. **Range and habitat:** Present year-round off entire coast, fewest individuals in winter. Mainly in open ocean but on occasion flocks of thousands may be seen close to shore. **Distinguished by:** Dark body and wings, *over-all sooty brown-black plumage,* broken only by whitish under-lining of wings. Feet patter on water in taking flight, especially when weather is calm, a characteristic of all shearwaters.

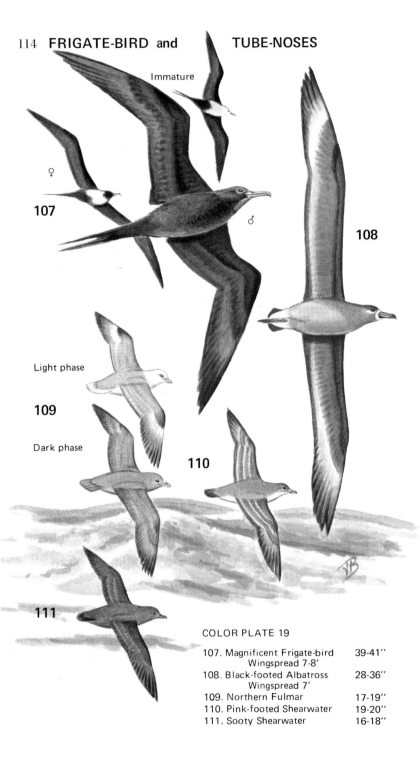

114 **FRIGATE-BIRD and** **TUBE-NOSES**

Immature

♀

107

108

Light phase

109

Dark phase

110

111

COLOR PLATE 19

107. Magnificent Frigate-bird   39-41''
    Wingspread 7-8'
108. Black-footed Albatross   28-36''
    Wingspread 7'
109. Northern Fulmar   17-19''
110. Pink-footed Shearwater   19-20''
111. Sooty Shearwater   16-18''

Below not to same scale.

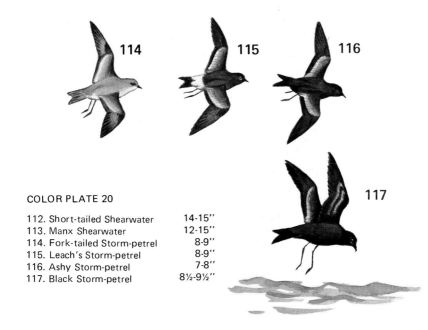

COLOR PLATE 20

112. Short-tailed Shearwater	14-15''
113. Manx Shearwater	12-15''
114. Fork-tailed Storm-petrel	8-9''
115. Leach's Storm-petrel	8-9''
116. Ashy Storm-petrel	7-8''
117. Black Storm-petrel	8½-9½''

112. SHORT-TAILED SHEARWATER, *Puffinus tenuirostris*. **Range and habitat:** Somewhat sporadic late fall and early winter visitor along full length of coast when few to many individuals may be seen. **Distinguished by:** Being very similar to Sooty Shearwater, but may be *slightly smaller*, and most have *darker lining on undersides of wings*. **Behavior:** Wing-beat quite rapid. More numerous than Sooty Shearwater in fall and winter.

113. MANX SHEARWATER, *Puffinus puffinus*. **Range and habitat:** Numbers vary through the year on ocean from central California south; most numerous in late summer and early fall. **Distinguished by:** *Upper parts dark brownish-black; underparts white*, especially under-surface of wings; bill blackish. Smaller than Pink-footed Shearwater, and with faster wing-beat.

Storm Petrels: Family Hydrobatidae. Small, dark, grosbeak-sized birds with long legs and short bills. California species with forked tails. The flitting flight over the ocean, especially in storms, is marvelous to watch, the birds often seeming to dance on the waves. Usually nest in burrows or under rocks on offshore islands. Petrels often follow ships, daintily skimming up thrown-out food from the water-surface, but their normal feeding is on zooplankton, small fish and crustacea.

114. FORK-TAILED STORM-PETREL, *Oceanodroma furcata*. **Range and habitat:** Along north two-thirds of coast; summer visitor mainly on islands off north coast; winter visitor and migrant elsewhere. **Distinguished by:** *Lighter colored* than other petrels along our coast; *bluish-gray above, whitish below*. Feet and bill dark. **Behavior:** Nests under rocks or burrows in soil on offshore islands; frequently glides. **Voice:** High pitched twitter.

115. LEACH'S STORM-PETREL, *Oceanodroma leucorhoa*. **Range and habitat:** Mainly offshore in summer and during migration; many breed off north coast. **Distinguished by:** *A dark petrel, usually with a white patch at base of tail, wings show white area in flight; bill and feet dark colored.* **Behavior:** During breeding season normally leaves nesting burrow only at night. **Voice:** In night flight over breeding grounds give pulsing falsetto hoots.

116. ASHY STORM-PETREL, *Oceanodroma homochroa*. **Range and habitat:** Generally fairly common migrant and summer visitor in open ocean off coast; less often seen in winter; most regular off central California coast. **Distinguished by:** *Being much like Black Petrel, but slightly smaller.* Over all grayish-black bird with a hint of gray in upper and lower wing-linings; feet and bill dark. **Behavior:** Best distinguished by more fluttery flight. **Voice:** Twitters at night, especially on offshore breeding islands.

117. BLACK STORM-PETREL, *Oceanodroma melania*. **Range and habitat:** Fairly common summer and winter off the coast of southern half of California; probably the most commonly seen of the petrels; generally in the open ocean, seldom near shore. **Distinguished by:** *A dark-plumaged bird with dark legs and feet.* **Behavior:** The largest of the petrels and the slowest in wing-beat looking almost lazy compared to others' swift fluttering. Quite active at night, as are most of the petrels. **Voice:** Often gives a ventriloquistic effect of *pook-pook-ah-pooh*.

Flight Silhouettes of Sea and Shore

1. Albatross
2. Frigate-bird
3. Pelican
4. Shearwater
5. Jaeger
6. Tern
7. Gull
8. Loon
9. Cormorant
10. Murre
11. Duck
12. Scoter
13. Petrel
14. Small Alcid

GULL PLUMAGES

Most people recognize the gregarious, noisy group of water birds they call *"seagulls"*. They associate most of them as scavengers along the waterfronts of the state. These birds appear to have a common pattern of coloration as adults—white head and body and gray wings with black tips. The more experienced students of birds will watch for variations in this basic color pattern as well as the variations in color of bill, feet and eyes from species to species.

Of the ten species of gulls most commonly found in California, all are easiest to identify in the adult stage. The usual seasonal plumage change in these adults is the appearance of some dusky spots or streaks on the head and neck during the winter (see illustration top left). At this time inland breeders such as the California Gull (see map at left) and northern breeders such as the Herring Gull join the common coastal resident species, the Western Gull, making winter the most fruitful time for observing the greatest variety of species.

If one finds identifying adult gulls a modest challenge, the problem of identification of immatures is very difficult by comparison. Feet and bill color so diagnostic in mature birds offer little help. Plumages among immatures are often similar between species and even may be variable within species. Gulls or Larids found in California typically take from two (Bonaparte's Gull) to three (California Gull) to four years (Herring Gull) to attain full adult plumage. The first year California Gull (see top left) is a mottled brown like most immature gulls while the second year bird (see center left)

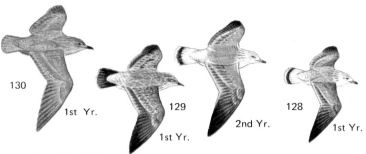

130
1st Yr.

129
1st Yr.

128
2nd Yr.

1st Yr.

128. Ring-billed Gull
129. Western Gull
130. Glaucous-winged Gull

JAEGERS

118 Immature

Dark Phase

Light Phase

120

119

COLOR PLATE 22

118. Pomarine Jaeger 20-23"
119. Parasitic Jaeger 16-21"
120. Long-tailed Jaeger 20-23"

assumes a generally lighter colored plumage. By the third winter the familiar white and gray adult plumage appears (see bottom left page 118).

It may help the watcher of gulls to get acquainted fairly well with the gray, white and black marked adults first, learning to differentiate the various species, and then watch to see which of the brown-marked immature gulls associate with the more easily identified adults. Admittedly this is far from fool-proof, as gulls of different species often mix together, but when just the adults of one species are noticed in one area the immatures that associate with them are most likely to be of that species. In such cases it would be a worthy problem in observation to note down or photograph the variations in color patterns shown by the immatures of a certain species and compare them with similar variations in color found with another species. Out of such close observation of details could come in time the ability to recognize the immatures of some or most of the gulls with greater certainty.

JAEGERS

Jaegers: Family Stercorariidae. Appear like dark-colored gulls, but have extra long central tail feathers; tails fan out as they change direction in flight, which is very swift and powerful. May attack sea birds to rob them of fish.

118. POMARINE JAEGER, *Stercorarius pomarinus.* **Range and habitat:** Offshore migrant chiefly fall, in deep sea and on rocky islets. **Distinguished by:** Central tail feathers broad with twisted tips. Two color phases: (1) Light phase most common with *upperparts dark brown or black except for creamy white sides of head and nape;* whitish areas in spread tail and stretched wing; underparts white except for brownish-black upper breast. (2) Dark phase is generally *blackish-brown except for whitish spots in out-stretched wings* and at base of tail. Immature has underparts mottled black and white. **Voice:** Harsh call.

119. PARASITIC JAEGER, *Stercorarius parasiticus.* **Range and habitat:** Coastal migrant, some wintering to south, in deep sea, shallow sea and along shore. **Distinguished by:** Very similar to 118, but *extended central tail feathers are shorter and flat,* are pointed in fall and winter, *being lost in spring and summer when tail becomes broadly rounded.* **Behavior:** Like other jaegers, it harries terns, gulls and other sea birds until they drop a fish they are carrying or disgorge the food, either of which the jaeger swoops down to pick out of the air. **Voice:** Usually quiet, but sometimes shrieks or wails.

120. LONG-TAILED JAEGER, *Stercorarius longicaudus.* **Range and habitat:** Occasional fall migrant offshore in deep sea. **Distinguished by:** Looks like both above birds, *but two central tail feathers extend 8-10" beyond others* and are pointed. **Behavior:** Very graceful and swift in flight. **Voice:** Usually quiet; a shrill call.

Gulls and Terns: Family Laridae. Gulls light on water, while terns usually plunge in head-first to catch fish. Gulls have generally square tails, while terns usually have forked and pointed tails. Gulls have stout hooked bills, while terns have stout but long pointed bills. Gulls have deliberate powerful flight, while the flight of terns is more bouyant and swift. Both have webbed feet. Immature gulls are much more brownish than adults, immature terns are generally more spotted than adults.

121. BLACK-LEGGED KITTIWAKE, *Rissa tridactyla.* **Range and habitat:** Irregular to common coastal winter visitor over open ocean and rocky islands. **Distinguished by:** *Solid black wing-tips cut sharply across ends of wings in adult;* white border on hind edge of wings behind light gray mantle; *except for gray back, rest of plumage is pure white in spring and summer.* In fall-winter, gray patch appears on back of neck. Immature similar to dark-headed gulls, but with short black legs, dark band on neck, black wing-tips and somewhat forked tail. **Behavior:** Graceful and bouyant flight. **Voice:** Moaning *aaaaaah* sound.

122. BONAPARTE'S GULL, *Larus philadelphia.* **Range and habitat:** Migrant and winter visitor, mainly along seashore, but also inland waters and cultivated areas. **Distinguished by:** *A small gull with red legs* and black bill; adult in spring with black head; some white by eye; neck white; light gray mantle; outer parts of wings white, ending in black tips; rest of year sides and top of head mottled with brownish-gray on white. Immature similar, brown blotches at bend of wing; black bar near end of tail. **Behavior:** Light and bouyant almost tern-like flight. **Voice:** Nasal *chrr.*

123. SABINES GULL, *Xema sabini.* **Range and habitat:** Migrant, usually offshore. **Distinguished by:** Similar to 122 in spring, *but black outer primaries and triangular white patch on hind wing are unique; our only gull with a distinctly forked tail;* head slate gray. In fall-winter head is white except for dark patch on back. Immature grayish-brown on mantle with wide black band at end of tail. **Behavior:** May hover over water, picking off small life from the surface; often solitary in habit. **Voice:** A hoarse rasping note; also low chattering calls.

124. MEW GULL, *Larus canus.* **Range and habitat:** Winter visitor along seacoast, in offshore waters, occasionally on bays. **Distinguished by:** *Small gull with greenish legs, short greenish-yellow bill,* white spot near end of black-tipped wing. Immature dark grayish-brown above, dark-speckled on white below, with black band on tail. **Behavior:** May pick food daintily off of water while fluttering in the air. **Voice:** Low mew.

125. HEERMANN'S GULL, *Larus heermanni.* **Range and habitat:** Summer-fall visitor along coastal sea and seashore; some winter visitors. **Distinguished by:** Adult dark gray with black tail, red bill and white head, *hind edge of inner part of wings white; black feet.* Rest of year head dark-mottled. Immature mainly sooty brown. **Behavior:** Breed along Mexican coast to south, then move north in summer, fall and winter. **Voice:** High *whee* call.

GULLS

121

Immature

Adult
Winter

121

124

125

122

Immature

Adult
Winter

Adult
Summer

Adult
Summer

Adult
Summer

Adult
Summer

Immature

Adult
Summer

Immature

Adult
Winter

Immature

Adult
Winter

124

Adult
Summer

Adult
Winter

123

Adult

Immature

125

COLOR PLATE 23

GULLS

128

126

127

129

130

126 Adult

127 Adult

128 Adult

Adult Winter

Immature

Immature

129 Adult

Immature

Immature

Adult

130

COLOR PLATE 24

126. Herring Gull   23-26''
127. California Gull   20-23''
128. Ring-billed Gull   18-20''
129. Western Gull   24-27''
130. Glaucous-winged Gull   24-27''

123

126. HERRING GULL, *Larus argentatus*. **Range and habitat:** Migrant and winter visitor, chiefly coastal along seashore and bays; some inland near water; occasionally on cultivated land. **Distinguished by:** *Adult is only large gull with black wing-tips, pinkish legs* and pearl gray mantle; whitish eye. Immature of first year is dark gray-brown; second year, broad dark band on tail tip merges into white of rump; much whiter than first year. **Behavior:** A very effective scavenger; is adept at picking up food from the water, coming down so lightly as to pick up a morsel without getting wet. It sometimes dives for fish like a tern, and may carry shellfish high in the air to drop them so they will break open on the rocks; skilled at soaring. **Voice:** Strikingly loud clear squeal or scream, like *kah-kak-kak* or *kee-kee-keeek*; plus a variety of other calls.

127. CALIFORNIA GULL, *Larus californicus*. **Range and habitat:** Common winter visitor along coast and widespread migrant in shallow sea and bay waters, and inland around cultivated fields, lakes and reservoirs; summer visitor on large inland lakes in N.E. **Distinguished by:** Adult very similar to 126, but *with sharply-cut black tip to underside of wing, also red or red and black spot on lower bill* and greenish legs. Immature as in 126, in first year bill is pinkish with black tip; second year dark tail. **Behavior:** Scavengers; like most gulls they regularly soar almost motionless on the wing. **Voice:** Loud squeal of *kyarrrr!* Other characteristic gull calls as well.

128. RING-BILLED GULL, *Larus delawarensis*. **Range and habitat:** Migrant and winter visitor along entire coast; on seashore and widespread inland around water and cultivation; greatest numbers south of S.F.; summer-visitor on inland lakes to the N.E. **Distinguished by:** Medium size, *black ring around yellow bill, very yellowish-green legs* and grayish mantle, in adult. Immature with brown speckling and spotting and *with narrow blackish band near tip of tail*. **Behavior:** Much as in 127; regularly walks with head up, tail down. **Voice:** Shrill squeals, anxious *kah*.

129. WESTERN GULL, *Larus occidentalis*. **Range and habitat:** Common resident along seacoast; seldom very far inland. **Distinguished by:** *Large size, very dark gray mantle* (which appears at distance as black area above white undersides); wings white at tips, then black, merging into dark mantle; *yellow bill with red spot near lower tip*. First year immature with dark wings and tail, dark gray-brown mottled elsewhere. Second year, underparts and *head whitish, dark back, primaries blackish*. **Behavior:** Common scavenger on bays and beaches, also catches fish at sea. **Voice:** Typical gull *kak-kak-kak* call.

130. GLAUCOUS-WINGED GULL, *Larus glaucescens*. **Range and habitat:** Migrant and winter visitor along coast much as 129. **Distinguished by:** *Mainly white or whitish with light gray mantle;* wing tips not dark, legs pink. Immature mostly brownish with some white specking in first year; second year a paler gray-brown, with primary wing feathers gray. **Behavior:** Generally similar to that of the above gulls. **Voice:** Like that of Herring Gull and Western Gull but not as loud.

Terns: **Family Laridae** (in part). More slender than gulls, with long narrow wings, slender and sharp-pointed bills, and usually forked or deeply-notched tails; flight pattern swallow-like. When foraging the bill is usually pointed downward as the tern watches for fish in the waters below. They dive from the air to seize the fish, often disappearing completely underwater and then surfacing. May hover before dropping to water below. California species typically possess plumage of gray, white and black; they are gregarious and aquatic; have short legs and webbed feet; and normally both sexes care for the young. Terns usually nest in colonies most often laying eggs in a slight depression on the ground such as on sand bars or beaches above the high tide line.

131. FORSTER'S TERN, *Sterna forsteri*. **Range and habitat:** Widespread migrant on seashore, bays and inland lakes and marshes; winter visitor along southern 2/3 of coast; summer visitor to N.E. and Great Valley. **Distinguished by:** *Tail deeply forked, black cap in adult,* upperparts gray, but silver linings appear on outer wings, pale gray tail is fringed with white; underparts white; *bill red with black at tip in spring.* Young birds and winter adults have black only in strip through eye. **Behavior:** Rather quarrelsome to birds of other species, sometimes attacking them viciously. Does less diving for food than other terns, often catching insects, crustaceans and small fish by swooping lightly to water's surface and picking them up; often hunts over marsh waters as well as open water. **Voice:** Young birds give a shrill squeal; older birds give a nasal, rasping *zaaaap* or *zrureep.*

132. COMMON TERN, *Sterna hirundo*. **Range and habitat:** Migrant along coast in shallow seas and bays and along seashore. **Distinguished by:** Very similar to 131, *but wing tips are appreciably darker and whitish tail is rimmed with gray* (the reverse of 131); *bill bright orange-red.* Immature has less black on head. **Behavior:** Feeds mainly on small fish in saltwater, diving often below surface. **Voice:** High piercing harsh *teye-arrrr!*

133. ARCTIC TERN, *Sterna paradisaea*. **Range and habitat:** Irregular to common southward migrant offshore in open ocean while undertaking its long journey from the Arctic to the Antarctic. **Distinguished by:** Very similar to 131 and 132, but is grayer below and underpart of wing shows less black near tip; *also entire bill is red in adult. Appears to have white streak between black cap and gray below.* The white tail is more like that of 132, being bordered outside with gray. **Behavior:** Dives for fish like other terns, and has swift powerful flight; seldom seen near land. Like other terns it is frequently attacked by Jaegers and forced to drop the food it has just seized. A group of terns seen hovering over the waves usually means a school of fish. **Voice:** Harsh squeal.

134. GULL-BILLED TERN, *Gelochelidon nilotica*. **Range and habitat:** Summer visitor to the S.E. and at Salton Sea and into Mexico. **Distinguished by:** *Much whiter than other terns,* but with black cap in summer and *black thick gull-like bill;* feet black. **Behavior:** Seldom dives into water after fish, but usually hunts arthropods on surface of shallow water or nearby land, dashing down to scoop them up with very swift flight. Flight acrobatic with many swift turns and zig-zags. **Voice:** A nasal 2-3 syllabled *kay-wek* call.

TERNS

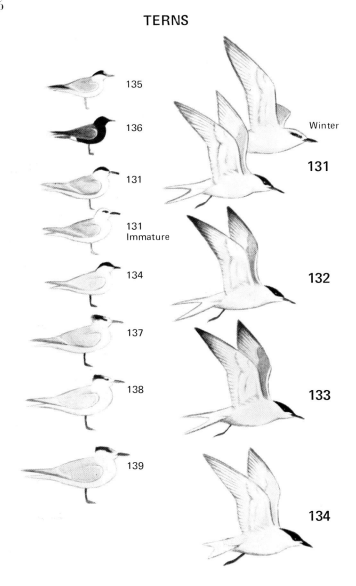

135

136

131

131
Immature

134

137

138

139

Winter

131

132

133

134

COLOR PLATE 25

131. Forster's Tern   14-15''
132. Common Tern   13-16''
133. Arctic Tern   14-17''
134. Gull-billed Tern 13-14½''

TERNS

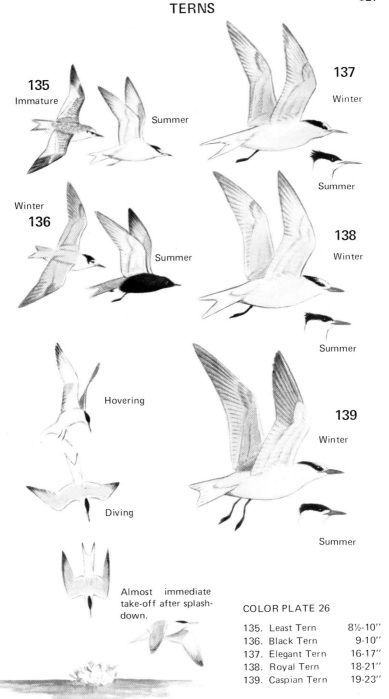

135 Immature

Summer

137 Winter

Summer

Winter **136**

Summer

138 Winter

Summer

Hovering

139 Winter

Diving

Summer

Almost immediate take-off after splash-down.

COLOR PLATE 26

135. Least Tern   8½-10''
136. Black Tern   9-10''
137. Elegant Tern   16-17''
138. Royal Tern   18-21''
139. Caspian Tern   19-23''

135. LEAST TERN, *Sterna albifrons.* **Range and habitat:** Summer visitor along coast southern half of state in open coastal water, bays, estuaries. **Distinguished by:** *Small size,* pale gray mantle on back and wings, but dark patches on forward outer parts of wings; black cap is cut by white forehead in adult; white below on neck and on *rather shallowly forked tail; bill and legs yellow.* Immature mottled blackish-gray above except for solid black areas on forward edges of wings; blackish on neck. **Behavior:** Feeds on small organisms found in or near the surface of the water, generally swooping down to skim the surface, but sometimes diving. The flight is graceful, and bouyant with rapid wing-beats. Often hovers in air. **Voice:** Sharp, paired *ket-ket* notes, rapidly repeated; also piercing *zreeeeeek* cry.

136. BLACK TERN, *Chlidonias niger.* **Range and habitat:** Summer visitor around inland waters; migrant inland and along seacoast to the south. **Distinguished by:** *Head and lower body black;* gray above. Winter adults and young birds have white heads with some dark markings; underparts white; *tail short and shallowly-forked.* **Behavior:** Does comparatively little diving, mainly catching insects on the wing or scooping them off the water surface or from the grass tops. The flight is darting and zig-zag, and it often hovers to watch for prey. **Voice:** Sharp nasal *kleek!* cry, or *kik.*

137. ELEGANT TERN, *Thalasseus elegans.* **Range and habitat:** Occasional fall visitor along coastal ocean waters and bays, southern half of state. **Distinguished by:** Plain gray mantle over wings and back, white below and on tail and neck; *black cap may be seen in early fall, changing later to black crest* at back of neck; *bill yellow.* **Behavior:** Little is recorded about this bird, but it does dive in the tern way for food. **Voice:** Call a nasal *car-zek.*

138. ROYAL TERN, *Thalasseus maximus.* **Range and habitat:** Primarily winter visitor over open ocean and along seashore southern half of state. **Distinguished by:** *Large size with deeply forked tail,* black crest at back of head; wing tips reach end of tail when folded; thick orange bill; light gray mantle on back and wings; white forehead. **Behavior:** Slower wing-beats are evident in flight; feeds by diving for small fish, usually well offshore; often seen flying in lines. Occasionally feed in the company of Brown Pelicans and may be seen robbing them of fish; normally dives for fish from a much greater height above sea than do most terns. **Voice:** Shrill *tseer* cry, also sharp *ker-ree* and *kak-kak.*

139. CASPIAN TERN, *Hydroprogne caspia.* **Range and habitat:** Migrant and winter visitor along coast and inland around lakes; summer visitor typically associated with lakes and marshes. **Distinguished by:** Larger than 138, with darker gray mantle on wings and back, tail forked about ¼ of length instead of ½ as in 138; when at rest the *wing-tips extend beyond end of tail; red bill much larger than Royals';* black cap covers forehead in summer; in winter head is speckled black on white except for slight crest of black at back of head. The red bill and black cap readily identify the Caspian Tern in a group of Gulls and the larger amount of dark to black that shows underneath on the wing-tips distinguishes it from the smaller Royal Tern. **Behavior:** Gull-like, such as alighting on water, sometimes soaring, and may rob other sea birds. **Voice:** Deep *kaa-aaarr* cry.

LAND BIRDS

(Including some birds that feed in water, such as kingfisher and dipper.)
VULTURES, HAWKS AND EAGLES: ORDER FALCONIFORMES.

Osprey: Family Pandionidae. A fish-eating hawk; hover high over water, then plunge down feet first to seize fish.

140. OSPREY, *Pandion haliaetus.* **Range and habitat:** Mainly summer resident and migrant around seacoast, lakes and rivers; winters more to the south. **Distinguished by:** Large size; white head with dark through cheeks and crown; *distinctive crook in wing in flight;* black patch on whitish underside of wing; plumage white below, dark brown above. **Behavior:** In foraging may plunge completely under water to capture fish; large piled nest of sticks in top of tree. **Voice:** Shrill cries; a whistled *kee-eek, kee-eek,* and a low *ak-ak-ak.*

Eagles: Family Accipitridae (in part). Wingspread 6' or more.

141. BALD EAGLE, *Haliaeetus leucocephalus.* **Range and habitat:** Resident primarily to the north, avoiding deserts and higher mountains, usually in vicinity of seashore, lakes and rivers. **Distinguished by:** *Adult has white head and tail* contrasting with dark brown body and wings. Immature dusky all over, but has some white in wing linings and some on base of tail underneath; in flight wings of eagles show flat profile. **Behavior:** Scavenges dead fish and similar food; dives from sky to seize fish in lake or bay, may steal food from birds such as Ospreys. **Voice:** Metallic shrill *kwee-kuck-ick-ick -ick* call.

142. GOLDEN EAGLE, *Aquila chrysaetos.* **Range and habitat:** Generally resident in open mountain and foothill terrain mainly between the humid coast and Sierra divide. **Distinguished by:** *Very long rounded wings; adult generally rich dark brown all over,* somewhat golden on head and neck. Immature best told below by wide dark band at end of white-based tail, and much white at base of primaries on dark wings. **Behavior:** Hurtles down at high speed to attack running prey, and levels off with glide before striking it. Two eagles sometimes harry the same prey. **Voice:** An occasional bark or a whistle.

Soaring Hawks: Family Accipitridae (in part). Rounded broad wings.

143. RED-TAILED HAWK, *Buteo jamaicensis.* **Range and habitat:** Widespread resident avoiding higher elevations in winter; most common in mixed woodland and grassland but frequenting many habitats. **Distinguished by:** *The rounded tail in the adult, red above;* immature has light gray tail usually with numerous dark bars; dark belly band common on both. **Behavior:** Nests in tall trees or on ledges, but hunts small animals in open country by diving from a soaring position in sky. Commonly perches on power poles. **Voice:** A descending squeal or scream.

144. RED-SHOULDERED HAWK, *Buteo lineatus.* **Range and habitat:** Resident west of Sierra divide mainly Central Valley and coastal half of southern California usually associated with woodlands along streams. **Distinguished by:** *Chestnut patch on shoulder, reddish brown underparts,* narrow white bands on dark tail. Immatures streaked below. **Behavior:** Often hunts from a perch in tree or on pole. **Voice:** High whistled call dropping in inflection.

OSPREY and BUTEOS

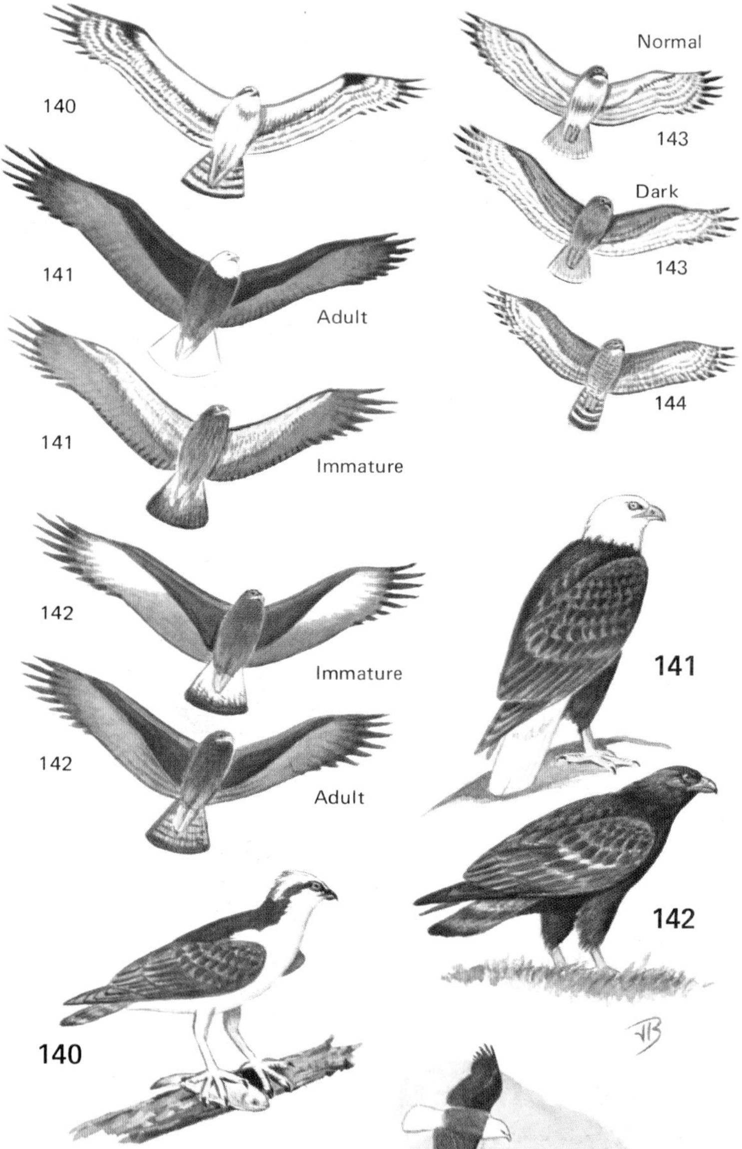
140
141
Adult
141
Immature
142
Immature
142
Adult
Normal
143
Dark
143
144
141
142
140

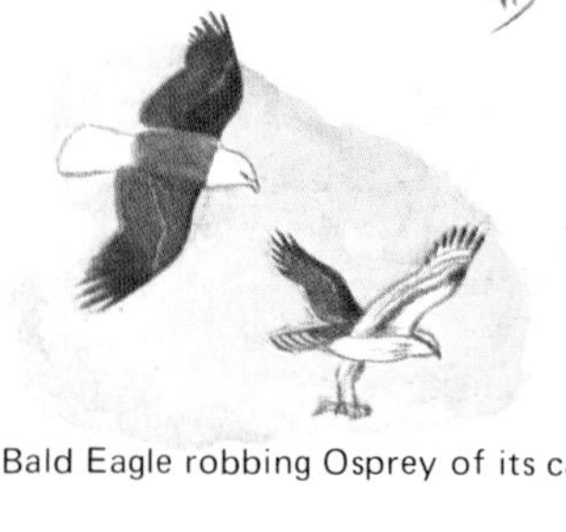

Bald Eagle robbing Osprey of its catch.

COLOR PLATE 27

140.	Osprey	22-26″
141.	Bald Eagle	30-32″
142.	Golden Eagle	30-40″
143.	Red-tailed Hawk	19-25″
144.	Red-shouldered Hawk	18-22″

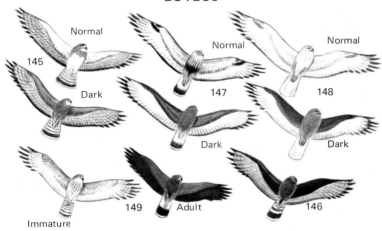

BUTEOS

Normal
145
Dark

Normal
147
Dark

Normal
148
Dark

Immature
149 Adult
146

143

145

147

144

148

146

149

COLOR PLATE 28

145. Swainson's Hawk   19-23"
146. Zone-tailed Hawk   18-22"
147. Rough-legged Hawk 20-22"
148. Ferruginous Hawk   22-24"
149. Harris' Hawk   17-24"

145. SWAINSON'S HAWK, *Buteo swainsoni*. **Range and habitat:** Summer visitor and migrant, chiefly in northeast, Central Valley and western, southern Californian dry open country with scattered trees. **Distinguished by:** Quite variable in coloration from black beneath to almost white with dark breast; underwing lining may be brownish with dark flight feathers; *tail banded with narrow bands*, broad at tip; *upper parts brownish*. **Behavior:** Often migrates in flocks; usually sits on low perches; rather sluggish flight with wings slightly uptilted. It hunts small mammals and grasshoppers by diving from lower flight height than the Red-tailed Hawk. **Voice:** A shrill but melodious whistle of *keeeeeeeeeeeer*.

146. ZONE-TAILED HAWK, *Buteo albonotatus*. **Range and habitat:** Rare winter transient near Mexican border, mainly in low mountainous country in desert scrub and savannah. **Distinguished by:** A dark hawk with *wide white tail bands in adult;* immature with wide dark band at end of tail; both with plain grayish-brown at base of wings, but breast of immature is white-spotted; *wings give two-toned effect like those of Turkey Vulture.* **Behavior:** Often soars with wings held up in shallow V like Turkey Vulture; slow, sluggish flight; dives from sky to catch small mammals, reptiles and birds. **Voice:** A light whistled squeal.

147. ROUGH-LEGGED HAWK, *Buteo lagopus*. **Range and habitat:** Sporadic winter visitor in northern 2/3 of state, mainly in grasslands, and savannah. **Distinguished by:** Body beneath light with blackish-brown belly with *a black patch on underside of whitish, black-bordered wing;* this is sometimes obscured in a dark phase. *Broad black band at tip of white tail distinctive.* **Behavior:** Hovers more than most buteo hawks, then dives on prey, usually a rodent. Often appears sluggish and sits for long times in a low tree, bush or even on the ground rising with heavy, slow wing-flaps when disturbed. It may hunt by flying low back and forth over grassy or marshy area, especially at dusk. **Voice:** Thin, whistle becomes blurred as it falls in tone.

148. FERRUGINOUS HAWK, *Buteo regalis*. **Range and habitat:** Primarily a winter visitor in interior of state, in open country such as grassland; a few breed to the N.E. **Distinguished by:** Best told by studying underparts in flight; *light phase appears mostly white below with reddish on legs* and bend of wing; dark phase has plain brown on body and inner half of wings, *but white on tail and on rest of wings except extreme dark tips*, upper parts brownish to brownish-red with white blotches; may have red-brown tail band above. **Behavior:** May poise motionless in strong wind; heavy slow flapping as the rule when not soaring; feeds on rodents. **Voice:** High-pitched, weak squeal.

149. HARRIS' HAWK, *Parabuteo unicinctus*. **Range and habitat:** Resident in S.E. California in woods and open country associated with river lands; also desert scrub. **Distinguished by:** *Very dark reddish-brown to brown main plumage contrasts sharply with white rump, tail base and white band at end of tail;* tail unusually long for a buteo; may show white colors beneath but reddish-brown at forward edge and bend of wing; reddish on shoulder and upper leg distinctive. **Behavior:** Hunts in thicker foliage or brush than most buteos, catching gophers, mice, small lizards and birds. **Voice:** Loud, rasping *kaaaar!*

American Vultures: Family Cathartidae. Powerful beaks for tearing flesh, but comparatively weak feet; carrion eaters. Soar in circles high in sky, like soaring hawks, but always show much black on uppersides; heads naked and appear smaller in proportion than those of hawks and eagles.

150. CALIFORNIA CONDOR, *Gymnogyps californianus*. **Range and habitat:** Resident in southern California mountains, mainly in Santa Barbara and Ventura Counties; occasional in southern Sierra, Only a few dozen pairs of this magnificent bird still exist. **Distinguished by:** *Large size, large white areas on undersides of black wings;* body black; bare head and neck yellowish-orange; heavy beak. Young birds are dusky on head, and have no white wing-linings, so appear all black, but are much larger than Turkey Vulture. **Behavior:** Majestic soaring flight, with such fine control in updrafts that they can waft themselves above the clouds in a matter of seconds. Hold wings in flatter plane when soaring than does vulture and normally does not tilt from side to side. Nests in caves or on ledges on cliffs. Wings flapped heavily to get bird off ground with some difficulty. **Voice:** Occasional hiss or grunt.

151. TURKEY VULTURE, *Cathartes aura*. **Range and habitat:** Widespread resident; in winter absent at higher elevations and to the far north. Some may migrate south in winter; most habitats except water. **Distinguished by:** *Black body, two-toned black and ashy-gray (on hind borders) wings; neck and head naked and red.* Immature have blackish heads. **Behavior:** When soaring, feathers at wing-tips often appear more widespread than hawks; wings held a bit above horizontal; often tilts and rocks body rather unsteadily. Often seen perched in trees or on fence posts in solemn row near dead or dying animals. **Voice:** A hiss or muffled grunt.

Kites: Family Accipitridae (in part). Long pointed wings and long tail, regularly hover in flight. Flight pattern very graceful.

152. WHITE-TAILED KITE, *Elanus leucurus*. **Range and habitat:** Resident from Sonoma County and Sacramento Valley south along streams, over marshes, savannah, grassland and oak woods. Somewhat restricted because of man's encroachment on habitat. **Distinguished by:** *White underneath, gray above; black wing patch; no other falcon-shaped bird has white tail;* immature has rusty band on tail, also reddish-brown marks on breast. **Behavior:** Swift flier and skilled at soaring; hovers then slips down (not plummetting like other hawks) and catches small reptiles, rodents and large insects. It rises from ground in swooping motion. Very shy about its nest, somewhat disturbed by man's presence. **Voice:** Harsh *hew* or whistled *pwe-pwe*.

Harriers·   Family Accipitridae (in part). Long rounded wings, long tail; regularly forage low to ground, harrying prey.

153. MARSH HAWK, *Circus cyaneus*. **Range and habitat:** Common summer visitor in marshlands and grasslands; widespread migrant and winter visitor. **Distinguished by:** *Obvious white rump patch;* ♂ *with gray back, throat and breast,* white belly marked with brown, tail with black bars. ♀ is brown-streaked on breast; brown above. **Behavior:** Tips of wings held high; tilts from side to side; hunts rodents. **Voice:** Excited *kek-kek-kek-key* cry and a whistle call.

134

VULTURES, KITE, MARSH HAWK

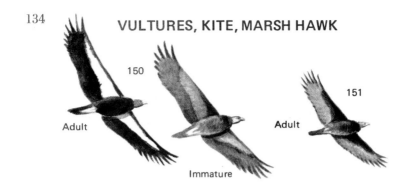

150

Adult

Immature

151

Adult

150   Adult

Immature

151

Adult

152

Immature

Hovering

Adult

Kite and Gull compared

153   ♂

♀

COLOR PLATE 29

150. California Condor 48-55''
      Wingspread 9'
151. Turkey Vulture   27-30''
      Wingspread 6'
152. White-tailed Kite 15-17''
153. Marsh Hawk   17-24''
      Wingspread 4'

FALCONS and ACCIPITERS

COLOR PLATE 30

154. Prairie Falcon   17-20"
155. Peregrine Falcon   15-21"
156. Pigeon Hawk   11-13"
157. American Kestrel   9-12"
158. Goshawk   21-24"
159. Coopers Hawk   14-20"
160. Sharp-shinned Hawk   10-14"

Falcons: Family Falconidae. Streamlined; long tails, pointed wings.

154. PRAIRIE FALCON, *Falco mexicanus.* **Range and habitat:** Resident mostly in open interior dry areas. **Distinguished by:** *Pale colors, except black patches at base of under-wings contrast sharply with white wings;* body below streaked with brown and white; pale brownish above; *dark brownish stripe down side of head.* **Behavior:** Very fast flier; captures prey by dashing into a bird flock; usually nests on cliffs. **Voice:** Loudly screeches.

155. PEREGRINE FALCON, *Falco peregrinus.* **Range and habitat:** Resident mainly along seacoast; migrant and winter visitor near marshlands, grasslands and inland cliffs. **Distinguished by:** ♂ *black cap and black sideburns against white throat;* other upper parts bluish-black with tail barred with black; reddish-brown streaked on white below; immature and ♀ more brownish. **Behavior:** Seldom soars; rapid flight enables it to catch birds on the wing (ducks), knocking the bird out of a flock in a power dive. **Voice:** Harsh *kek-kek-kek.*

156. PIGEON HAWK, *Falco columbarius.* **Range and habitat:** Common winter visitor over much of state mainly west of Sierra divide; usually woodland, primarily scattered oaks. **Distinguished by:** *Looks like miniature Peregrine Falcon with dark cap and bluish back* in ♂ but *has no sideburns on face;* underparts white, streaked with black; bands on tail conspicuous; ♀ and immature brownish or brownish-streaked all over. **Behavior:** Usually dashes low over the ground or into bushes with steady wing-beats to catch small birds, mice and large insects. In flight often skims low over ground then rises suddenly to perch. **Voice:** Quiet, may chatter.

157. AMERICAN KESTREL, *Falco sparverius.* **Range and habitat:** Common resident in most of state in most land habitats except dense woodland. **Distinguished by:** *Both sexes have reddish brown upper parts barred with black;* two black streaks on side of head, orange crown and wide black bar at end of reddish tail; ♂ *has blue wings.* **Behavior:** Often hovers, then plunges earthward to capture prey; tail moves up and down when bird alights. **Voice:** Shrill *killy-killy* or *kee-kee.*

Accipiter or Bird Hawks: Family Accipitridae (in part). ♀ largest.

158. GOSHAWK, *Accipiter gentilis.* **Range and habitat:** Resident in high mountain coniferous forests; winters in lowland, open woodlands. **Distinguished by:** ♂ *with black cap, white eye-stripe, black blotch back of eye and bluish-black back and wings;* grayish underparts; ♀ brownish. **Behavior:** Very secretive in activities. **Voice:** Shrill *kac-kac-kac.*

159. COOPER'S HAWK, *Accipiter cooperii.* **Range and habitat:** Resident in open woodlands over most of state except higher mountains. **Distinguished by:** *Much like Sharp-shinned, but larger and with rounded tail.* **Behavior:** Similar to above hawk, but does more hunting with swift rush near ground. **Voice:** Loud *keck-keck.*

160. SHARP-SHINNED HAWK, *Accipiter striatus.* **Range and habitat:** Breeds in woodlands of mountains mainly north half of state; widespread migrant and winter visitor elsewhere. **Distinguished by:** *Square-tipped tail with wide blackish bands;* ♂ more bluish above than brown ♀. **Behavior:** Flies near tree tops in early morning, soars higher later. **Voice:** Shrill *kee-kee.*

OWLS: ORDER STRIGIFORMES. Large eyes face forward.

Barn Owl: Family Tytonidae. Light colors; face heart-shaped and monkey-like.

161. BARN OWL, *Tyto alba.* **Range and habitat:** Common resident, mainly at lower elevations, seldom in dense woods, open deserts and at higher elevations; associated with open country and scattered trees, often associated with presence of man in woods, cultivated areas, grasslands. **Distinguished by:** *Yellowish-brown and white general colors;* white breast and belly speckled with brown; white specks on brown back and wings. **Behavior:** Often lowers head and moves it quickly back and forth; nests in buildings, cliffs or dense trees; flies very quietly dropping out of the night onto the backs of its prey, mainly small mammals. **Voice:** Hiss or wheezy screech.

Other Owls: Family Strigidae. Large-headed, short-necked birds of prey with hooked bills and strong talons. Largely nocturnal; forward facing eyes surrounded by "discs" of feathers. Quiet flight somewhat moth-like.

162. SNOWY OWL, *Nyctea scandiaca.* **Range and habitat:** Occasional winter visitor in northern California along coast and in Sierra in grasslands, cultivated areas, marshes and seashores. **Distinguished by:** *Only all-white owl, but flecked with black above and on belly;* yellow eyes and black bill. **Behavior:** Often perches near or on ground; often hunts by day for rodents or rabbits. Flight strong and steady but not swift; may glide for some distance. It rarely perches in trees, but chooses a high point to watch for prey. **Voice:** Quiet most of time; an *ow-ow* call.

163. SPOTTED OWL, *Strix occidentalis.* **Range and habitat:** Fairly common resident of mountains of south coastal slopes, west edge of Sierra and northwest in coniferous forests, oak woods and inland cliffs. **Distinguished by:** *Large size, no horns, dark brown color of back and wings thickly covered with white spots;* yellowish-brown underparts spotted or horizontally barred with white. **Behavior:** Shy and retiring; sleeps during day, usually hidden deep in foliage of a tree; moves jerkily along a limb when disturbed. **Voice:** High-pitched barking *wu-wu*, of 3 to 4 notes; or a whistled *wheeeeee!*

164. GREAT GRAY OWL, *Strix nebulosa.* **Range and habitat:** Rather uncommon resident in northern parts of Sierra Nevada in mountain and subalpine forests. **Distinguished by:** *Largest of our owls with 5' wingspread; dark brown above, but marked with gray and white;* light gray breast streaked vertically with dark brown; very large head, and seemingly long tail. **Behavior:** Flies with apparently labored flappings of its broad, rounded wings. **Voice:** Deep echoing *hoo-hooo-oo-oo;* or single, *whoo!*

165. GREAT HORNED OWL, *Bubo virginianus.* **Range and habitat:** Widespread common resident in almost all land habitats. **Distinguished by:** *Large size and large wide-apart tufts of feathers or "horns"; upper parts dark brown or blackish* with light brown underparts barred crosswise with light brown; *wingspread 4½'.* **Behavior:** Preys on many kinds of animals, some, as large or larger than itself; it even may attack skunks and porcupines. **Voice:** Deep *hoo, hoo-hoo, hoo, hoo* cry of 4 or 5 notes.

LARGE OWLS

Pale Phase   Rusty Phase

161

163

164

162

165

COLOR PLATE 31

161. Barn Owl   14-20''
162. Snowy Owl   21-26''
163. Spotted Owl   16½-19''
164. Great Gray Owl   25-32''
165. Great Horned Owl 18-25''

MEDIUM and SMALL OWLS

139

Screech Owl hiding during daylight.

Marsh Hawk and Short-eared Owl compared.

162

153

166

161

(18-32")

(14-17")

(7-11")

(5-8")

Seen overhead the common barn owl is often mistaken by the beginner for the larger and rare snowy owl.

169 168
171 170 161 161
172 173 166 162
           167 163
                164
                165

167

168

166

167

165

169

170

COLOR PLATE 32

166. Short-eared Owl   14-17"
167. Long-eared Owl   14-16"
168. Screech Owl   7-10"
169. Flammulated Owl   6½-7"
170. Burrowing Owl   9-11"

166. SHORT-EARED OWL, *Asio flammeus*. **Range and habitat:** Widespread migrant and winter visitor in meadows, marshes and open irrigated areas; some breeding west of deserts. **Distinguished by:** *Yellowish-brown color, streaked and spotted with blackish; ear tufts quite short and black;* black rings around eyes; blackish patches show on wings when flying; black patch shows on underwing in flight. **Behavior:** Often flies by day, especially when cloudy; floppy, almost moth-like flight, differs from hawks; swoops back and forth low over ground with slow wing-beats when foraging, suddenly dropping to seize prey; wings often tilted upward similar to Marsh Hawk's; sometimes soars high above ground or flies high in circles with steady flapping. **Voice:** Loud nasal *teee-yow*, like a bark; also hoots.

167. LONG-EARED OWL, *Asio otus*. **Range and habitat:** Widespread resident in state except nothern humid coastal area; mainly associated with woods along streams adjacent to open areas. **Distinguished by:** *Long narrow ears or horns are close together on head;* general color above *blackish with white marks;* below whitish with lengthwise black marks; *face disk tawny, wings unusually long and pointed* for owl. **Behavior:** Regularly alights close to tree trunk and freezes position there; preys on small rodents mainly at night; usually nests in tree in thick growth near stream, sometimes several owls having nests close together, most often using nests built by other large birds. Flight is buoyant and light. Attacks prey mainly from short distance; quite vocal when alarmed at nest; may feign injury and shriek to lead enemy away. **Voice:** Soft *coo*, also varied whistles, hoots, low moans and described by some to whine like a cat.

168. SCREECH OWL, *Otus asio*. **Range and habitat:** Common widespread resident in open woodlands, coniferous forests, cultivated areas and in suburbs. **Distinguished by:** *Small size with wide-apart distinctive ear tufts combined with general gray and white marked coloration;* may appear in reddish-brown phases; young birds lack ear tufts and are generally gray. **Behavior:** Regularly hide in thick foliage; drop down on mice or other small prey rather than gliding or swooping very far; nest in woodpecker holes or other cavities. **Voice:** A series of whistles becoming tremulous and quavering, usually descending.

169. FLAMMULATED OWL, *Otus flammeolus*. **Range and habitat:** Found in mountains mainly as summer visitor in coniferous forests and some oaks. **Distinguished by:** Looks like *small gray Screech Owl with very short ear tufts;* the only small owl in California *with dark eyes.* **Behavior:** *As in 168.* Usually this gentle, shy little owl perches close to the trunk of the oak, pine, or madrone tree. **Voice:** Soft mellow hoot or *hoo-hoo.*

170. BURROWING OWL, *Athene cunicularia*. **Range and habitat:** Common widespread resident of open grasslands and desert scrub generally at low elevations. **Distinguished by:** *V-shaped band over eyes, unusually long naked legs for an owl;* short tail; *sandy brown in color with many white marks.* **Behavior:** Frequent quick bobbing and bending motions; regularly nest in ground squirrel holes in open country; often seen standing by entrance to burrows; hunt mainly in daylight by short swoops. **Voice:** Shaky chuckle and coo.

171. ELF OWL, *Micrathene whitneyi.* **Range and habitat:** Summer resident mainly S.E. along Colorado River Valley in desert scrub. **Distinguished by:** *Small sparrow-sized owl, brown above and flecked with yellow-brown;* tail barred with white spots and *much shorter than* other little owls; underparts faintly striped; *no ear tufts.* **Behavior:** Usually roosts by day in holes formerly dug out by woodpeckers in a giant saguaro cactus but hides also in plants such as mesquite or palo verde. Flies rapidly down from perch to capture prey such as large insects, or may fly along low to ground seeking prey; becomes active soon after dusk. **Voice:** Quite variable, a musical *whee-kee-kee*, repeated is one of the most common.

172. PYGMY OWL, *Glaucidium gnoma.* **Range and habitat:** Common resident around coniferous forests, oak, piñon-juniper and mixed woodlands. **Distinguished by:** *Conspicuous long dark-brown tail, barred with white; a black neck patch edged with white;* numerous white spots on head, back and wings; the *black streakings on the backs are not found in other small earless owls.* **Behavior:** Often active in daytime; flight undulating and shrike-like with abrupt rise to a perch at the end, all with rapid wing-beats; when perched often tilts and wags tail; forages usually by darting suddenly from a hiding place. **Voice:** Soft whistled repeated *tewk-tew-kew.*

173. SAW-WHET OWL, *Aegolius acadicus.* **Range and habitat:** Rather uncommon resident mainly of mountain forests and oak woods in many parts of state. **Distinguished by:** *Wide brown markings on whitish undersides,* except in juvenile which is brown below; *open wing shows rows of white spots,* but closed wing shows irregular white blotches against brown; *no ear tufts;* tail not conspicuous as in 172. **Behavior:** Nocturnal by habit; often described as being a tame owl; at mating time are very noisy with their whistles, and can be decoyed by imitating its call; hunts mainly small rodents, but also a few small birds. Often approach a campfire at night. **Voice:** A variable slow or rapid whistle, *too-too* repeated endlessly; also saw-filing sound.

KINGFISHERS: ORDER CORACIIFORMES, Family Alcedinidae.

174. BELTED KINGFISHER, *Megaceryle alcyon.* **Range and habitat:** Common resident in state near water, breeding mainly in northern half, wintering mainly in southern half. **Distinguished by:** *Bluish-gray above, white below* with grayish breast band, ♀ has second rusty band; *bushy crest;* stout bill and large head. **Behavior:** Wing-beats irregular and deep; dives head-first into water after fish; may hover before diving; often fly rapidly up and down a stream. **Voice:** Loud rattle.

ROADRUNNER, CUCKOOS: ORDER CUCULIFORMES. Family Cuculidae. (in part).

175. ROADRUNNER, *Geococcyx californianus.* **Range and habitat:** Resident mainly from north central California south, usually associated in areas of open ground with scattered vegetation. **Distinguished by:** *Long pointed tail and conspicuous legs; a large gray-brownish-streaked* bird, often with crest erected; toes arranged two forward and two behind. **Behavior:** Fast runner, rarely flying; chases lizards, snakes and large insects, killing by blow of powerful bill. **Voice:** Series of low *coos*, dropping in pitch; also rattling *brrrrrrrrrr!*

LITTLE OWLS

172

173

171

KINGFISHER and ROADRUNNER

♂   ♀

174

♂

COLOR PLATE 33

171. Elf Owl   5-6″
172. Pygmy Owl   7-7½″
173. Saw-whet Owl   7-8″
174. Kingfisher   11-14″
175. Roadrunner   20-24″

175

WHITE-RUMPED WOODPECKERS

COLOR PLATE 34

176.	Red-shafted Flicker	12-14"
177.	Gilded Flicker	12-13"
178.	Yellow-shafted Flicker	12-13"
179A.	Yellow-bellied Sapsucker	8-9"
179B.	"Red-breasted" form	8-9"
180.	Williamson's Sapsucker	9-10"
181.	Acorn Woodpecker	9-10"

WOODPECKERS: ORDER PICIFORMES. Family Picidae. Typically fly with undulating flight pattern, folding wings on down glide and rapidly stroking them on up-sweep; strong chisel-like bill; may drum with bill during courtship; stiff tail props body on tree trunk; toes arranged two forward, two back.

176. RED-SHAFTED FLICKER, *Colpates auratus.* **Range and habitat:** Common resident west of deserts in most open wooded area; often around buildings, orchards, parks. **Distinguished by:** *Salmon-red under wings and tail; red "mustache" mark below cheek of ♂;* all 3 California flickers have whitish breasts with many black spots, a black crescent on breast, and *no white on brownish wings; white rump is conspicuous in flight.* **Behavior:** Flickers are familiarly seen foraging on the ground, but they also dig in trees; often duck head vigorously when alighting. **Voice:** Many notes, including *wick-wick, kee-er, flick-ak-flick-ah.* (Three forms; see also 177-178.)

177. GILDED FLICKER, *Colaptes auratus.* **Range and habitat:** Resident in S.E. along Colorado River Valley in desert scrub and streamside woods. **Distinguished by:** Looks like 176, except for *yellow wing and tail linings; no red crescent in back of head* as in 178. **Behavior:** Similar to 176, but nests in holes in cactus. **Voice:** Similar to 176, but higher shrill *ti-yerr.*

178. YELLOW-SHAFTED FLICKER, *Colaptes auratus.* **Range and habitat:** Unusual transient, scattered in state, habitat like 176. **Distinguished by:** Looks like 176, except for *yellow wing and tail linings and red crescent-shaped mark on back of neck* (different habitats than 177); black instead of red "mustache" on ♂. **Behavior and Voice:** Like 176 (may hybridize with 176).

179A. YELLOW-BELLIED SAPSUCKER, *Sphyrapicus varius* (in part). **Range and habitat:** Summer visitor in woodlands of N.E. California; winter visitor in S.E. **Distinguished by:** Adult ♂, *with white, red and black-striped face and black bib on breast;* immature brown mottled on back, breast and head; both this and race below have distinctive longitudinal white wing stripe and mottled back. **Behavior:** Cuts even rows of holes in trees and return to feed on sap; sometimes flies out like a flycatcher to catch insects in the air; **Voice:** Nasal *chrrrr* or squeal.

179B. RED-BREASTED SAPSUCKER, *Sphyrapicus varius.* **Range and habitat:** Common summer visitor in mountain coniferous forests, streamside and mixed woodlands; also cultivated areas; winter visitor in lowlands south to San Diego. **Distinguished by:** *Bright red hood.* Otherwise as 179A.

180. WILLIAMSON'S SAPSUCKER, *Sphyrapicus thyroideus.* **Range and habitat:** Common resident in higher mountain forests; some winter in nearby lowlands. **Distinguished by:** *Upper parts generally black except for white stripes behind and on wing;* ♀ with brownish head. **Behavior:** As with 179. **Voice:** A nasal *weee-er.*

181. ACORN WOODPECKER, *Melanerpes formicivorus.* **Range and habitat:** Widespread common resident associated with oaks. **Distinguished by:** *Yellow throat, white rump,* only lowland woodpecker showing *wide white wing patches in flight.* **Behavior:** Regularly stores acorns in bark of trees. **Voice:** Repeated *wik-up* or *jay-cup* call.

182. GILA WOODPECKER, *Centurus uropygialis.* **Range and habitat:** Resident in streamside woodland and desert scrub of S.E. California. **Distinguished by:** *Our only desert woodpecker with plain gray-brown belly, head and neck and white wing patches showing on opened wings;* ♂ has red cap, head of ♀ plain; back, rump, tail and wings all barred with black and white. **Behavior:** Very active and noisy, often jerking its head about when perched. Its frequently dug nest holes in Saguaro cacti, willow and cottonwood trees are also used as homes by other birds and animals. Feeds on insects; also fruit of cacti, mistletoes, etc. **Voice:** Rough, low *chrrr-chrrrrrr* and *pic* call.

183. LADDER-BACKED WOODPECKER, *Dendrocopos scalaris.* **Range and habitat:** Primarily a resident in desert scrub and streamside woodlands of S.E. California. **Distinguished by:** *Two black streaks on white face, one V-shaped; yellowish-white belly and sides with faded dark spots;* ♂ with red crown; ♀ with black crown; backs and wings of both with black and white bars; *tail black and not barred.* **Behavior:** Agave, yucca and willow trees seem favored for nesting. **Voice:** Has long rattling cry, also a high-pitched *tchik.* It drums in spring on dry branches.

184. NUTTALL'S WOODPECKER, *Dendrocopos nuttallii.* **Range and habitat:** Resident in hilly country over most of state west of deserts and Sierra Divide, seeming to favor oak and streamside woodlands and cultivated trees. **Distinguished by:** The only woodpecker of its area with *white cross stripes on black back;* ♂ with red on back of head; ♀ with black on top and back of head; *both with black blotch surrounded by white behind eye.* **Behavior:** Eats harmful insects in trees and on ground, plus a few wild fruits and seeds. Often flies up to underside of branch where it hangs upside-down like a nuthatch, foraging for food. Rather quarrelsome. **Voice:** Very high-pitched buzzing cry of *szee-szee-szee-szee;* also a sharp *prrrrt* plus a rattling call.

185. DOWNY WOODPECKER, *Dendrocopos pubescens.* **Range and habitat:** Widespread resident west of deserts and Sierra Divide associated with riparian trees; some association with oak and cultivated trees. **Distinguished by:** *Small size, small bill and white back; single black stripe across white face;* top of head and *neck black in* ♀, *but with red patch on nape of* ♂; outer tail feathers with black bars. **Behavior:** Hops about jerkily on branch, often rearing back a little in search for food, mainly insects. **Voice:** Metallic kink; also rapidly descending notes like whinny of horse; drums bill lightly.

186. HAIRY WOODPECKER, *Dendrocopos villosus.* **Range and habitat:** Resident in open woods of foothills and mountains (generally avoiding deserts and Central Valley). **Distinguished by:** *A large copy of 185; but outer tail feathers plain white.* **Behavior:** Bolder and noisier than 185. **Voice:** Loud kink; long loud rattling cry at same pitch; loud rolling drumming.

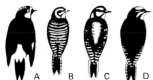

BOLD PLUMAGE PATTERNS

A. White-rumped (seen best in flight, 181)
B. Striped-backed (183, 184)
C. White-backed (185, 186)
D. Black-backed (189)

Striped-backed

White-backed

COLOR PLATE 35

182. Gila Woodpecker   8-10''
183. Ladder-backed Woodpecker   7-7½''
184. Nuttall's Woodpecker   6½-7''
185. Downy Woodpecker   6½-7''
186. Hairy Woodpecker   9-10''

WOODPECKERS

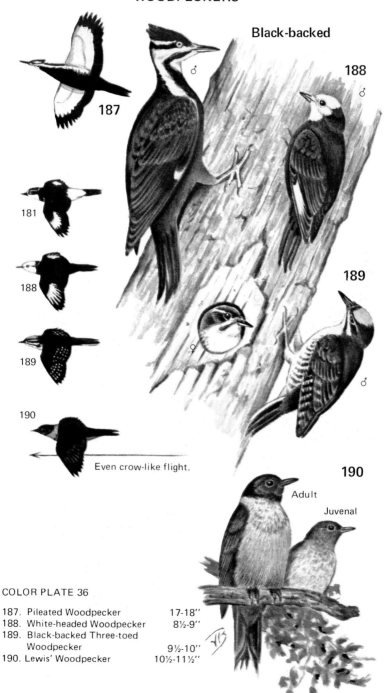

Black-backed

Even crow-like flight.

187. PILEATED WOODPECKER, *Dryocopus pileatus*. **Range and habitat:** Resident in thick coniferous forests from southern Sierra and Sonoma Co. north. **Distinguished by:** *Large size*, general black color, *flaming red, pointed crest; white zig-zag streak down side of neck;* red streak behind bill, *and black streak through eye on white side of head; long conspicuous bill;* white patch on wing most apparent underneath in flight, ♀ lacks red "whisker" mark. **Behavior:** Strong but irregular flapping of large wings in flight. When digging for larvae in trees, it gives a powerful blow with its large bill, striking so hard that the sound carries far through the forest; large chips are chiseled out creating a conspicuous pile at base of tree. Large holes are left in trees. May work on fallen logs. **Voice:** Common call is loud *wi-wi-wii*, or *kek-kek-kek;* also makes deep rolling heavy drumming.

188. WHITE-HEADED WOODPECKER, *Dendrocopos albolarvatus*. **Range and habitat:** Common resident of middle elevation mountain coniferous forests of southern California, Sierra Nevada and west into higher inner coast ranges to the north. **Distinguished by:** *White throat and head, red on nape of neck, black on rest of body* except for *white patch on outer wing feathers.* **Behavior:** Bold, easily watched flying to and from its nest hole in some tree or stump; in foraging alights sideways or even upside down. Nest usually lined with small wood chips. Hunts insects and their larvae in the bark of conifers by prying off layers of the bark and so exposing the prey; sometimes flies up into air like a flycatcher to catch insects. Flight usually direct, heavy and slow. **Voice:** Shrill *wick* or *chik*, often rapidly repeated; also a sharp rattling cry. Drums rather lightly.

189. BLACK-BACKED THREE-TOED WOODPECKER, *Picoides arcticus*. **Range and habitat:** Resident mainly in high Sierra and Cascades in lodgepole and red fir forests. **Distinguished by:** *Solid black back, yellow crown in ♂, black bars on white sides, three toes instead of four on feet.* Black wings are barred with white, tail black with white outer tail feathers. **Behavior:** Leaves evidence of its presence by peeling off large sections of bark from dead trees to get at the insects underneath. Feeds mainly on wood-boring beetles and their larvae, but also on ants and other insects and rarely on fruits and seeds. Often holds head to one side as if listening for insect activity in tree. The swift flight is made with broad undulations. **Voice:** Sharp *pick* or *kick;* drumming loud and rolling.

190. LEWIS' WOODPECKER, *Asyndesmus lewis*. **Range and habitat:** Resident in open oak woodland and mountain coniferous forests south to about latitude 35°; a number winter to the south. **Distinguished by:** *The only dark woodpecker with rose-red belly and cheeks;* gray neck and breast collar. **Behavior:** Flies with even slow crow-like flight; often flies up from perch to catch insect in flycatcher fashion, bobbing head when it alights again. Feeds on insects more on ground and in air than most woodpeckers. **Voice:** Very quiet most of the time, but may give short *chrrr* in spring; sometime sharp metallic *ik-ik-ik* is heard.

RAVEN, CROW AND MAGPIES

PERCHING BIRDS: ORDER PASSERIFORMES (in part). Have three toes in front and one long one behind for perching; most singing birds are found in this order, and most are small or medium-sized.

Crows, Magpies and Jays: Family Corvidae. The Crows and Ravens are the largest of all perching birds. All have heavy general type bills related to their omnivorous diet.

191. COMMON RAVEN, *Corvus corax*. **Range and habitat:** Resident widespread along N.W. coast, in foothills of interior and deserts, occasionally to higher mountains. Habitats occupied must provide open country for foraging and walls or cliffs for nesting. **Distinguished by:** *Black all over like crow, but larger size and with very ruffled appearing throat feathers;* in flight *tail appears wedge-shaped,* not squarish as with crow. **Behavior:** Does more soaring and less flapping than crows, and more feeding on carrion; soars on flat wings instead of partly uptilted as in crow. Ravens in pairs or groups often appear to play with each other in the sky. **Voice:** Deep croaking *krruach* cry; also a hoarse *kor-kor-kor,* deeper than crow's call.

192. COMMON CROW, *Corvus brachyrhynchos*. **Range and habitat:** Common resident in many parts of state, generally avoiding deserts and higher mountains; occupying valleys and foothills with open areas and scattered trees nearby. **Distinguished by:** *All black color; smooth throat, smaller size than Raven,* and tail appears squarish in profile. **Behavior:** When flying, told from Raven or hawk by frequently flapping its wings, and less soaring. Crow flocks appear well-organized, sending out scouts and putting up guards to watch for enemies and sound off when they come near. A flock usually roosts in a grove of trees at night, starting out in the early morning to visit feeding places in long wavering lines, returning at dusk to sleep. **Voice:** Loud *caw-caw-caw.*

193. BLACK-BILLED MAGPIE, *Pica pica*. **Range and habitat:** Resident of valleys near open streamside woods and scattered shrub growth east of Sierra and Cascades. Usually within short distance of thickets. Presence of water critical. **Distinguished by:** *Long flowing greenish-black tail, short blackish-blue-green and white wings, black hood, white belly and black bill.* **Behavior:** Builds a huge domed nest of sticks in a bush or tree. As magpie walks, its tail may be slightly elevated and often twitched. Feeds on great variety of foods, mainly insects; commonly scavenges for dead animals, often along highway. **Voice:** A staccato *eck-eck-eck,* also a nasal *maogh.*

194. YELLOW-BILLED MAGPIE, *Pica nuttalli*. **Range and habitat:** Common resident in and near Central Valley and Coast Ranges, Ventura Co. north to San Francisco Bay; open ground with scattered large trees, or open groves or trees along stream courses favored; oaks, sycamores and cottonwoods most often frequented. **Distinguished by:** Similar to 193 but the *bill and bit of bare skin behind eye yellow.* **Behavior:** Much like 193 but build bulky nests in trees, many to a tree. They fly with their long narrow tail straight out behind. When they walk the tail is held slightly elevated. When they alight they jerk their tail upward, wren-like; very gregarious and are nearly always in talkative groups. **Voice:** Similar to the Black-billed Magpie with little emphasis or resonance; a very vocal bird.

CORVIDS

191

195

196

198

197

192

199

Soaring
flight

198

Straight
flight

193

193

The two native magpies of North America are separated by the Cascade and Sierra-Nevada Mountains. The Black-bill (blue on map) ranges over much of the West (and also northern Eurasia). The Yellow-bill (orange on map) is confined entirely to lowland California.

194

COLOR PLATE 37

191.	Common Raven	21-27″
	Wingspread	4-4½′
192.	Common Crow	17-20″
193.	Black-billed Magpie	17-22″
	Tail	9-12″
194.	Yellow-billed Magpie	16-18″
	Tail	9-10″

Juvenile

195

196

197

198

199

Scrub Jays have a habit of storing acorns and other nuts in autumn. These plantings frequently sprout and may **eventually** crowd out the trees which sheltered them as seedlings.

COLOR PLATE 38

195.	Gray Jay	11-13''
196.	Pinon Jay	9-11¾''
197.	Steller's Jay	12-13½''
198.	Scrub Jay	11-13''
199.	Clark's Nutcracker	12-13''

195. GRAY JAY, *Perisoreus canadensis*. **Range and habitat:** Resident from Mendocino Co. north in coastal forests and in a few places in coniferous forests of higher mountains of north central and N.E. corner of state. **Distinguished by:** *Fluffy gray in appearance with white forehead and throat,* black on back of head; *short rounded wings and long rounded tail;* immature, dark gray above, blackish on head; breast dark gray, white streak by mouth. **Behavior:** Travels in flocks most of year, keeping in touch by soft whistles; flock may mob predators. Is rather bold often being found around camps or other forest establishments, scavenging; in the forest it lives on a wide variety of foods. **Voice:** Harsh screaming calls of *ker-weep,* also weakly-whistled *wheeeyooo,* or soft *shuck.*

196. PIÑON JAY, *Gymnorhinus cyanocephalus.* **Range and habitat:** Resident east of Cascade-Sierra ranges, south into higher mountain ranges of desert and southern California; mainly in piñon-juniper woodlands; rare on west side. **Distinguished by:** *Dull blue except for streaked bluish-white throat; long pointed bill.* **Behavior:** Usually flies in loose flocks, often foraging on the ground; rear part of flock often flies in leap-frog motion over to the front; flight by flapping and glide, not pitching up and down as in most jays. May catch flying insects like a flycatcher. On ground it usually walks or runs rather than hopping. **Voice:** Mewing *quew-wa-ch;* repeated nasal *qweh-qweh!*

197. STELLER'S JAY, *Cyanocitta stelleri.* **Range and habitat:** Common resident over much of state in foothill and mountain coniferous forests, oak, streamside and mixed woodlands. **Distinguished by:** *Head, upper back and chest dark black-brown, rest of body deep blue;* the only jay in California with *a crest;* wings and tail lightly barred. **Behavior:** Very secretive about hiding its nest but very conspicuous in action otherwise; feeds more on fruits, nuts and seeds than on insects, but also occasionally robs a bird nest. Regularly associates with campgrounds. **Voice:** Many harsh notes, including rapid *chey-chey-chey!;* copies harsh cry of Red-tailed Hawk; has loud *kweeck-kweech* and a call like a squeaky gate.

198. SCRUB JAY, *Aphelocoma coerulescens.* **Range and habitat:** Common widespread resident of oak, streamside and mixed woods, chaparral, piñon-juniper woods, and cultivated areas, north and west of deserts generally at lower elevations. **Distinguished by:** *Back brown, rest of upper parts blue;* underparts light gray, except for *dark blue band across breast;* no crest. **Behavior:** When perched, often hangs tail straight down; flies with pitching motion in long shallow curves; bobs head energetically when it alights. Feeds on wide variety of food. **Voice:** Harsh *chey-chey-chey!* higher and usually slower than Steller's; also harsh *krr-wheeek.*

199. CLARK'S NUTCRACKER, *Nucifraga columbiana.* **Range and habitat:** Common resident in higher mountain forests and alpine meadows. **Distinguished by:** *Black tail with white outer tail feathers;* white patches on black wings; body grayish; throat white; bill long and pointed. **Behavior:** Flight and habits rather crow-like; may wander to low country in winter; otherwise mostly a rather nomadic timber line bird. **Feeds extensively** on pine nuts. **Voice:** Harsh grating caw or *kraaaa.*

CHICKEN-LIKE BIRDS: ORDER GALLIFORMES. Bill chicken-like; wings typically short and rounded; in flying burst up suddenly from the ground into full flight, usually traveling only short distance close to ground. Primarily ground birds, foraging with much scratching with feet. See courtship, p. 40.

Grouse: Family Tetraonidae.

200. BLUE GROUSE, *Dendragapus obscurus.* **Range and habitat:** Common resident mainly associated with fir forests of northwest and north central parts of California as well as higher parts of the Sierra. **Distinguished by:** ♂ with dark gray general color; *tail blackish with broad light gray band at tip; orange patch of skin above eye;* ♀ with dark bands at end of tail, otherwise mottled brownish. **Behavior:** In winter dwells mainly in fir forests feeding on fir needles, high up in trees. In summer it comes down on the ground to feed and nest. May fly with burst of speed and then plane out of sight. **Voice:** Loud cackling *cuk-cuk-cuk* when disturbed; ♂ gives ventriloquial calls; may boom using neck sacs.

201. RUFFED GROUSE, *Bonasa umbellus.* **Range and habitat:** Scattered resident in extreme N.W. part of state in streamside and canyon bottom woodlands. **Distinguished by:** *General reddish-brown color above; broad black band at tip of tail; black feathers form ruff on neck;* underparts yellowish-brown with brown bars; sometimes has a phase with mostly gray color. **Behavior:** ♂ struts on log, making loud booming noise with beating wings; spreads tail feathers in courtship (see p. 40). **Voice:** Sharp *quit-quit* when alarmed; ♀ *clucks.*

202. SAGE GROUSE, *Centrocercus urophasianus.* **Range and habitat:** Resident in N.E. of state and east of Sierra south to about Owens Valley. Closely associated with sagebrush. **Distinguished by:** *Distinctive long tail with stiff pointed feathers;* general grayish-brown colors mottled white; black on belly; ♂ has *black on chin with white between it and black throat.* **Behavior:** ♂ shows off to ♀ by strutting with spread tail, making popping noise, or bubbling, while air sacs in neck are greatly inflated. Soft leaves and shoots of the sagebrush are main food. Normally run from disturbance but may rise in heavy, wobbling flight. **Voice:** Gutteral, deep *cuk-cuk-cuk* call.

Pheasant: Family Phasianidae (in part).

203. RING-NECKED PHEASANT, *Phasianus colchicus.* **Range and habitat:** Introduced resident typically found associated with cultivated fields grassland and streamside woodlands. Mainly Central Valley, but occuring elsewhere. **Distinguished by:** *Very long pointed black-barred brown tail;* ♂ *beautifully colored purple, green, reds, with white ring on neck;* ♀ mottled brown with white around eye. **Voice:** Sudden loud squawking cry.

Turkey: Family Meleagrididae.

204. TURKEY, *Meleagris gallopavo.* **Range and habitat:** Introduced resident now found mainly in mountains of parts of Santa Cruz, Monterey and Kern counties. **Distinguished by:** *Very large size, bare head and upper neck;* much like domestic turkey. **Behavior:** Seldom fly, spending most time on ground. Quite timid. **Voice:** Male gobbles.

154

CHICKEN-LIKE GAMEBIRDS

COLOR PLATE 39

200. Blue Grouse   16-19"
201. Ruffed Grouse   15-19"
202. Sage Grouse   21-30"
203. Ring-necked Pheasant   20-33"
204. Turkey   36-48"

SMALLER CHICKEN-LIKE GAMEBIRDS

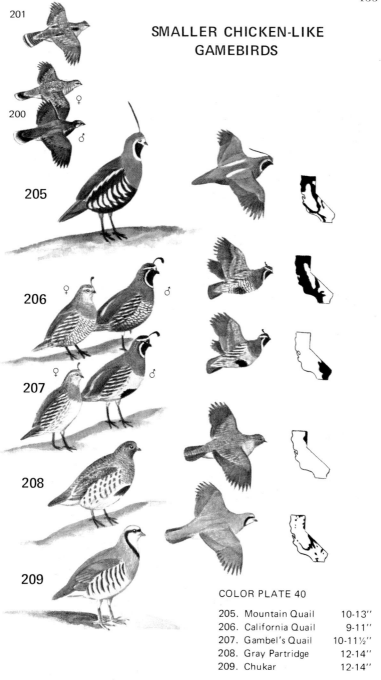

201

200

♀

♂

205

206 ♀ ♂

207 ♀ ♂

208

209

COLOR PLATE 40

205. Mountain Quail   10-13"
206. California Quail   9-11"
207. Gambel's Quail   10-11½"
208. Gray Partridge   12-14"
209. Chukar   12-14"

Quails and Partridges: Family Phasianidae (in part).

205. MOUNTAIN QUAIL, *Oreortyx pictus.* **Range and habitat:** Common resident of most mountains except in central coastal region; associated with brushy vegetation and a mixture of open mixed woodland and brush. **Distinguished by:** Distinctive *straight plume; bluish hood except for white streak down neck and around face* and *reddish-brown throat;* wings and tail brownish-gray; white streaks on sides of back and on lower sides of body. **Behavior:** Hard to flush, as seeks cover in thick brush or woods. Feeds on seeds, leaves, and other parts of plants but takes some insects in warm seasons, feeding mainly in early morning and evening, resting during midday in brush. Flight noisy and swift when flushed. **Voice:** A loud resonant *tu-yoork* or *ti-wcook; cut-cut* of ♀ to young; also has tremulous whistles.

206. CALIFORNIA QUAIL, *Lophortyx californicus.* **Range and habitat:** Resident in most of California except central Sierra and S.E. deserts, generally associated with interrupted brushland and adjoining open grassy areas. **Distinguished by:** *Black plume curves forward from reddish-brown crown, which is surrounded by white ring in* ♂; also has black throat, rimmed by white; breast blue, belly brown blotched with white; white streaks on sides. ♀ with duller colors and gray throat streaked with white. **Behavior:** Usually seen in larger flocks than above, and much more inclined to fly if disturbed; flocks break up during breeding season and sexes pair up. Precocial young are closely watched by parents, and readily respond to calls. A sentinel usually stands watch over a feeding flock. **Voice:** Rallying cry of *quer-ca-go!* a clucking *tik-tik* in flock; ♀ calls young with a sharp *pt-pt-ptpt!*

207. GAMBEL'S QUAIL, *Lophortyx gambelii.* **Range and habitat:** Resident in drier S.E. associated with desert thickets and nearby open ground; daily drinking water limiting. **Distinguished by:** Same general appearance as 206, but ♂ has *large black blotch on otherwise unmarked whitish belly,* while ♀ *has pure white belly.* Both sexes have white-streaked reddish-brown sides. **Behavior:** As with most quail, ♂ courts ♀, displaying top-knot, tail and wing-feathers, while loudly challenging rivals. When disturbed usually runs and hides in brush rather than flushing. **Voice:** Similar calls to 206.

208. GRAY PARTRIDGE, *Perdix perdix.* **Range and habitat:** Introduced resident in far N.E. corner of state in grasslands and cultivated areas. **Distinguished by:** *Quail-like but no top-knot;* general brownish and gray color, with *gray flanks marked with crescents or wavy lines;* dark reddish-brown patch on white belly. Rusty on sides of tail in flight. **Behavior:** In vigorous fights between males they buffet each other with their wings. Usually run from enemies rather than fly, but are strong fliers; feeds more on insects than do quail. **Voice:** *Kee-uck* clucking notes, the first more shrill and nasal, the second rasping.

209. CHUKAR, *Alectoris chukar.* **Range and habitat:** Introduced resident in more arid mountain ranges mainly in eastern and southern parts of state in desert scrub, sagebrush and streamside vegetation. **Distinguished by:** Sexes alike; *cream-colored face with black border; whitish on sides with moon-like markings;* legs reddish. **Behavior:** Explodes into flight when flushed, lands swiftly running; rather aggressive in behavior: **Voice:** Calls *chuka, chuka.*

PIGEONS, DOVES: ORDER COLUMBIFORMES, *Family Columbidae*. Distinguished by small heads, short legs, pointed wings, fanned or tapered tails and swift flight; also bob heads when walking. They are mainly seed, grain, acorn and fruit eaters.

210. BAND-TAILED PIGEON, *Columba fasciata*. **Range and habitat:** Widespread resident generally west of Sierra crest entire length of state. In summer oak and mixed woods of mountains; in winter oak woods of lower elevations. Move a good deal depending on acorn crop. **Distinguished by:** *Broad gray band across end of wide tail,* white crescent on back of neck of adults; bluish-gray *back and wings contrast with blackish tips of wings;* bill yellow with dark tip. **Behavior:** Roost mainly in trees; feeds on nuts and berries, especially acorns; forage in trees, bushes and on ground; usually moving in flocks. Flocks rise with a loud whirr of wings when disturbed and fly off rapidly. Usually draws head and neck close to breast when at rest, otherwise small head thrust out. **Voice:** The repeated owl-like soft-sounding *ooo-cooo* or *whoo-ooo-cooo* is hollow-noted.

211. ROCK DOVE (domestic pigeon), *Columba livia*. **Range and habitat:** Widespread introduced resident, generally associated with man in both rural and urban situations. **Distinguished by:** Many variations in color, from almost pure white to quite dark, but the commoner dark colored doves always show a *white rump, two long curved black bars on the inner half of each wing,* and a *wide black bar at the end of the tail.* Most of upper parts mainly grayish-blue except for black tinged outer wing coverts; *head and lower body usually purplish-gray and iridescent.* **Behavior:** A ground feeder, but usually roosts in trees or buildings; glides with wings somewhat raised up. **Voice:** Seems to gurgle as it gives a soft *cooo-rooo-cooo.*

212. SPOTTED DOVE, *Streptopelia chinensis*. **Range and habitat:** Introduced resident found mainly in Santa Barbara to San Diego region in cultivated lands, cities and streamside woodland. **Distinguished by:** In the adult the *dark general colors are offset by beaded or lace-like pattern of black and white on the back and sides of the neck,* and by the *white side tips of the long rounded tail.* Immature more yellowish-brown on neck and breast and without neck pattern. **Behavior:** Favors bushes and trees, feeding on berries, seeds and nuts. **Voice:** Soft, *coo-whoo-coo-coo* or low whistles with a rising inflection.

213. WHITE-WINGED DOVE, *Zenaida asiatica*. **Range and habitat:** Primarily a summer resident in S.E. California, in desert scrub and streamside woodlands. **Distinguished by:** Only dove with *large white wing patches contrasting with general dark olive-brown colors of body; tail rounded* instead of pointed (as in Mourning Dove) and with outer tail feathers *white at tips.* **Behavior:** Nests in colonies in thickets such as mesquite or low trees. When courting, ♂ flies up high, spreads its wings to soar and tipping its wings from one side to the other slides down towards the ♀. Often gathers in flocks to feed in the stubble fields. **Voice:** Cooing, crowing call, rather harsh, of *coo-uh-kuk-oo-coo-coo-ee-coooo!*

PIGEONS

COLOR PLATE 41

210. Band-tailed Pigeon   14-16"
211. Rock Dove   14-16"
212. Spotted Dove   13-14"
213. White-winged Dove   11-12½"

DOVES and CUCKOO

214

215

216

217

COLOR PLATE 42

214.	Mourning Dove	10½-13"
215.	Ringed Turtle Dove	10-13"
216.	Ground Dove	5½-6½"
217.	Yellow-billed Cuckoo	12½-13½"

214. MOURNING DOVE, *Zenaida macroura.* **Range and habitat:** Common resident, widespread except higher mountains in summer, in winter more generally lower elevations in Central Valley and southern 2/3 of state; frequents open ground in mixed woodland, grassland and brushy areas. **Distinguished by:** *Long central pointed tail feathers of brown; other tail feathers gray, tipped with white;* back brown, wings grayish; pinkish-brown breast; reddish-brown head small; red feet. **Behavior:** Fly in pairs during breeding season, otherwise in flocks, rather swiftly, with tail flashing white; wings whistling. Like most doves, they walk with a dainty motion with body only a little off the ground. They are commonly seen resting on telephone lines. **Voice:** Soft plaintive heart-tugging *coo-coo-cuk-coo* of ♂ heard in spring and summer.

215. RINGED TURTLE DOVE, *Streptopelia risoria.* **Range and habitat:** Introduced resident concentrated in western half of southern California, in cultivated areas, buildings, parks and streamside woodlands. **Distinguished by:** *Narrow black ring circles back and sides of whitish neck; much paler brown in general color* than Mourning Dove; tail shorter, wider and more rounded with white in outer corners. Shows dark outer wing feathers in flight, contrasting with sandy appearance of rest of body and wings. **Behavior:** Makes a rather flimsy stick platform for its nest in a tree. **Voice:** Purring *hooo-cooo-hrooo.*

216. GROUND DOVE, *Columbina passerina.* **Range and habitat:** Resident in S.E. California in streamside woodlands, cultivated areas and desert scrub, generally not too far from water. **Distinguished by:** *Very small size, short dumpy appearance, short dark tail and wings that flash reddish-brown in flight;* body gray to dark colors. **Behavior:** Flies with very rapid wing-beats; usually nests on or near to ground, building frail saucer-like nest of grasses and rootlets. Feeds mainly on ground on seeds, bobbing head as it moves; often appears rather tame. **Voice:** Single soft whistled *coo-coo-coo;* closer the notes may sound doubled, like *coo-oo-coo-oo,* each with rising inflection.

CUCKOOS, ROADRUNNERS: ORDER CUCULIFORMES (in part).

Cuckoos: Family Cuculidae (in part). Slender birds with long pyramid-shaped and stepped profile tails, and rather short rounded wings. Upper mandible curves down.

217. YELLOW-BILLED CUCKOO, *Coccyzus americanus.* **Range and habitat:** Scattered summer visitor in valleys west of Sierra and south to Mexico border; typically associated with willow and cottonwood habitat along water courses. **Distinguished by:** *Color brown above, but reddish-brown on outer wings; yellow lower bill,* upper bill dark and curved downward; long blackish tail feathers with large white spots; body white below. **Behavior:** A rather sluggish flier, but its extreme secretiveness generally keeps it out of sight. The nest is usually a slightly-built saucer of twigs well-hidden in a bush or small tree. When alighting on a branch often slowly raises its tail. **Voice:** Explosive and loud for such a shy bird, the song a rapid series of throaty notes, like *kak-kuk-ka-ka-kak, kyeow-kowp-kowp!* It also may give some soft low dove-like notes of *coo-coo-coo.*

SWIFTS AND HUMMINGBIRDS: ORDER APODIFORMES (in part).

Swifts: Family Apodidae. Swiftly beating wings give "twinkling" effect; wings characteristically curve downward, especially when sailing between bursts of wing-beats; insects captured in flight. Long narrow wings and short tails diagnostic.

218. VAUX'S SWIFT, *Chaetura vauxi.* **Range and habitat:** Summer visitor along coast north of Monterey associated mainly with open coniferous forest; widespread migrant. **Distinguished by:** *Brownish-black general color; ashy below and specially whitish about throat*, small size for swift. Tail very short and inconspicuous. **Behavior:** Nests in trees in forests; flies with zigzag rapid twistings over forest clearings. **Voice:** Faint rapid *chip-chip* notes.

219. WHITE-THROATED SWIFT, *Aeronautes saxatalis.* **Range and habitat:** Widespread summer visitor except along N.W. coast; resident to the south; mainly in open country, roosting in cliffs. **Distinguished by:** *White on throat and middle of breast and flanks*, rest of bird blackish. **Behavior:** Nests in crevices in cliffs; flocks fly in criss-crossing high-speed patterns high in sky. **Voice:** High *jee-jee-jee* twitter.

220. BLACK SWIFT, *Cypseloides niger.* **Range and habitat:** Summer visitor along central California coast, central and south Sierra and some southern California mountains; around cliffs and open areas. **Distinguished by:** Mainly all *black color and slightly forked tail.* **Behavior:** Sudden sharp turns in flight, with plunges and upward sweeps at high speed; nests on remote cliffs. **Voice:** Twittering *pik-pik.*

NIGHTHAWKS AND POOR-WILLS: ORDER CAPRIMULGIFORMES. **Family Caprimulgidae.** Mainly night or dusk-flying insect feeders with small bills but large mouths, and large flat heads; eyes become very large; flight mothlike; usually nest on ground.

221. POOR-WILL, *Phalaenoptilus nuttallii.* **Range and habitat:** Widespread in scattered brush country generally avoiding N.W. and Central Valley; summer visitor to the north, resident to the south. **Distinguished by:** Rather *squat, dumpy appearance;* dark brown colors, except for *white bar on throat and white-tipped outer tail feathers;* wings rounded. **Behavior:** Usually crouches on ground in dusk, springing up suddenly to catch passing insect. **Voice:** Soft *poor-will* call.

222. LESSER NIGHTHAWK, *Chordeiles acutipennis.* **Range and habitat:** Summer visitor from north central California south, in dry brushy country. **Distinguished by:** *Dark colors with white throat band,* white band near tail tip and *whitish bars near tips of long narrow wings.* **Behavior:** Flies at dusk, near ground or close to tree tops, darting from side to side to catch insects with wide mouth. **Voice:** Mewing *waa-waa-woo,* and purring sound.

223. COMMON NIGHTHAWK, *Chordeiles minor.* **Range and habitat:** Summer visitor in open coniferous forest of high mountains and on N.W. coast; scattered elsewhere. **Distinguished by:** Looks like 222, but *white patch on wing farther from wing-tip.* **Behavior:** Active during day in sky as well as at dusk; dives earthward making sound with wings. **Voice:** Nasal *pee-ent!* cry.

SWIFTS and GOATSUCKERS

Pattern comparison between swifts and swallows as seen from a distance.

COLOR PLATE 43

218.	Vaux's Swift	4-5''
219.	White-throated Swift	7-8''
220.	Black Swift	6-7''
221.	Poor-will	7-8''
222.	Lesser Nighthawk	8-9''
223.	Common Nighthawk	8½-10''

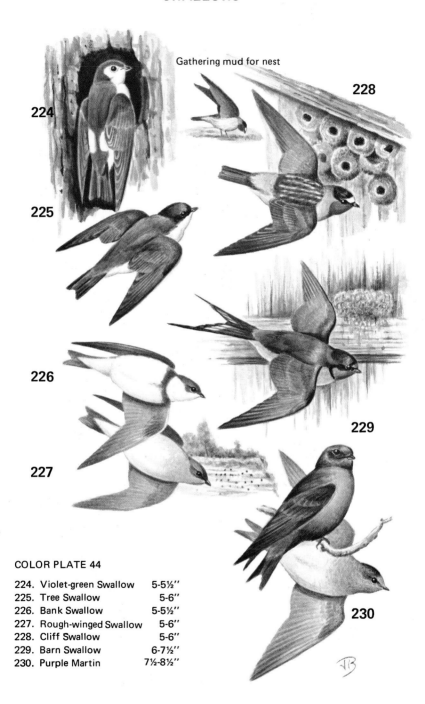

Gathering mud for nest

224

228

225

226

227

229

230

COLOR PLATE 44

224. Violet-green Swallow   5-5½"
225. Tree Swallow   5-6"
226. Bank Swallow   5-5½"
227. Rough-winged Swallow   5-6"
228. Cliff Swallow   5-6"
229. Barn Swallow   6-7½"
230. Purple Martin   7½-8½"

PERCHING BIRDS: ORDER PASSERIFORMES (in part; see Jays, Crows)

Swallows: Family Hirundinidae. Long pointed wings and usually notched or deeply-forked tails are characteristic; legs and bill short; mouth wide, capturing insects in flight; regularly seen perching on wires.

224. VIOLET-GREEN SWALLOW, *Tachycineta thalassina.* **Range and habitat:** Widespread abundant migrant and summer visitor in low mountainous areas; some winter from Santa Barbara south; in open country where canyons and cliffs present; open woods and forest edges. **Distinguished by:** *Iridescent greenish or purplish-black back and wings;* white of underparts extends up on *sides of face and on sides of rump.* **Behavior:** Nests in cavities; graceful, sweeping pursuit of insects with rapid flapping of wings. **Voice:** 2-3 weak *tseep-seet* notes.

225. TREE SWALLOW, *Iridoprocne bicolor.* **Range and habitat:** Common widespread summer visitor and migrant, mainly in interior valleys near water, providing trees present for nesting; a few may winter to the far south. **Distinguished by:** ♂ with *bright green or blue-black above, bright white below;* ♀ and immature with upper parts brown. **Behavior:** Commonly nest in cavities. **Voice:** *Tsee-tee* or a twitter.

226. BANK SWALLOW, *Riparia riparia.* **Range and habitat:** Migrant and summer visitor in lower elevations mainly of southern half of state; open country associated with soil banks. **Distinguished by:** *Brown above, white below; a dark band across white breast.* **Behavior:** Large colonies; dig holes for nests in cliffs or banks usually near water. **Voice:** Soft *brrrt* or *bzzz-bzzzz.*

227. ROUGH-WINGED SWALLOW, *Stelgidopteryx ruficollis.* **Range and habitat:** Summer visitor and migrant mainly of lower elevations; associated with low earth and rock banks. **Distinguished by:** *Brown above; breast and throat brownish-gray,* no distinct collar; *white belly.* **Behavior:** Nests in banks, but in small groups or alone. **Voice:** Harsh weak *prrrt* call.

228. CLIFF SWALLOW, *Petrochelidon pyrrhonota.* **Range and habitat:** Abundant widespread summer visitor and migrant except higher mountains, drier deserts; around inland cliffs, buildings, open country with water source nearby. **Distinguished by:** *Only square-tailed swallow; orange-brown rump; top of head steely-blue;* dark throat and whitish forehead. **Behavior:** Build gourdlike mud nests under overhangs. **Voice:** Alarmed *kyeeer;* low *chrrrr,* squeaks.

229. BARN SWALLOW, *Hirundo rustica.* **Range and habitat:** Common migrant and summer visitor, mainly in lower country north of Bakersfield; in cliffs, buildings, open country with water in vicinity; uncommon in southern California; a few winter in S.E. **Distinguished by:** *Forked tail; bluish-black above, orange-brown below and on forehead.* **Behavior:** Has open mud nests on cliffs or in buildings. **Voice:** Soft twitter or shrill *eet-eet.*

230. PURPLE MARTIN, *Progne subis.* **Range and habitat:** Widespread irregular summer visitor in open wooded areas of lowlands into low mountains; may associate with man. **Distinguished by:** *Deeply notched tail;* ♂ *bluish-black all over;* ♀ brownish. **Behavior:** Frequently soars. **Voice:** Lilting song ends in gutteral trill; call gutteral twitter.

Tyrant Flycatchers: Family Tyrannidae. Large heads, short legs and broad bills are distinctive; have habit of perching on conspicuous perch, then suddenly darting out to catch flying insect, usually returning to same perch.

231. EASTERN KINGBIRD, *Tyrannus tyrannus.* **Range and habitat:** Uncommon summer visitor along Nevada border in open country with scattered trees or shrubs, streamside vegetation and cultivated areas; scattered migrant elsewhere. **Distinguished by:** Generally *dark upper parts, grayish to white below, white-tipped black tail.* **Behavior:** May quiver in flight, as though using only wing-tips; like most kingbirds it dives and strikes at crows, hawks, owls and other birds. **Voice:** Shrill, dry sputtering *zee-zee-zee* or *hit-hit-hitter.*

232. WESTERN KINGBIRD, *Tyrannus verticalis.* **Range and habitat:** Widespread common summer visitor primarily in interior valleys and adjacent hills with widely scattered trees; common in open cultivated areas. **Distinguished by:** *Black tail bordered by white on sides; yellowish beneath, pale gray head and back, whitish throat* (not as sharply defined as Cassin's); wings brownish. **Behavior:** Very similar to that of 231. Puts saucer-like nest of grass, twigs, etc. on branch or building ledge. **Voice:** Very noisy with many shrill notes, including a peevish, sharp *whit,* and a *whig-er-whig.*

233. CASSIN'S KINGBIRD, *Tyrannus vociferans.* **Range and habitat:** Resident mainly in inner coast range valleys south from San Benito Co. in open country with widely scattered trees or other suitable perches. In summer some move to parts of arid S.E. **Distinguished by:** Similar to 232, but *black tail without white sides,* and has a *dark olive-gray back; distinct white patch on throat.* **Behavior:** Often sits still for a long time; usually quieter than above birds. **Voice:** Harsh low *chrr-kee-deeyar* call; also high *kee-ee-ee.*

234. ASH-THROATED FLYCATCHER, *Myiarchus cinerascens.* **Range and habitat:** Common summer visitor and migrant, primarily in dry low country in chaparral or brushy areas with scattered trees; some in cultivated areas; a few winter in the south. **Distinguished by:** Similar to Western Kingbird, but with *reddish-brown tail, dark back, 2 white bars on wing and pale yellowish-white belly.* **Behavior:** A quiet sedate bird; nests in cavities. **Voice:** Sharp, short *key-whrrr, prrrrt* and *pwit* calls, bickering cries between rivals.

235. SAY'S PHOEBE, *Sayornis saya.* **Range and habitat:** Generally a widespread resident in drier interior valleys and hills, greatest numbers in southern half of state east and west of Sierra; open areas with scattered vegetation. Many localities in winter. **Distinguished by:** *Dark to grayish-brown above, reddish-brown belly, grayish-brown throat and breast.* **Behavior:** Feeds close to or on ground. **Voice:** *Phee-ee* call; also repeated *pt-see-ar.*

236. BLACK PHOEBE, *Sayornis nigricans.* **Range and habitat:** Common resident in most middle to low elevations mainly west of Sierra divide; primarily associated with water, nearby tree-shrub vegetation and banks. **Distinguished by:** *Upper parts and breast black; belly white.* **Behavior:** Often perches alone, frequently wags tail; nest cup of mud and grass put on cliff ledge, trees or on building beams. **Voice:** *Fee-bee!* or *tsee-see-tee* calls.

231

234

232

235

236

Compare Tails
and Throats.

233

A

A number of birds occasionally "fly-catch" but the Tyrannids systematically use this method. Their distinctive foraging behavior starts from a lookout perch from which they launch out and capture flying insects. An audible "click" can often be heard as the aerial prey is snapped up. Frequently they return to the same perch to await another insect.

Most flycatchers nest in the forks or crotches of tree branches (A.); some use man-made structures such as building beams beneath buildings and bridges (B.); the Ash-throat is the only California flycatcher that is a hole-nester (C.).

232　238
233　239
234　240-44
237

COLOR PLATE 45

231. Eastern Kingbird　　　　　　8-9"
232. Western Kingbird　　　　　　8-9½"
233. Cassin's Kingbird　　　　　　8½-9"
234. Ash-throated Flycatcher　8-8½"
235. Say's Phoebe　　　　　　　　7-8"
236. Black Phoebe　　　　　　　　6½-7"

237

♂   ♀

239

238

EMPIDONAX
GROUP

240-244

These almost identical small flycatchers are best identified by voice
and habitat.

♀   **245**

♂

B   C

235
236   **234**
244

Hutton's
Vireo

The Ruby-crowned
Kinglet and Hutton's
Vireo are easily con-
fused. See page 182.

♂   **246**

♀

COLOR PLATE 46

237. Olive-sided Flycatcher   7-8''
238. Western Wood Pewee   6-6½''
239. Vermilion Flycatcher   5½-6½''
240-44. Empidonax Flycatchers 5½-6''
245. Ruby-crowned Kinglet   4-4½''
246. Golden-crowned Kinglet   3½-4''

237. OLIVE-SIDED FLYCATCHER, *Nuttallornis borealis*. Range and habitat: Widespread summer visitor in open coniferous forests, streamside woods and eucalyptus groves. Distinguished by: Very similar to 238, but *larger and slightly darker; two dark chest patches are separated by wide white stripe; two white patches on sides of rump* show in flight. Behavior: Prefers forest solitudes; defends territory. Voice: *Pee-pee* or *pee-peet-peer.*

238. WESTERN WOOD PEWEE, *Contopus sordidulus*. Range and habitat: Widespread summer visitor and migrant common in wooded streamsides, oak woods, open coniferous forests and cultivated areas. Distinguished by: *No white eye-ring, 2 white wing-bars; breast separated by light line down middle.* Behavior: Flits tail with each call. Voice: Nasal *pee-weeee!*

239. VERMILION FLYCATCHER, *Pyrocephalus rubinus*. Range and habitat: Resides in desert scrub and streamside woods of S.E.; unusual visitor to S.W. Distinguished by: ♂ *bright scarlet crown and underparts;* ♀ and immature brown above; black tail; *faded white wing-bars; orange-yellow tinge on lower belly.* Behavior: ♂ defends nest heroicly, otherwise appears tame. Voice: Sharp *pssk;* ♂ utters weak *pet-a-see* in flight, repeats while head jerks.

The following 6 species of small Empidonax flycatchers are identified by habits, habitats, and voice in breeding season. All appear as in colorplate.

240A. ALDER (TRAILL'S) FLYCATCHER, *Empidonax alnorum*. Range and habitat: Widespread common summer visitor in willow thickets and wet, bushy mountain meadows; less habitat restriction in migration. Behavior: Retiring; keeps out of sight. Voice: Low *see-bee-do* notes, sharp *wee-oo-o-wit.*

240B. WILLOW FLYCATCHER, *Empidonax traillii*. Range and habitat: Same as 240A. Behavior: Shy. Voice: *Wheep-a-deear* or explosive *sitz-beep.* Call, a sharp *twhit.*

241. HAMMOND'S FLYCATCHER, *Empidonax hammondii*. Range and habitat: Widespread transient; summer visitor in red fir and lodgepole pine forests. Behavior: Spends most of time high in trees. Voice: A rapidly repeated *seh-put;* a burring *tsoor-rr-pp*, and a rising *tseeep.*

242. DUSKY FLYCATCHER, *Empidonax oberholseri*. Range and habitat: Summer visitor in higher mountains, in chaparral with scattered trees and open forest usually feeding in top branches. Behavior: One of two Empidonax flycatchers that wag tail; Dusky moves tail rapidly forward, then quickly back. Voice: Rapid whistles of declining pitch with sharp rising note.

243. GRAY FLYCATCHER, *Empidonax wrightii*. Range and habitat: Common summer visitor in piñon-juniper and sagebrush east of Sierra crest; transient winter visitor south in thickets. Behavior: Wags tail with a quick flick backward. Voice: A strong *chee-weep* or soft high *cheeep.*

244. WESTERN FLYCATCHER, *Empidonax difficilis*. Range and habitat: Common summer visitor in mixed woods near water at mid to low elevations; widespread transient. Behavior: Both ♂ and ♀ devoted parents. Voice: Rising *tss-eet* wheezy note; soft *Wheet* or *sss-seet, speek.*

Kinglets and Gnatcatchers: Family Sylviidae. Small very active birds.

245. RUBY-CROWNED KINGLET, *Regulus calendula*. Range and habi-

tat: Summer visitor in high elevation coniferous forests; winter visitor in lowland woodlands and thickets. **Distinguished by:** *Small size, white eye-ring.* **Behavior:** Nervous flicking of wings. **Voice:** Soft shrill *ti-dee-dee*, song.

246. GOLDEN-CROWNED KINGLET, *Regulus satrapa.* **Range and habitat:** Summer resident in high mountains and from Bay area north along coast in coniferous forests; widespread common winter visitor in lowlands west of Sierra south to Los Angeles latitude in fairly dense vegetation. **Distinguished by:** *Small size,* bright *orange-yellow crown bordered by black and with a white band above eye.* **Behavior:** Continuous flicking of wings. **Voice:** High thin *see see see* call; song uses same notes rising, then dropping away.

247. BLUE-GRAY GNATCATCHER, *Polioptila caerulea.* **Range and habitat:** In summer resides in low to mid elevations, central California in chaparral thickets; resident western southern California; common winter visitor in southern lowlands and S.E. deserts. **Distinguished by:** *White eye-ring, bluish-gray back and head* (except forehead of ♂ black in spring and summer) long black tail with white sides, mainly white underneath. **Behavior:** May do some flycatching. **Voice:** Song a quiet warble; note a sibilant *speeeee.*

248. BLACK-TAILED GNATCATCHER, *Polioptila melanura.* **Range and habitat:** Resident in S.E. deserts and on coast, from Ventura Co. south in desert scrub and chaparral. **Distinguished by:** Similar to above, but *tail largely black underneath, and black cap in ♂.* **Behavior:** Both gnatcatchers flip their tails erratically. **Voice:** Harsh *chee-ee-eee;* mewing *pee-e-ee* call.

Creepers: Family Certhiidae. Small, short-legged, down-curved bill.

249. BROWN CREEPER, *Certhia familiaris.* **Range and habitat:** Common in coniferous forests and woodlands. **Distinguished by:** *Slender, brown and white downward-curved bill.* **Behavior:** Tail used as prop in climbing trees to hunt insects. **Voice:** High-pitched lisping *tsee-tsee-sisisi-tsee.*

Chickadees, Titmice, Bushtits: Family Paridae. Feed on insects on twigs.

250. PLAIN TITMOUSE, *Parus inornatus.* **Range and habitat:** Common resident at low to mid elevations in open woodland, mainly oak, and piñon-juniper, also cultivated trees; irregular east of Sierra. **Distinguished by:** *Small gray bird with a crest.* **Behavior:** Very inquisitive, active, constantly foraging for food in cracks. **Voice:** *Sick-a-dee* or soft melodious *sweety-sweety.*

251. VERDIN, *Auriparus flaviceps.* **Range and habitat:** Common resident in desert scrub (such as mesquite) of S.E. **Distinguished by:** *Black line between bill and eye contrasts with yellow head and throat;* rest of upper parts ashy-gray except for *reddish-brown patch on bend of wing.* **Behavior:** Jerky flight between bushes; may forage upside down on twigs like chickadee. **Voice:** Soft *tzee-tee-ee* song; or sharp buzzing *tzzeee*, and staccato *tsik-tsik-tsik.*

252. BUSHTIT, *Psaltriparus minimus.* **Range and habitat:** Widespread; resides in bushes and trees of oak, piñon-juniper and streamside woods, chaparral and cultivated areas except high Sierra and low deserts. **Distinguished by:** *Tiny gray-backed bird with comparatively long tail.* **Behavior:** Flies in small twittering flocks, moving nervously from bush to tree gleaning insects; pairs build elaborate hanging nests. **Voice:** Lisping high twitter.

♀

250

247   ♂

248   ♂

251   ♀

249   ♂   252

Nest under loose bark.

COLOR PLATE 47

247. Blue-gray Gnatcatcher   4½-5"
248. Black-tailed Gnatcatcher   4-4½"
249. Brown Creeper   5-5½"
250. Plain Titmouse   5-5½"
251. Verdin   4-4½"
252. Bushtit   4-4½"

CHICKADEES and NUTHATCHES

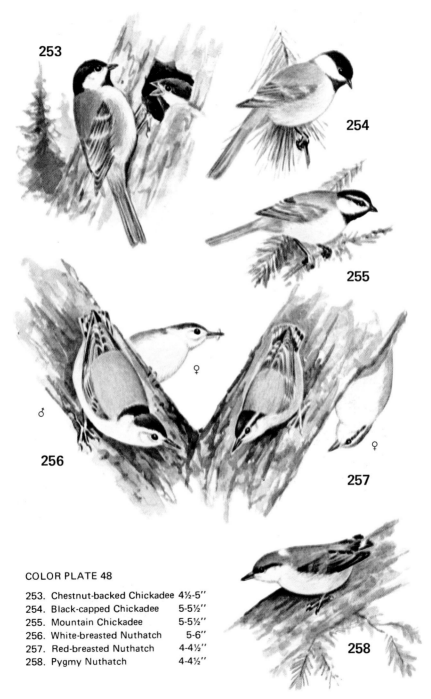

253. CHESTNUT-BACKED CHICKADEE, *Parus rufescens*. **Range and habitat:** Resident along coastal slopes from San Luis Obispo Co. north, in coastal forest, streamside and oak woodlands and cultivated areas among trees. **Distinguished by:** *Reddish-brown back and sides, black cap and throat and white cheeks.* **Behavior:** Very active, often hanging upside down while feeding, as do other chickadees; may forage high in foliage but usually nest in cavities fairly close to ground; readily associate with other small birds, but readily scold an owl or other enemy. **Voice:** Many varying notes, including a rasping *sick-sick-a-dee-dee!*, a harsh *see-see* or *zzee-zzee*, a sharp startled *sik-ah!*

254. BLACK-CAPPED CHICKADEE, *Parus atricapillus*. **Range and habitat:** Resident in N.W. corner of state mainly associated with deciduous trees along water courses. **Distinguished by:** *White sides of head contrast with black top of head;* pale to dark gray back, wings edged with white on gray-black, sides buff. **Behavior:** Similar to that of 253; nests usually made by digging out hole in dead tree branch where wood is very friable. **Voice:** Prolonged whistle; also has *tee-dee-dee* and *dee-dee-dee* notes, and a *tsick-a-dee*.

255. MOUNTAIN CHICKADEE, *Parus gambeli*. **Range and habitat:** Common resident in coniferous forests of mountains entire length of state; occasional winter visitor at lower levels in oak woods. **Distinguished by:** *Black head cap broken by white stripe over eye; white cheeks contrast with black throat, rest of upper parts gray.* **Behavior:** Similar to 253 and 254; forages in peripheral twigs and foliage; usually does not dig own nest hole. **Voice:** A sweet 3-4 noted song *see-dee-dee*, with plaintive down-drop; *sip* or *see*.

Nuthatches: Family Sittidae. Forage for insects up and down bark of trees; often climb down trunk head first; nest in holes.

256. WHITE-BREASTED NUTHATCH, *Sitta carolinensis*. **Range and habitat:** Widespread common resident in foothill and mountain oak woodland and coniferous forest; generally avoid N.W. coast, Central Valley and lower deserts. **Distinguished by:** *Bluish-gray back, black cap and back of neck and white breast;* area under tail reddish-brown, white at sides of tail. **Behavior:** Typically forage on trunks and larger limbs; occasionally forage close to or on ground; do not dig own nest holes. **Voice:** Nasal *yank yank* calls.

257. RED-BREASTED NUTHATCH, *Sitta canadensis*. **Range and habitat:** Common resident in high mountain coniferous forests, especially fir; mainly north half of state some to higher mountains of the south; occasional winter visitor at lower levels in mixed trees. **Distinguished by:** *Black top of head and black streak through eye with white above and below; breast and belly reddish-brown.* **Behavior:** Typically forage in upper most part of trees often with mixed band of other small birds; dig own nest holes. **Voice:** Repeated nasal *yank yank* calls, higher than 256.

258. PYGMY NUTHATCH, *Sitta pygmaea*. **Range and habitat:** Common resident mainly in pines of most mountains and along central coast; some winter movement into adjacent areas. **Distinguished by:** *Gray-brown cap runs down over eye; white throat; gray back.* **Behavior:** Jerking, bobbing flight; usually forage high in trees, typically in small flocks; continuously call to one another; dig own nest holes. **Voice:** Staccato *tee-dee;* weak *ket-ket*.

Wrens: Family Troglodytidae. Small; restless brown-backed birds with sharp slender bills for insect-eating; tails barred and often cocked up.

259. WINTER WREN, *Troglodytes troglodytes.* **Range and habitat :** Common resident in N.W. coastal forest, south to Monterey Co. and in mountain forest west slope central Sierra; winter visitor as far south as Los Angeles. **Distinguished by:** *Very small for a wren, very stubby tail;* dark brown above, barred, brownish belly; light line over eye. **Behavior:** Does much bobbing; extremely active, generally near ground, with tail cocked over the back. **Voice:** Song of rapid high-pitched clear quavering notes; hard *kt-kt* call.

260. HOUSE WREN, *Troglodytes aedon.* **Range and habitat:** Widespread common summer visitor in most wooded or brushy areas; some winter visitors north to mid California latitudes. **Distinguished by:** *Similar to 259, but larger, longer tail, and underparts lighter and less barred, general brownish color, faint streak through eye.* **Behavior:** Aggressive and bold, with much scolding. **Voice:** Gurgling and stuttering song, first loud then soft.

261. BEWICK'S WREN, *Thryomanes bewickii.* **Range and habitat:** Common resident in foothills and lowlands in most brushy and wooded areas, generally avoiding higher Sierra and desert areas. **Distinguished by:** Unstreaked *brown above, white below; white stripe over eye; long tail has narrow base and is barred with white tips on outer tail feathers, also much white underneath.* **Behavior:** Regularly flick tail from side to side. **Voice:** Varied calls; harsh scolding note; song of high notes followed by *buzz* and *trill.*

262. LONG-BILLED MARSH WREN, *Telmatodytes palustris.* · **Range and habitat:** Resident along coast, N.E. corner of state, Central Valley and along Colorado River; in most marshlands; in winter more scattered in south. **Distinguished by:** *Black and white striped back; sides of back and top of head reddish-brown; bright white stripe over eye.* **Behavior:** Easy to approach; perches on reeds. **Voice:** Gurgling sibilant song; harsh *chrr-chrr.*

263. CAÑON WREN, *Catherpes mexicanus.* **Range and habitat:** Resident in mountains, primarily of south inner coast and Sierra, mainly canyon walls with rocky outcrops. **Distinguished by:** *Reddish-brown belly in marked contrast with white breast and throat; upper parts brownish, speckled with black and white.* **Behavior:** Bobs hind parts up slowly, then quickly brings them down again; slips in and out of rock crevices. **Voice:** Song starting in staccato, then drawn-out double *teu* notes, ending with deep *two-two-two.*

264. ROCK WREN, *Salpinctes obsoletus..* **Range and habitat:** Widespread resident in rocky country, generally avoiding N.W. coast; some move south in winter. **Distinguished by:** *White breast lightly streaked with brown, yellowish-brown tip of tail; grayish-brown above; white streak over eye.* **Behavior:** Energetic; active performer. **Voice:** Harsh chant of *too-too, kee-poo.*

265. CACTUS WREN, *Campylorhynchus brunneicapillus.* **Range and habitat:** Common resident in arid areas of southern Calif. in thickets of cactus scrub or trees. **Distinguished by:** *Very large wren with heavy dark spotting on whitish underparts; much white streaking on brown back and wings.* **Behavior:** Builds covered nest in thorny vegetation. **Voice:** *Chu-chu* call; *kut-kuk.*

WRENS

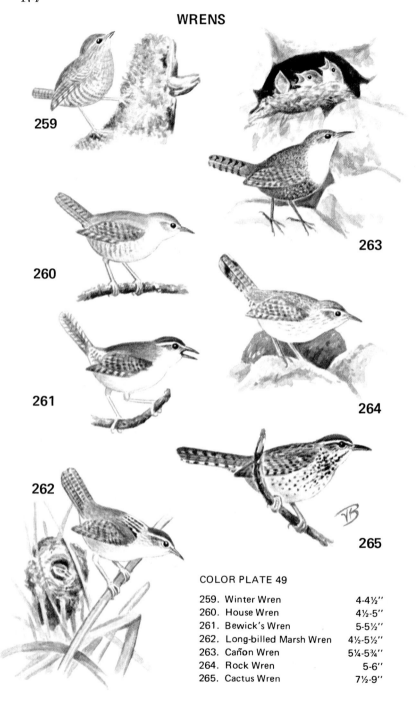

COLOR PLATE 49

259.	Winter Wren	4-4½''
260.	House Wren	4½-5''
261.	Bewick's Wren	5-5½''
262.	Long-billed Marsh Wren	4½-5½''
263.	Cañon Wren	5¼-5¾''
264.	Rock Wren	5-6''
265.	Cactus Wren	7½-9''

WRENTIT and DIPPER

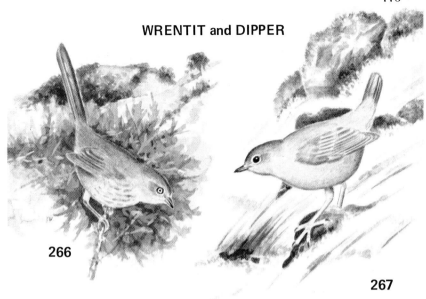

266

267

WARBLERS
(without wing-bars)

269

268

270

COLOR PLATE 50

266.	Wrentit	6-6½"
267.	Dipper	7-8½"
268.	Orange-crowned Warbler	4-5"
269.	Nashville Warbler	4-5"
270.	Lucy's Warbler	4-4½"

Wrentits: Family Chamaeidae. Brown wren-like birds with very long tails, appear rather weak in flight, hopping through thick brush when disturbed.

266. WRENTIT, *Chamaea fasciata.* **Range and habitat:** Common resident of chaparral and other brushy country and streamside woodlands of coastal ranges and west slope of Sierra and Cascades. **Distinguished by:** Lax plumage, *very long, round-tipped, cocked up brown tail; overall brown colors and whitish eye;* breast and throat streaked buffy brown. **Behavior:** Most secretive in dense bushes, but seems curious and will come out to look around if one stands still and make a squeaking noise; often seen in pairs. **Voice:** Soft *prrr, prrr* notes; song starts with slow loud notes and changes to rapid staccato of trilling notes, dropping in pitch.

Dipper or Water Ouzel: Family Cinclidae. Strong legs plus waterproofing oil glands aid these birds in pursuit of insect life underwater.

267. DIPPER, *Cinclus mexicanus.* **Range and habitat:** Common resident along permanent mountain streams, primarily northern half of state. **Distinguished by:** *Short tail with chunky body, which is dark slate-gray in spring and summer, but paler gray below for rest of year;* dark bill, pale legs; upper eyelid whitish. **Behavior:** Walks underwater on bottom foraging for insect prey; often bobs nervously or dips up-and-down on rocks; mossy nest usually placed on rocks close to water, often hidden behind spray of waterfall. Flies with rapidly beating wings, close to water. **Voice:** Spirited song of trills and clear flute-like notes, often with repeated high phrases. Alarm *bzzit, tzeet!*

Wood Warblers: Family Parulidae. Bright-colored, actively flitting.

268. ORANGE-CROWNED WARBLER, *Vermivora celata.* **Range and habitat:** Common summer visitor at low and middle elevations over much of state except S.E.; in chaparral, streamside and mixed wooded areas and coniferous forests. Widespread migrant; some wintering individually mainly in southern half of state. **Distinguished by:** *Greenish-gray-yellowish colors; lightly streaked on breast;* orange crown is rarely seen; no white. **Behavior:** Appears extremely restless and lively, moving quickly among outermost twigs and foliage of tree, especially broad-leaved trees. **Voice:** A weak, frequently repeated trill, becoming very soft at end; faint chip call.

269. NASHVILLE WARBLER, *Vermivora ruficapilla.* **Range and habitat:** Summer visitor in foothills and mountains of north 2/3 of state, in open mountain forests, mixed and oak woods, all with scattered bushy understory. Widespread in migration. **Distinguished by:** *Bright yellow throat and underparts, distinct white eye-ring, ashy-gray top and sides of head, olive-green back.* **Behavior:** Nests on or near ground. **Voice:** Sharp *tsp;* song shrill *see-lit.*

270. LUCY'S WARBLER, *Vermivora luciae.* **Range and habitat:** Common summer visitor in mesquite thickets primarily near Lower Colorado River. **Distinguished by:** *Only warbler with a chestnut-colored rump; reddish-brown crown; ashy-gray upper parts; white eye-ring;* underparts whitish or brownish-white. **Behavior:** Very wary and well-camouflaged bird; nests in cavities. **Voice:** Song begins with musical but staccato *whee-chit, whee-chit-chit-chet,* ending with buzzing *zweee!*

271. COMMON YELLOWTHROAT, *Geothlypis trichas.* **Range and habitat:** Common resident in marshy areas of southern California; summer visitor in valleys of north and central California in marshes and adjacent vegetation; some winter in central California; widespread in migration. **Distinguished by:** *Black mask and yellow throat in* ♂; yellowish-brown upper parts; belly whitish. ♀ mainly dull olive-brown above, but has yellow throat, and is brownish across chest. **Behavior:** Forages and nests (grassy cup) usually close to or on ground. **Voice:** *Tchek* note like Marsh Wren's but higher, softer; *wit-chee-chee* song.

272. WILSON'S WARBLER, *Wilsonia pusilla.* **Range and habitat:** Common migrant in most parts of state; common summer visitor length of state in coastal belt and higher mountains of interior primarily in thickets associated with moisture. **Distinguished by:** ♂ *has black cap; black eye on yellow face;* both sexes are olive-green above and *sharp yellow below.* **Behavior:** Especially fond of willows; a very active bird with frequent side-flipping of its notched tail; often flies up from branch to catch flying insect like a flycatcher; normally forages in lower foliage often near ground. **Voice:** Song begins with rapid *chit-chit-chit*, getting louder and faster, dropping at end; hoarse *chup* cry.

273. AMERICAN REDSTART, *Setophaga ruticilla.* **Range and habitat:** Regular but uncommon migrant in streamside woodlands and cultivated areas with trees. **Distinguished by:** ♂ *with black back, head and throat; salmon-orange wing and tail patches; white belly;* ♀ with gray head, grayish-white throat, and yellow instead of orange markings. **Behavior:** Very active in catching insects like a flycatcher; regularly works understory vegetation. **Voice:** Usually 2 different kinds of songs, alternated, one starting *see-see-see,* the other *seetsa-seetsa-seetsa,* often sibilant.

274. YELLOW WARBLER, *Dendroica petechia.* **Range and habitat:** Common migrant and summer visitor primarily in streamside woodlands and cultivated areas; in most of state except higher Sierra and S.E. **Distinguished by:** *A yellow warbler with light reddish-brown streaks below and dark markings on wings and tail.* **Behavior:** Usually forages at middle heights in trees. Appears tame and calm in nature. **Voice:** Light *see-see-weetee-see* song; final note slurring higher; a *tsick* call note.

275. MACGILLIVRAY'S WARBLER, *Oporornis tolmiei.* **Range and habitat:** Summer resident in coast ranges from San Benito Co. north, across to and down Sierra in thick low vegetation near water or damp ground; widespread migrant. **Distinguished by:** ♂ *with dark gray hood, broken white ring around eye, olive back, yellowish belly;* ♀ has paler hood, also immature. **Behavior:** Preference for dense vegetation close to ground shown. Slips elusively through foliage; very secretive. **Voice:** Variable song may start as a rocking chant of *siddle, siddle* or *sweeter-sweeter,* repeated; ends low or high.

276. YELLOW-BREASTED CHAT, *Icteria virens.* **Range and habitat:** Migrant and common summer visitor in streamside woods and associated vegetation in most parts of state exclusive of high Sierra. **Distinguished by:** Very large yellow-breasted warbler with bright white spectacle-like eye-rings. **Behavior:** Most activities carried on in dense tangles of vegetation close to ground; may sing at night. **Voice:** Loud, harsh and clear, whistled notes; mimics.

WARBLERS (faint or no wing-bars)

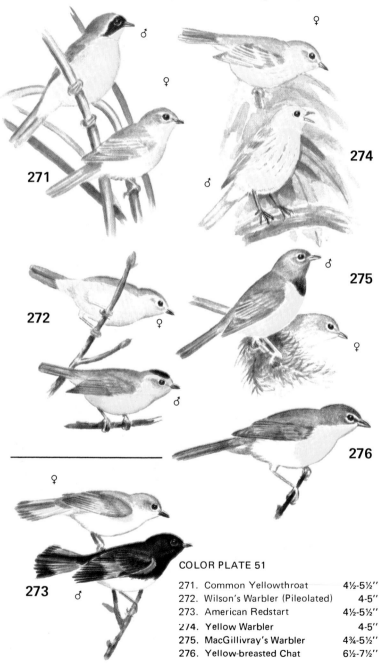

COLOR PLATE 51

271. Common Yellowthroat — 4½-5½"
272. Wilson's Warbler (Pileolated) — 4-5"
273. American Redstart — 4½-5½"
274. Yellow Warbler — 4-5"
275. MacGillivray's Warbler — 4¾-5½"
276. Yellow-breasted Chat — 6½-7½"

WARBLERS (with wing-bars)

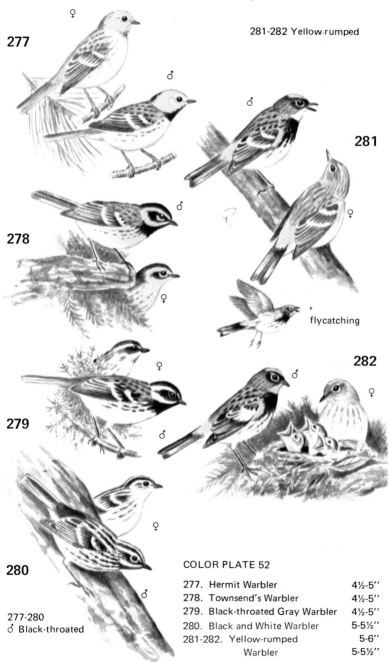

281-282 Yellow-rumped

277

281

278

flycatching

282

279

280

277-280
♂ Black-throated

COLOR PLATE 52

277.	Hermit Warbler	4½-5''
278.	Townsend's Warbler	4½-5''
279.	Black-throated Gray Warbler	4½-5''
280.	Black and White Warbler	5-5½''
281-282.	Yellow-rumped	5-6''
	Warbler	5-5½''

277. HERMIT WARBLER, *Dendroica occidentalis*. **Range and habitat:** Common summer visitor in Sierra, Cascades and coast ranges south to San Francisco Bay area, in dense coniferous forests; widespread in migration. **Distinguished by:** ♂ *with yellow head except for black throat; gray back streaked with black; underparts unstreaked white.* ♀ with dull yellow head; top of head mottled blackish, whitish throat, dusky spotted below. **Behavior:** Forages most of time in middle heights to tree tops of conifer trees. Nests at 24-40′ heights; deliberate in movements. **Voice:** *Tskk* call; variable song, *tweeky, tweeky, tweeky, tsuk, tsuk.*

278. TOWNSEND'S WARBLER, *Dendroica townsendi.* **Range and habitat:** Common winter visitor along coast from S.F. Bay Region south, in oak woods, coniferous forests and cultivated areas with trees; widespread in migration. **Distinguished by:** *Adult ♂ in spring and summer with black crown, dark patch back of eye, encircled with yellow, black throat.* Adult ♀ and ♂ in winter have more greenish heads and yellowish throat with black dots or streaks. **Behavior:** Normally forages in upper foliage of dense trees; lower levels in migration. Prefers firs to nest in. **Voice:** Similar to that of 279, but usually ending with a long drawn out *eeee-zzzeeeee.*

279. BLACK-THROATED GRAY WARBLER, *Dendroica nigrescens.* **Range and habitat:** Common summer resident in foothills and mountains, avoiding lower deserts in oak woods, coniferous forests and some chaparral; widespread migrant; a few remain to winter. **Distinguished by:** ♂ *gray with black and white striped face and black throat;* ♀ similar except throat whitish. **Behavior:** Rather quiet usually foraging in dense peripheral foliage. **Voice:** Variable wheezy song, *tzeedle-tzeedle* or *zee-zee, zee-zee,* more *z* sounds than others.

280. BLACK AND WHITE WARBLER, *Mniotilta varia.* **Range and habitat:** Occasional migrant, primarily coastal, and winter visitor to the south associated with a variety of broad-leaved trees. **Distinguished by:** *Similar to 279, but has white stripe down middle of crown, and much more white on back and under outer part of tail.* **Behavior:** Distinctive method of feeding up and down trunk and on larger branches, sometimes going down trunk face first like a nuthatch. **Voice:** Thin wiry *tee-see, tee-see* whistle.

281-282. YELLOW-RUMPED WARBLER, *Dendroica coronata.* **Range and habitat:** Common summer visitor in mountain coniferous forests; common migrant and winter visitor in varied habitats such as oak woods, coniferous forests, grasslands, cultivated areas and desert scrub; most abundant in west central and N.W. areas. **Distinguished by:** *Adults with yellow cap, side breast patches and rump; throat yellow or white.* **Behavior:** Very active; forage in foliage, often flycatch on the wing, may feed on the ground. **Voice:** Song a warble, beginning *tseet-tsee-tseet,* then trill; call a *chip* or *tsep.* (Formerly separated as Myrtle Warbler and Audubon's Warbler.)

Vireos: Family Vireonidae. Distinctive large heads, rather plain colors; forage rather slowly for insects among foliage, not flitting about rapidly as do warblers, nor flying out from branches like flycatchers; bill thicker than in the warblers, and with little hook at end.

283. HUTTON'S VIREO, *Vireo huttoni*. **Range and habitat:** Common resident west of Sierra crest mainly in live oaks, also streamside woodlands, coastal coniferous forest and cultivated areas with trees. **Distinguished by:** *Incomplete white eye-ring broken by black spot above eye;* gray or greenish above, with blackish wings and tail whitish marked; underparts grayish-whitish-yellow; white wing-bars clear and sharp. **Behavior:** Secretive and quiet in moving through the foliage; tame around its nest, often allowing touching without flying away. These actions differentiate it from the Ruby-crowned Kinglet, which looks much like it, but is much more active and nervous in its movements. **Voice:** Repeated peevish *tsu-weep* note, or *thay-thee, thee-tee.*

284. BELL'S VIREO, *Vireo bellii*. **Range and habitat:** Summer visitor to coastal slopes and valleys to central California, inland through Central Valley, in Owens Valley and along Colorado River; primarily in low streamside vegetation. **Distinguished by:** *Light gray or greenish-gray back, complete white eye-ring or spectacles, faint whitish wing-bars on blackish-green wings.* **Behavior:** Usually forages low-down in dense part of streamside tangle of foliage, appearing quite shy. **Voice:** Song a soft husky whistle or warble, often repeated, sounding like *seedle-seedle-seedle, see;* ending as if with a plaintive question.

285. GRAY VIREO, *Vireo vicinior*. **Range and habitat:** Summer visitor in foothills, mountains in southern third of state primarily in dry chaparral, some sagebrush, piñon-juniper. **Distinguished by:** *Drab gray or greenish-gray upper parts, with faint single whitish wing-bar on dark gray wings; whitish below; faint eye-ring.* **Behavior:** More lively than most vireos, often flipping tail; keeps to interior of brush most of time; occasionally scratches on ground for food like a towhee. **Voice:** Loud musical song, sounding like *see-wee, see-wee, chey-wee, chrrr-weeet,* frequently repeated.

286. SOLITARY VIREO, *Vireo solitarius*. **Range and habitat:** Common summer visitor over much of state in foothills and mountains in coniferous forest, oak woods and streamside woodland; widespread in migration. **Distinguished by:** *Bright white spectacle-like eye-rings, white throat and wing-bars;* gray head; dark grayish-green above; white below and with yellowish sides. **Behavior:** Leisurely, lazy movements; quite tame when approached on nest. **Voice:** Variable song, but of clear quality, with *chee-wee* and *wheee-wee* notes; also has nasal *tee-wah* call.

287. WARBLING VIREO, *Vireo gilvus*. **Range and habitat:** Common summer visitor mainly in deciduous streamside and mixed woodlands over state except east of Sierra and S.E. deserts; widespread migrant. **Distinguished by:** *Dull grayish-brown general color, paler below, with white eye-stripe.* **Behavior:** Feeds mainly in middle to high branches of trees. **Voice:** A musical even-toned endlessly repeated slow warble; also a scolding querulous *twew!* and a mewing *twee.*

182

VIREOS

283

284

285

Vireo

Kinglet

Warbler

Flycatcher

Small olive-brownish birds

287

286

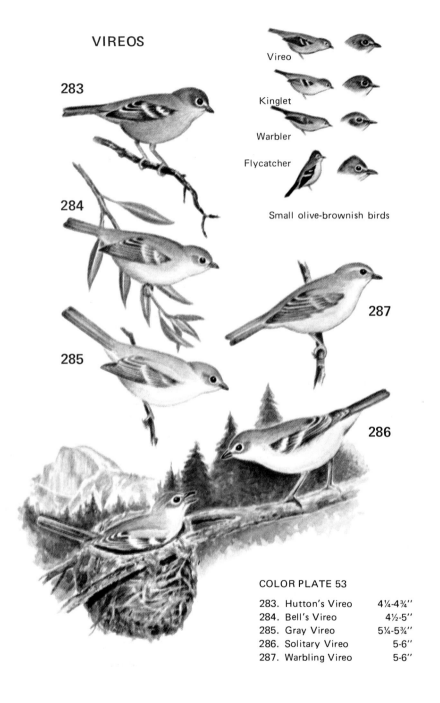

COLOR PLATE 53

283. Hutton's Vireo   4¼-4¾"
284. Bell's Vireo   4½-5"
285. Gray Vireo   5¼-5¾"
286. Solitary Vireo   5-6"
287. Warbling Vireo   5-6"

183

HUMMINGBIRDS

COLOR PLATE 54

288. Anna's Hummingbird   3½-4''
289. Costa's Hummingbird   2¾-3½''
290. Black-chinned Hummingbird   3½-4''
291. Calliope Hummingbird   2¾-3¼''
292. Broad-tailed Hummingbird   4-4½''
293. Rufous Hummingbird   3¼-4''
294. Allen's Hummingbird   3-3½''

SWIFTS AND HUMMINGBIRDS: ORDER APODIFORMES (in part).

Hummingbirds: Family Trochilidae. Very small birds; often hover with wings moving at high speed, probing blossom with long bill and tongue. Very quarrelsome; some feathers iridescent; voice a squeek or lisping *chip* or *tsip*.

288. ANNA'S HUMMINGBIRD, *Calypte anna.* **Range and habitat:** Common resident in western and central valleys and foothills north to S.F. Bay area, interiorly to Redding, mainly mixed woodland, chaparral, eucalyptus and cultivated areas, occasional winter visitor elsewhere. **Distinguished by:** ♂ *with iridescent red throat and forehead;* rest of body mainly green, but black on wings and tail edges; ♀ with white throat slightly touched with rosered. **Behavior:** When perched, head moved constantly from side-to-side.

289. COSTA'S HUMMINGBIRD, *Calypte costae.* **Range and habitat:** Summer visitor mainly drier parts of southern third of state and to Owens Valley associated with brush such as sages and desert scrub; some winter in Colorado Desert. **Distinguished by:** *Throat and head of ♂ violet-purple; throat feathers stand out conspicuously on each side.* ♀ greenish-bronze above, white below. **Behavior:** ♂ in courtship makes U-shaped dive, and hiss with wings.

290. BLACK-CHINNED HUMMINGBIRD, *Archilochus alexandri.* **Range and habitat :** Summer visitor in lower elevations in so. and interior parts of state; woodlands, brushy and cultivated areas. **Distinguished by:** ♂ has *white band below black chin and throat; throat appears purple in certain lights.* ♀ as in 289. **Behavior:** ♂ whirrs back and forth in shallow courting arc.

291. CALLIOPE HUMMINGBIRD, *Stellula calliope.* **Range and habitat:** Summer visitor in high mountains over much of state, in mixed forest and brushland; lowlands in migration. **Distinguished by:** *Head and back of ♂ golden-green; brilliant lilac feathers on throat, appearing streaked against white background.* ♀ and immature bronze-green above; dark-speckled white throat. **Behavior:** ♂ makes shallow U-shaped courting dive.

292. BROAD-TAILED HUMMINGBIRD, *Selasphorus platycercus.* **Range and habitat:** Summer visitor in mountains along east central border of state in chaparral, piñon-juniper, sagebrush and cultivated areas. **Distinguished by:** ♂ *with whitish underparts and rosy-purple throat;* ♀ greenish above, whitish below, with some buff on sides and sides of tail. **Behavior:** Both sexes make almost constant rattling trilling sound with wings.

293. RUFOUS HUMMINGBIRD, *Selasphorus rufus.* **Range and habitat:** Common spring migrant mainly in foothills, lowlands west of Sierra; migrant south in mountains; in most wooded and brushy areas. **Distinguished by:** ♂ *with bright coppery-red throat; both sexes have bright reddish-brown feathers on tail; ♂ reddish-brown on back.* **Behavior:** ♂ makes courting dive to few inches from ♀ with shrill sound.

294. ALLEN'S HUMMINGBIRD, *Selasphorus sasin.* **Range and habitat:** Common summer visitor along coast, mainly north of Ventura area in most brushy and wooded areas; some resident on south coastal islands. **Distinguished by:** ♂ *like 293 but with green back; ♀ looks like 293.* **Behavior:** ♂ dives from high up, in wide J-shaped arc in courtship, swinging back and forth.

PERCHING BIRDS: ORDER PASSERIFORMES (in part).

Mockingbird and Thrashers: Family Mimidae. Most have long rounded tails, generally narrowest at base; slender, often downward-curved bill. Usually sing loudly from prominent perches; most mimic to some extent.

295. SAGE THRASHER, *Oreoscoptes montanus.* **Range and habitat:** Common summer visitor in sagebrush, desert scrub, chaparral and cultivated areas east of Sierra and Cascades; winter visitor in brushland of deserts, coastal southern foothills and southern end of San Joaquin Valley. **Distinguished by :** *Straight slender bill, streaked whitish breast,* grayish-brown above with *darker stripes down back; two narrow white wing-bars; outer tail feathers white-tipped.* **Behavior:** When perched it may jerk up its tail; runs under bushes when startled; forages on ground. **Voice:** Long even warbling song; *kuk-kuk* call.

296. BENDIRE'S THRASHER, *Toxostoma bendirei.* **Range and habitat:** Summer visitor in Mohave and Colorado desert scrub. **Distinguished by:** *Straight bill, comparatively short for a thrasher;* pale brownish above; faint grayish-brown streaks on whitish-brown breast; *yellow eye.* **Behavior:** Often nests in cacti; builds a finely woven nest. **Voice:** Song a steady 2-note warble.

297. MOCKINGBIRD, *Mimus polyglottos.* **Range and habitat:** Common resident in open country with mixed scattered bushes and trees; lower elevations west of Sierra divide, Mexican border north to Sonoma Co. coastal, Shasta Co. interiorly. **Distinguished by:** *Gray above and whitish below;* white on side edges of dark gray tail; *white patches on dark gray wings flash in flight.* **Behavior:** The expressive tail usually held up jauntily; often sings at night. **Voice:** Typical song is of high clear flute-like notes, phrases repeated several times, but also copies songs of many other birds, has harsh *charr!*

298. CALIFORNIA THRASHER, *Toxostoma redivivum.* **Range and habitat:** Common resident in brushy country, streamside woods and cultivated areas west of Sierra and deserts and north to Humboldt Co. **Distinguished by:** Overall brown to gray-brown, *slight reddish-brown below; light streak over eye; long down-curved bill.* **Behavior:** Often thrashes dry leaves and soil under bushes with bill to find insects; when alarmed, runs rapidly under brush with long tail held up. **Voice:** Song a long drawn-out series of musical and harsh phrases; phrases usually repeated once. Gives a sharp *week* cry.

299. LE CONTE'S THRASHER, *Toxostoma lecontei.* **Range and habitat:** Resident in deserts and at south end and west side of San Joaquin Valley and in open areas with scattered bushes such as desert scrub. **Distinguished by:** *Overall pale light grayish-brown with dark tail; down-curved bill; dark eye.* **Behavior:** Nests in thorny plants; runs on ground a great deal. **Voice:** Loud musical song; *huh-weep* call.

300. CRISSAL THRASHER, *Toxostoma dorsale.* **Range and habitat:** Common resident to the S.E. in thickets of desert scrub and sagebrush. **Distinguished by:** General brownish-gray color, but *white throat bordered by dark stripe; underside of tail base reddish-brown.* **Behavior:** Spends much time on ground under low scrub vegetation. **Voice:** Song similar to that of 298, but sweeter and softer; a *chee-deeray* call note.

MOCKINGBIRD and THRASHERS

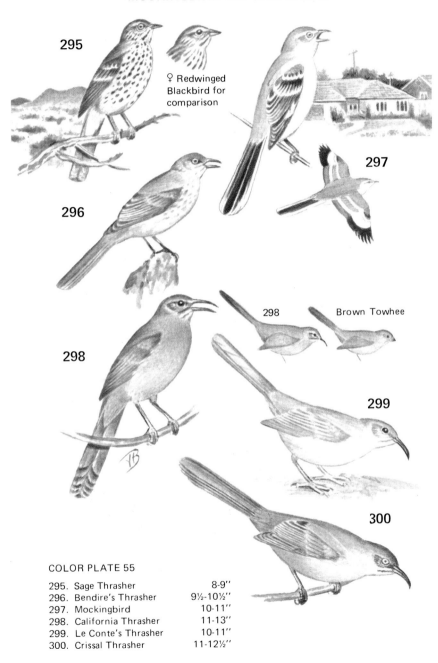

295

♀ Redwinged
Blackbird for
comparison

296

297

298

298   Brown Towhee

299

300

COLOR PLATE 55

295. Sage Thrasher	8-9"
296. Bendire's Thrasher	9½-10½"
297. Mockingbird	10-11"
298. California Thrasher	11-13"
299. Le Conte's Thrasher	10-11"
300. Crissal Thrasher	11-12½"

SHRIKES, PHAINOPEPLA, WAXWINGS, PIPIT

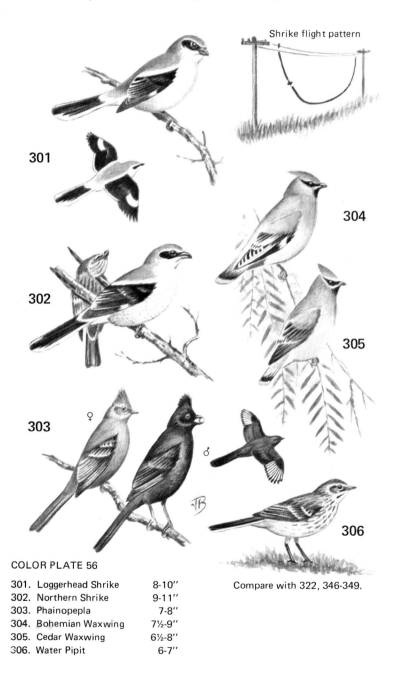

Shrike flight pattern

301

304

302

305

303

♀

♂

306

COLOR PLATE 56

301.	Loggerhead Shrike	8-10''
302.	Northern Shrike	9-11''
303.	Phainopepla	7-8''
304.	Bohemian Waxwing	7½-9''
305.	Cedar Waxwing	6½-8''
306.	Water Pipit	6-7''

Compare with 322, 346-349.

Shrikes: Family Laniidae. Upper bill strongly hooked for tearing prey, (small birds, mammals, insects) which are often impaled on barbed wires or thorns; forage alone from wire or branch or by hovering low over ground. Flight is undulating and rather low with sudden swoop upward at end to perch.

301. LOGGERHEAD SHRIKE, *Lanius ludovicianus.* **Range and habitat:** Resident in much of state except higher mountains and N.W., in open country with scattered perching sites such as found in savannah, desert shrub, sagebrush, and cultivated areas. **Distinguished by:** *Black eye mask, white blotches on dark wings, and white edges on dark tail; grayish above and whitish below.* **Behavior:** Very rapid wing-beats. Sits absolutely still while watching for prey. **Voice:** Harsh *treee* call; repeated *cle-lip* or *chee-rrr* notes.

302. NORTHERN SHRIKE, *Lanius excubitor.* **Range and habitat:** Occasional winter visitor, chiefly in N.E. in open country providing scattered trees. **Distinguished by:** *Similar to 301, but whitish-gray underparts are marked with faint but dark wavy lines, and black mask does not extend from eye over top of bill.* **Behavior:** Seldom seen on ground; may flick tail about. **Voice:** Mixture of chattering, whistling, warbling notes.

Silky Flycatchers: Family Ptilogonatidae. Pointed erect crests, long tails.

303. PHAINOPEPLA, *Phainopepla nitens.* **Range and habitat:** Resident in drier areas of south; summer visitor north into Sacramento Valley; winter, scattered records elsewhere; inhabit dry areas with scattered groups of trees often containing mistletoe. **Distinguished by:** *♂ all glossy black except for white outer wing patches; ♀ grayish with dark wings and tail and pale wing patches.* **Behavior:** Gregarious; tail often jerked on perch; may flycatch on the wing. **Voice:** Wheezy soft and broken song; a repeated *quart.*

Waxwings: Family Bombycillidae. Sleek appearance; pointed crest.

304. BOHEMIAN WAXWING, *Bombycilla garrulus.* **Range and habitat:** Sporadic winter visitor primarily inland in north, in areas where plants provide suitable berry food. **Distinguished by:** *General greenish-gray color, tail bluish with yellow band at tip; black throat and mask; white, black and yellow areas on wing of ♂; reddish-brown under base of tail.* **Voice:** Rough *zree.*

305. CEDAR WAXWING, *Bombycilla cedrorum.* **Range and habitat:** Summer visitor to the N.W.; widespread migrant and winter visitor elsewhere, mainly in areas of trees and shrubs providing berry food. **Distinguished by:** *Similar to 304, but more yellowish below, white under tail; most have red "wax" on secondaries of wings, but no yellow.* **Behavior:** Both waxwings move in flocks, following the wild fruit crops. **Voice:** High pitched monotonous whistling note, often quavering, in flight or perched.

Pipits: Family Motacillidae. Sparrow-like birds with thin bills; walk methodically on ground.

306. WATER PIPIT, *Anthus spinoletta.* **Range and habitat:** Widespread migrant and winter visitor mainly in low open country, such as grassland, marsh and cultivated areas. **Distinguished by:** *Gray-brown above, white outer tail feathers; white throat and line above eye, brownish below.* **Behavior:** Bobs tail up and down. **Voice:** 1-2 sharp *seep-seep* notes.

Thrushes, Bluebirds: Family Turdidae. Medium slender bills for omnivorous diet (insect and plant foods); young have spotted breasts; excellent singers.

307. AMERICAN ROBIN, *Turdus migratorius.* **Range and habitat:** Commonly breeds northern 2/3 of state and at higher elevations of southern California; associated with open woods and grassland, particularly with cultivated areas; widespread winter visitor at lower elevations. **Distinguished by:** ♂ *in spring and summer has rusty-red breast, head darker than back;* ♀ *has dark grayish head and back; breast pale reddish-brown.* **Behavior:** Tail often pumped up and down; typical thrush habit of running over ground in short dash and then pausing to strike at prey. **Voice:** Song of rising and falling sets of notes, low, loud *pip-pip* calls.

308. VARIED THRUSH, *Ixoreus naevius.* **Range and habitat:** Resident to the N.W. in dense coniferous forest; wintering south along coast to Monterey area and some to the interior and coastal south in relatively dense wooded areas. **Distinguished by:** *Broad dark band across reddish breast, pronounced light streak above eye,* orange wing-bars. **Behavior:** Shy and retiring; inconspicuous. **Voice:** *Chooak* call; long musical notes, higher than low.

309. WESTERN BLUEBIRD, *Sialia mexicana.* **Range and habitat:** Summer visitor over northern and western parts; winter widespread at lower elevations; found in most land habitats providing open wooded areas. **Distinguished by:** *Only* ♂ *bird of this size with tail, head, throat and wings dark blue; back and breast reddish.* ♀ *more brownish.* **Behavior:** Takes perch with view and sits quietly. **Voice:** Staccato *pu-pu-pu;* weak *chew-chew* song.

310. MOUNTAIN BLUEBIRD, *Sialia currucoides.* **Range and habitat:** Common high mountain, summer visitor primarily in Sierra-Cascade, some to the north, west and south in open country with scattered low shrubs and trees; widespread in lowlands in winter. **Distinguished by:** ♂ *pale blue azure except for white belly;* ♀ *brownish with blue on tail region and wings.* **Behavior:** Often hovers. **Voice:** *Turr* note; simple *cu-cu-cu* low warbling whistle.

311. HERMIT THRUSH, *Catharus guttata.* **Range and habitat:** Summer visitor in coniferous forests; widespread winter visitor at lower altitudes in bush and wooded areas. **Distinguished by:** *Reddish-brown on tail,* olive-brown back, *spotted white breast.* **Behavior:** Frequently raises tail slowly. **Voice:** Lovely flute-like song.

312. SWAINSON'S THRUSH, *Catharus ustulata.* **Range and habitat:** Common summer visitor in dense coniferous, mixed and streamside woods; widespread common migrant. **Distinguished by:** *All olive-brown above; buffy eye-ring; spotted breast.* **Behavior:** More often heard than seen. **Voice:** Very soft, beautiful song, spiralling slowly upward in pitch; *wheet* call.

313. TOWNSEND'S SOLITAIRE, *Myadestes townsendi.* **Range and habitat:** Common resident in mid to high mountain coniferous forests, coming lower in winter to areas of scattered trees and shrubs providing berry crop. **Distinguished by:** *Brownish-gray above, with white spectacles; pale gray below; long dark white-edged tail.* **Behavior:** Frequently flycatches from conspicuous perch. **Voice:** Long, loud warbling song; creaking *eesk* call note.

190

THRUSHES

307 Juvenile Adult

♂ 308

♀

311

309 ♂ ♀

♂ ♀

312

310

COLOR PLATE 57

307. American Robin   10-11''
308. Varied Thrush   9-10''
309. Western Bluebird   6-7''
310. Mountain Bluebird   6½-8''
311. Hermit Thrush   6½-8''
312. Swainson's Thrush   6½-8''
313. Townsend's Solitaire   8-9''

313

BLACKBIRDS

314 — Adult Winter / Immature

Adult Summer

♂ ♀ 315

316 ♂ ♀

319 ♂

317

318

♀

♂ Summer

320

COLOR PLATE 58

314. Starling 7½-8½"
315. Brewer's Blackbird 8-10"
316. Brown-headed Cowbird 6½-8"
317. Redwinged Blackbird 7-9½"
318. Tricolored Blackbird 7-9"
319. Yellow-headed Blackbird 8-10½"
320. Bobolink 6-8"

Starlings: Family Sturnidae. Introduced bird; often in aggressive flocks.

314. STARLING, *Sturnus vulgaris.* **Range and habitat:** Introduced species now quite widespread in towns, cultivated areas, grassland and open woods. **Distinguished by:** In spring and summer *glossy-purplish-black with green tints,* particularly on head; *bill yellow.* In fall and winter plumage brownish-black, *speckled with white;* immature brownish with white streaks and white throat. Body shape like meadowlark. **Behavior:** Swift direct flight; bold, aggressive birds. **Voice:** Whistled harsh squeaky; jumbled song; may mimic.

Blackbirds, Orioles, Meadowlarks: Family Icteridae (in part).

315. BREWER'S BLACKBIRD, *Euphagus cyanocephalus.* **Range and habitat:** Abundant widespread resident in grassland, streamside woods, cultivated areas and open coniferous forest. **Distinguished by:** ♂ *black with purplish reflections on head,* green elsewhere; *eye white.* ♀ brownish-gray; dark eyes. **Behavior:** Moves head back and forth when walking. **Voice:** Metallic *teck* note; song of wheezy rusty-hinge-like whistles, rather unmusical.

316. BROWN-HEADED COWBIRD, *Molothrus ater.* **Range and habitat:** Widespread resident except for N.W. coast and parts of higher Sierra; primarily in streamside woods, grasslands and cultivated areas. **Distinguished by:** ♂ *black with brown head and neck; short stout bill;* ♀ uniformly brown-gray. **Behavior:** Tail often lifted high; ♀ lays eggs in nests of other birds. **Voice:** *Chuck* note; *heee-eeet* when taking flight; creaky gurgling whistled song.

317. REDWINGED BLACKBIRD, *Agelaius phoeniceus.* **Range and habitat:** Abundant resident where there usually is standing water, as in freshwater marshes, moist grasslands and cultivated areas. **Distinguished by:** ♂ *entirely black with red and buff patch on wing* (may have all red patches). ♀ streaky white on brown. **Behavior:** Fly, feed and roost in large noisy flocks. **Voice:** Loud *keck* note; metallic, gurgling *onk-ka-la-reeeee* song.

318. TRICOLORED BLACKBIRD, *Agelaius tricolor.* **Range and habitat:** Resident but somewhat nomadic in S.W., west central and central California in freshwater marshes, grasslands and cultivated areas. **Distinguished by:** *Like common Redwing, but ♂ has white edge to red wing patch.* **Behavior:** Very gregarious even nesting close together. **Voice:** Song like 317, but coarser.

319. YELLOW-HEADED BLACKBIRD, *Xanthocephalus xanthocephalus.* **Range and habitat:** Summer visitor primarily in interior valleys and to the east in freshwater marshes and moist cultivated areas; widespread migrant except on N.W. coast; occasional winter visitor mainly to the south. **Distinguished by:** ♂ with general black color, *but yellow head, neck and chest; white patch wing.* ♀ brown with white throat, yellow breast and streaky upper belly. **Behavior:** On ground, sedate, seldom hop; flight like 317, deliberate, slow and wings whistle. **Voice:** *Kik* or *kak* call; raspy creaky song.

320. BOBOLINK, *Dolichonyx oryzivorus.* **Range and habitat:** Uncommon summer visitor in N.E. corner of state, in grasslands. **Distinguished by:** ♂ *black below and on head; yellow on back of neck,* basically dark below light above; in fall and winter ♂ similar to ♀, *yellowish-white below with brown streaks on sides,* brownish above with light streaking. **Behavior:** Sings in hovering flight. **Voice:** Distinctive bubbling gurgling song, like the name.

Meadowlarks: Family Icteridae (in part).

321. WESTERN MEADOWLARK, *Sturnella neglecta*. **Range and habitat:** Widespread abundant resident in open country, mainly grasslands and cultivated areas. **Distinguished by:** Streaked brown color, *white outer tail feathers; black V on yellow breast.* **Behavior:** Habit of turning brown back to observer; nests on ground in grass. **Voice:** Bubbling whistled song of 7-10 notes; *chuck* call.

Larks: Family Alaudidae. Often sing high in air.

322. HORNED LARK, *Eremophila alpestris*. **Range and habitat:** Resident over most of state except western parts of Sierra and N.W. area, in open terrain with low sparse vegetation. **Distinguished by:** *Black patch below yellow throat; yellow forehead* with black stripes above and below, *small black "horns" on head* **Behavior:** Flies low with undulating flight. **Voice:** Weak tinkling song *tsp-tsp, see-dee-dee;* clear *"see"* note.

Orioles: Family Icteridae (in part). Nests usually hung below branches.

323. SCOTT'S ORIOLE, *Icterus parisorum*. **Range and habitat:** Summer visitor to S.E. deserts; in dry piñon-juniper woods and desert scrub. **Distinguished by:** ♂ *with black head, neck, back, wings and tail; rest yellow;* ♀ as in 323 and 324, but more yellowish-green. **Behavior:** Feeds and moves quietly, no flitting. **Voice:** High clear song of whistled phrases, like meadowlark.

324. NORTHERN ORIOLE, *Icterus galbula*. **Range and habitat:** Common widespread migrant; common summer visitor in streamside and oak woods, savannah, and cultivated areas, except north coast and mountain forests. **Distinguished by:** ♂ *with black upper back and top of head, throat and line through eye;* wings dark with white patches; *body orange.* ♀ *yellow with gray back and wings.* **Behavior:** Vigorously defends nest. **Voice:** *Kit-kit-ick, kit-ick* calls; *whee, wheet* whistled song varied; may chatter.

325. HOODED ORIOLE, *Icterus cucullatus*. **Range and habitat:** Summer visitor at lower elevations, mainly to the south, in streamside woods, savannah and cultivated areas (favor palms for nesting); a few may winter in S.W. **Distinguished by:** *Orange crown and body* with black throat, back, wings and tail. ♀ as in 323. **Behavior:** Head lowered as bird leans forward nervously to watch stranger. **Voice:** Song of deep whistled notes; call a chattered *eek.*

Tanagers: Family Thraupidae. Tree dwellers with thick, fairly long bills.

326. WESTERN TANAGER, *Piranga ludoviciana*. **Range and habitat:** Widespread migrant in most wooded areas; common summer visitor to forested mountains. **Distinguished by:** ♂ *with yellow body, black wings and tail; bright red head;* bars on wings both yellow and white. ♀ greenish-gray, but light bars on black wings. **Behavior:** Flies in straight line with rapid wing-beats. **Voice:** Song rises and falls like Robin and Black-headed Grosbeak; *pri-tic* call.

327. SUMMER TANAGER, *Piranga rubra*. **Range and habitat:** Summer visitor along Colorado River; in streamside woods. **Distinguished by:** ♂ *reddish all over;* ♀ greenish-yellow. **Behavior:** Solitary habits; concealment revealed by loud voice. **Voice:** Song robin-like; musical *ki-yik* or *pit-ik.*

BILL COMPARISONS

Oriole

Tanager

Cardinal

FRINGILLIDS

A. I. II. III.
C. A. B. C. D. E.
B.

AN OUTLINE OF CALIFORNIA FINCHES

I. ♂ brightly colored
 A. Grosbeaks and bunting (red, yellow, blue, and orange).
 B. Reddish finches (crimson to pink).
 C. Goldfinches (small; yellow and black markings — except siskin which acts like goldfinch).
II. ♂ predominantly brown or gray.
 A. Juncos (head black or gray; bill pale; white-edged tail).
 B. Streak-breasted Sparrows
  1. Most commonly found in open fields.
  2. Most commonly found in brush or woodland.
 C. Crowned Sparrows
  1. Open fields
  2. Brush and woodland.
 D. Capped, "whiskered" and black fronted Sparrows.
 E. Towhees (large, long-tailed ground feeders).
III. House Sparrow (Ploceid) (Extremely common around human habitations); introduced weaver finch.

COLOR PLATE 60

328. Cardinal	8-9"
329. Black-headed Grosbeak	6½-8"
330. Evening Grosbeak	7-8½"
331. Blue Grosbeak	6½-8"
332. Lazuli Bunting	5-5½"

Grosbeaks, Sparrows, Finches and Buntings: Family Fringillidae. Largest family of N.A. birds; all have short conical stout bills, for breaking seeds, nuts.

328. CARDINAL, *Cardinalis cardinalis.* **Range and habitat:** Introduced resident in southern California, particularly Los Angeles County area. **Distinguished by:** *The only bright red ♂ bird with a crest; stout bill is red, encircled with black feathers.* ♀ has red bill, crest, wings and tail, but rest of body yellowish-gray. **Behavior:** Forages in fencerows and edges of woods; associated with man in towns. **Voice:** Soft *chip* note; song a drawling whistle, repeated and often varied.

329. BLACK-HEADED GROSBEAK, *Pheucticus melanocephalus.* **Range and habitat:** Widespread common summer visitor, generally avoiding S.E. deserts; associated with great diversity of vegetation, including streamside (favors cottonwoods and willows) and oak woods, coniferous forests with oaks, piñon-juniper and cultivated areas. **Distinguished by:** *♂ with black head, reddish-brown neck and breast, yellow on belly, black and white wings and tail.* ♀ duller, with a striped white and black face and streaked black on brownish body, but not breast. Both have large pale conical bills. **Behavior:** Do much feeding on ground, becoming quite tame in public camps, scavenging food at tables; may "flycatch" in air; ♂ takes very active roll in raising young. **Voice:** Sharp *spick* note; liquid mellow song of lifting and falling notes, often quite powerful; sweet *wee-we-you* call.

330. EVENING GROSBEAK, *Hesperiphona vespertina.* **Range and habitat:** Resident in coniferous forests (especially firs) of central and north sections of state; some may move west and south to lower elevations in winter. **Distinguished by:** *♂ with top of head, tail and wings (except for white patches) black; tail forked; yellow forehead and line over eye; body yellow;* ♀ brownish-gray with yellowish wash; black wing feathers edged with white; black tail tipped with white. Both sexes have very large pale bills. **Behavior:** Undulating flight; very tame, often seen hopping on ground. **Voice:** *Tseer-ip* call or whistled *tseee-ah;* song is a rough warbled *tseer-ip-grrreea.*

331. BLUE GROSBEAK, *Guiraca caerulea.* **Range and habitat:** Summer visitor in Central Valley and coastal southern California, Owens Valley and to the S.E., mainly in fairly dense streamside thickets, cultivated areas and chaparral. **Distinguished by:** *♂ is only dark blue bird with two reddish-brown wing bars and very thick bill.* ♀ has yellowish-brown bars on brownish-black wings; light brown body. **Behavior:** Jerks body nervously among low weeds; most activity takes place near ground. **Voice:** *Peenk* note; song rapid lifting falling short-noted warble that doesn't carry too far.

332. LAZULI BUNTING, *Passerina amoena.* **Range and habitat:** Widespread common summer visitor except for S.E. deserts, generally associated with brushy vegetation and low trees near water; widespread as a migrant. **Distinguished by:** *♂ has blue head, upper parts and tail; white wing-bars and reddish-brown narrow band on breast and sides; white belly; conical sparrow-like bill.* ♀ brownish with white wing-bars. **Behavior:** Tail frequently jerked nervously, ♂ often flies high when singing. **Voice:** *Tsik* note; shrill high song starts with 2 notes, *weet-weet* or *hew-hew.*

333. PINE GROSBEAK, *Pinicola enucleator*. **Range and habitat:** Resident mainly in central high Sierra in open coniferous forests up to subalpine. **Distinguished by:** *Much larger than other finches, but similar with red on head, rump and breast of ♂; white bars on dark wings.* ♀ generally brownish-grayish-yellowish with dark tail and wings (barred white). Both sexes with large conical bill. **Behavior:** Undulating flight; seem restless and tame; forage quietly either in trees or on ground. **Voice:** Whistled *tee-tee* notes, sharp *preeer*, many twitterings and whistles; whistled song of varied notes.

334. RED CROSSBILL, *Loxia curvirostra*. **Range and habitat:** Common resident of high mountains in coniferous forests, (mainly pine); winter visitor irregularly to lower elevations in coastal forests and mixed woods. **Distinguished by:** *Bill with crossed tips; ♂ dull red all over except black wings and tail.* ♀ dull grayish-green with dark wings and tail, some yellowish on head and rump. **Behavior:** Noisy birds, often seen clinging to pine cones, prying them open to get out seeds; may feed on ground. **Voice:** Loud *pip-pip* call; warbled *tu-tee-tu-tee*, *tay-tay* song.

335. PURPLE FINCH, *Carpodacus purpureus*. **Range and habitat:** Common widespread resident in mountains, mainly west of Cascade-Sierra crest, in oak woods and coniferous forests; winter visitor to lowlands in oak and streamside woods and cultivated areas with trees. **Distinguished by:** *♂ brown with rose-red on rump, breast and head, whitish below; more uniformly reddish than other small finches.* ♀ with streaked grayish-brown body, whitish with streaks below, *pale stripe over eye and dark blotch behind eye.* **Behavior:** ♂ flies high to sing. **Voice:** Swift warbling song; metallic *pick* call.

336. CASSIN'S FINCH, *Carpodacus cassinii*. **Range and habitat:** Common resident in high mountains, in open drier coniferous forests; occasional straggler downslope. **Distinguished by:** *♂ similar to 335, but bright red crown contrasts with brown hind neck; also paler red on breast.* ♀ has narrower brown streaks on white breast than 335, and less plain white stripe over eye. **Behavior:** Often forages on ground. **Voice:** Startled *tay-dee-yeep* alarm; rolling vibrant warble often ends in *chrrrrr*; a more open song than 335.

337. HOUSE FINCH, *Carpodacus mexicanus*. **Range and habitat:** Widespread abundant resident, mainly at low to middle altitudes, in open country and towns, associated with practically all land habitats. **Distinguished by:** *♂ similar to 336 and 335, but head looks flatter and smoother, and red color less widespread, being more restricted to rump, breast and head.* ♀ very similar to 336 and 335, but no dark blotch behind eye or white streak over eye. **Behavior:** Very gregarious; a most conspicuous bird of orchard, field and garden. **Voice:** Rather long loose musical song, ending usually in nasal *chee-wheer*; frequent *chip* call.

338. GRAY-CROWNED ROSY FINCH, *Leucosticte tephrocotis*. **Range and habitat:** Resident in high Sierra and Mt. Shasta area near or above timber line, in rocky areas, alpine meadows, with scattered conifers. **Distinguished by:** *♂ head cap gray in back, black in front; rose tints on brown body and wings.* ♀ duller, less rose. **Behavior:** Nest in rocks; forage on snow fields. **Voice:** Coarse *cheep-cheep* or *chee-chee* calls.

REDDISH FINCHES

♂ House Finches vary in color from crimson through orange-red to pale yellowish.

COLOR PLATE 61

333.	Pine Grosbeak	7½-9½''
334.	Red Crossbill	5-6½''
335.	Purple Finch	5-6''
336.	Cassin's Finch	6-6½''
337.	House Finch	5-6''
338.	Gray-crowned Rosy Finch	5½-7''

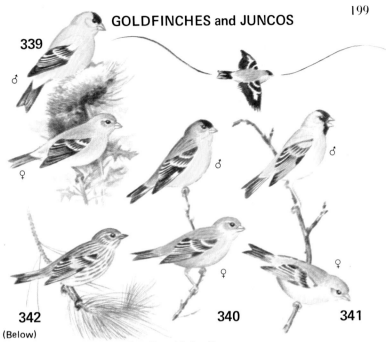

339

♂

♀

♂

♀

342

340

341

(Below)
Three similar looking small yellow birds: (from top) Goldfinch, Wilson's and Yellow Warblers. Note bills and build.

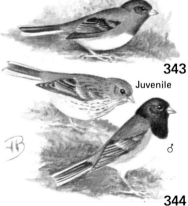

343
Juvenile

♂

344

COLOR PLATE 62

339. American Goldfinch	4½-5½''	
340. Lesser Goldfinch	3½-3¾''	
341. Lawrence's Goldfinch	4-4½''	
342. Pine Siskin	4½-5''	
343-344. Dark-eyed	5½-6¼''	
Junco	5-6''	
345. Gray-headed Junco	5-6''	

345

339. AMERICAN GOLDFINCH, *Spinus tristis.* **Range and habitat:** Common resident in low country west of Sierra-Cascade axis, north to south, in streamside woods, and brush near open country ard in cultivated areas. **Distinguished by:** ♂ *bright yellow body and head, with black cap; black wings with white bars; black tail* with white base; in winter the black cap is lost. ♀ lacks black cap; is greenish-yellow. **Behavior:** Flies deep undulating pattern. Flocks often sing in concert. **Voice:** *Prrr-kik-er-ree* call; canary-like song.

340. LESSER GOLDFINCH, *Spinus psaltria.* **Range and habitat:** Widespread resident in most land habitats, except higher mountains. **Distinguished by:** ♂ with *greenish-black back, black cap, black and white wings, yellow below;* ♀ and immature duller. **Behavior:** Typically in flocks often mixed with other goldfinches. **Voice:** Rising or falling *tee-yeer* note, musical song.

341. LAWRENCE'S GOLDFINCH, *Spinus lawrencei.* **Range and habitat:** Summer visitor mainly south and central California, in oak woods, mountain and coastal forest, grasslands, chaparral, cultivated areas; irregular winter visitor mainly to south. **Distinguished by:** ♂ with *head and neck black in front, gray behind* and on back; *yellow on breast,* rump and parts of black-marked wings. **Behavior:** More nomadic than 339 and 340. **Voice:** *Tink!* call; song harsher and lower-pitched than 339 or 340, with *key-yearrr* notes.

342. PINE SISKIN, *Spinus pinus.* **Range and habitat:** Common resident in coniferous forests and cooler woodlands of coast and interior up to subalpine; widespread migrant and winter visitor. **Distinguished by:** *Strongly streaked above and below; yellow blotch in wing* and yellow in tail seen when outstretched; bill pointed. **Behavior:** In flocks, often mixed with goldfinches. **Voice:** Talkative twitter of *tee-di-di;* sharp wheezy goldfinch-like song.

Juncos: Non-striped sparrow-like birds; black or gray-colored heads and necks; outer tail-feathers flash white in flight; bills pale; usually nest on ground; forage on ground usually in shade and in flocks.

343-344. DARK-EYED JUNCO, *Junco hyemalis.* **Range and habitat:** Resident in mountains over much of state; winters in many areas at lower elevations; centers around understory of open forests and woodland. **Distinguished by:** *Dull brownish or reddish-brown back, buff on sides, white belly* and *black head* and neck in ♂; ♀ grayer on head. Also this species can be a *uniform slate gray above and on breast,* contrasting sharply with *white belly* in ♂. **Voice:** Level insect-like trilling song; also has twittering and clicking noises. Call a hard *tek.*

345. GRAY-HEADED JUNCO, *Junco caniceps.* **Range and habitat:** Occasional summer visitor, mainly in desert mountains of central California and Nevada border, in mountain coniferous forests; winter visitor in south coast in oak woods. **Distinguished by:** *Reddish-brown back* and *pale gray sides, breast and head, pale pinkish bill;* white belly. **Voice:** Song a light *chipping* trill.

346. VESPER SPARROW, *Pooecetes gramineus.* **Range and habitat:** Common summer visitor in N.E. California in sagebrush; migrant and winter visitor west central and southern California primarily in open country with scattered grass and bushes. **Distinguished by:** *Brown above with dark streaks;* chestnut patch at bend of wing; *white outer tail feathers;* whitish underparts streaked with blackish-brown; *white eye-ring.* **Behavior:** If approached, runs quickly among low plants; nests on ground. **Voice:** Song of two clear whistled notes, followed by varied rising notes, song sparrow-like; a characteristic song at twilight in the summer.

347. SAVANNAH SPARROW, *Passerculus sandwichensis.* **Range and habitat:** Widespread winter visitor and migrant; summer visitor east side Sierra-Cascades and along coast length of state in grassland, meadow and marsh. **Distinguished by:** *Brown-streaked white breast without central spot; notched short tail;* darker race is dark brown, lighter race is light brown; a *yellowish stripe usually over eye;* brown cheek patch bordered by white lines. **Behavior:** Hops and runs about ground, flying only short distance when flushed. **Voice:** Sibilant soft *tsee-tsee-tsee-zee-tzee* with last note low; soft *tseep* or loud *tsup* call.

348. LARK BUNTING, *Calamospiza melanocorys.* **Range and habitat:** Occasional winter visitor and migrant in southern California, mainly east of mountains in open grasslands, shrubs and cultivated areas. **Distinguished by:** ♂ in late spring *all bluish-black except for white patch on wing.* ♂ in fall and winter, ♀ and immature like brown and white-streaked sparrows; more white on brown wings than most sparrows; small bluish bill. **Behavior:** Most activity on or near ground. **Voice:** Quiet *whoo-yee* call; song of warbles and trills.

349. LAPLAND LONGSPUR, *Calcarius lapponicus.* **Range and habitat:** Irregular winter visitor to N.E. California, in open grasslands. **Distinguished by:** In winter both sexes are *brownish with narrow dark streakings,* most evident on back and sides; *reddish-brown on nape of neck; black strip down middle of tail with white on both sides.* **Behavior:** Walks or creeps, rarely hop like sparrow; most activity on or near ground. **Voice:** Dry rattling call, often given in flight; song vigorous.

350. SONG SPARROW, *Melospiza melodia.* **Range and habitat:** Widespread common resident, generally absent in high Sierra and deserts, in streamside vegetation, marshes, brushy thickets and cultivated areas. **Distinguished by:** *Dark streaks on whitish underparts combine to form central large breast spot,* as in 352; much variation in color of races. **Behavior:** Keeps close to brushy vegetation. **Voice:** *Tchik* call; song starts with 3 or so soft *seet-seet-sweet* notes, followed by variety of trills and runs.

351. LINCOLN'S SPARROW, *Melospiza lincolnii.* **Range and habitat:** Primarily a widespread winter visitor and migrant in mixed shrub and grass vegetation; summer resident in most higher mountains in meadows near streams. **Distinguished by:** *Fine blackish-brown streaking across a buff-colored band on breast.* **Behavior:** Activities restricted to cover on or close to ground. **Voice:** Gurgling song, starting low, rising, then dropping low again at end. Soft to loud *tsee* or *tsep* call.

STREAKED-BREASTED SPARROWS OF GRASSLAND and OPEN-AREAS

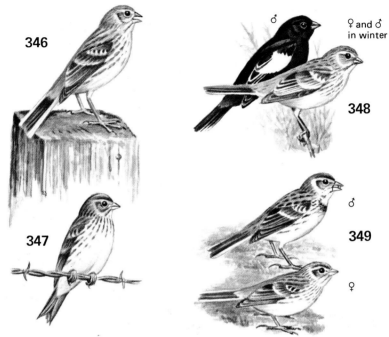

STREAKED-BREASTED SPARROWS OF BRUSH, WOODS, MARSH and STREAMSIDE

COLOR PLATE 63

346. Vesper Sparrow   5-6¼"
347. Savannah Sparrow   5-6"
348. Lark Bunting   5½-7½"
349. Lapland Longspur   6-7"
350. Song Sparrow   5-7"
351. Lincoln's Sparrow   5-6"
352. Fox Sparrow   6½-7½"

Fox Sparrow   Hermit Thrush

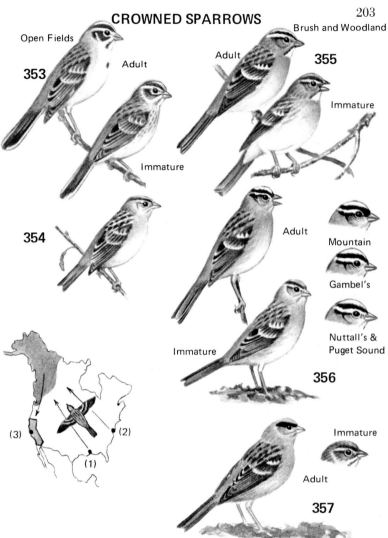

CROWNED SPARROWS

203

Open Fields

353

Adult

Adult

354

Immature

Brush and Woodland

Adult

355

Immature

Adult

Mountain

Gambel's

Immature

Nuttall's &
Puget Sound

356

(3)

(2)

(1)

Immature

Adult

357

In experiments under the direction of Dr. L. Richard Mewaldt, 411 White and Golden-crowned Sparrows were displaced from their normal wintering area in San Jose, California (3) to Baton Rouge, Louisiana (1) in the winter of 1961-62; 26 returned to San Jose the following year. In the winter of 1962-63, 660 were released at Laurel, Maryland (2). Fifteen are known to have returned to San Jose the following winter. Their journey probably took them first N.W. to their nor-

mal northern breeding grounds (red area) and then south to California.

(See Mewaldt, 1964. Science, Vol. 146, No. 3646, pp. 941-942.)

COLOR PLATE 64

353. Lark Sparrow   5½-6½''
354. Grasshopper Sparrow   4-5''
355. White-throated Sparrow   6-7''
356. White-crowned Sparrow   6-7''
357. Golden-crowned Sparrow   6-7''

352. FOX SPARROW, *Passerella iliaca.* **Range and habitat:** Widespread winter visitor in chaparral and understory vegetation; summer resident in high mountains in brushy areas. **Distinguished by:** *Large sparrow with upper parts dark;* heavily streaked on breast forming *large spot in middle;* underparts white. **Behavior:** Does much vigorous scratching in litter under bushes, jumping forward, then kicking back with both feet at same time. **Voice:** Two soft sweet notes starts song of *swee-chu* followed by loud trills. Metallic *sisp* note.

STRIPED-HEADED SPARROWS

353. LARK SPARROW, *Chondestes grammacus.* **Range and habitat:** Widespread resident over much of state in open country with scattered trees and bushes mainly foothills and interior valleys. **Distinguished by:** *Striped crown; reddish ear patches;* single *black spot on grayish breast;* rounded tail is white at corners. **Behavior:** Flies in long shallow pitches; most activities on ground. **Voice:** Variable song, with buzzes, clear notes and trills.

354. GRASSHOPPER SPARROW, *Ammodramus savannarum.* **Range and habitat:** Scattered resident in lower elevations west of Sierra-Cascade axis south; typically in grassland and open cultivation. **Distinguished by:** *Small sparrow* with seemingly *flat head* and very *short tail; pale stripe down middle of head;* generally brown color; clear buffy breast. **Behavior:** Short flights; seeks shelter on ground. **Voice:** *Tichick* call; buzzing, insect-like song like *zit-tick-zzeee,* or dry trill.

355. WHITE-THROATED SPARROW, *Zonotrichia albicollis.* **Range and habitat:** Occasional winter visitor west of Sierra, mainly along central and southern coast in open areas associated with streamside thickets, open chaparral and cultivated shrubs. **Distinguished by:** *White throat, white and black striped head,* yellow area in front of eye and plain grayish breast and cheeks mark adults. **Behavior:** Individuals usually found in flocks with 356 and 357. **Voice:** Harsh *tzeet* or *kink* notes; plaintive, whistling song.

356. WHITE-CROWNED SPARROW, *Zonotrichia leucophrys.* **Range and habitat:** Common resident along central coast; common summer visitor N.W. coast and high eastern mountains; widespread winter visitor in most parts of state below snow line; widespread migrant; associated with low scattered bush-type vegetation, edges of thickets, cultivated shrubs. **Distinguished by:** *Adult with black and white stripes on head;* throat and breast grayish. Four races vary in head striping and bill color (see illust). *Immature with dark and light brown stripes on head.* **Behavior:** 356 and 357 similar; flocking, ground feeding. **Voice:** Repeated metallic *pink* call; song of several clear plaintive notes followed by buzzing trill.

357. GOLDEN-CROWNED SPARROW, *Zonotrichia atricapilla.* **Range and habitat:** Winter visitor in lowlands of western and southern California; in open areas such as associated with streamside thickets, broken chaparral and cultivated shrubs; migrant in most parts of state. **Distinguished by:** *Yellow band through crown of black-sided head;* plain gray neck, breast and belly. **Behavior:** 356 and 357 similar; flocking, ground feeding. **Voice:** Plaintive 3-noted song, coming down scale like "three blind mice".

358. RUFOUS-CROWNED SPARROW, *Aimophila ruficeps*. **Range and habitat:** Resident in coast ranges and western Sierran foothills, central California south in brush or grassy slopes (preference shown for California sage, *Artemisia*). **Distinguished by:** *Reddish-brown unstreaked crown, black streak on each side of whitish throat,* plain dusky-gray breast and sides. **Behavior:** Stays on or close to ground most of time out of sight in cover. **Voice:** Musical *dreer-dreer* notes or *churr-churr* repeated; song of quick gurgled notes. Little carrying power to song.

359. CHIPPING SPARROW, *Spizella passerina.* **Range and habitat:** Widespread summer visitor except in deserts, in open areas of coniferous forests up to higher elevations; oak woodland and orchards in lowlands. **Distinguished by:** Small *reddish-brown crowned sparrow bordered with white stripes above eye; dark stripe through eye;* clear grayish-white underparts. **Behavior:** When alarmed flies to low tree branches; forages mostly on ground. **Voice:** *Sip* note; song a dry insect-like trill.

360. BREWER'S SPARROW, *Spizella breweri.* **Range and habitat:** Summer visitor in mountains of southern California and eastern part of Sierra, in brushy growth, typically sagebrush; common migrant and winter visitor to the south in brushland. **Distinguished by:** *Light brown crown finely-streaked with black;* brown patch behind eye bordered by black lines above and below; *clear whitish breast.* **Behavior:** Hops about on ground foraging primarily under bushes. **Voice:** Weak *sip* note; song a series of buzzing trills and runs at different-pitched notes.

361. BLACK-CHINNED SPARROW, *Spizella atrogularis.* **Range and habitat:** Summer visitor in inner coast foothills, from S.F. Bay area south, also in foothills of S.W. Sierra and desert hills to east; in brushland such as chaparral and sagebrush. **Distinguished by:** *Black chin and throat contrast with pink bill;* body and tail mostly dark grayish; *back streaked; no white in tail.* **Behavior:** Forages and nests close to ground in dense brush, such as chamise. Very shy. **Voice:** Faint *tchip;* song of plaintive sweet liquid notes, ending in rough trill.

362. BLACK-THROATED SPARROW, *Amphispiza bilineata.* **Range and habitat:** Common resident in open desert scrub uplands of S.E.; summer visitor in Great Basin area to north; occasional in mountains of S.W. California. **Distinguished by:** *More black on throat than 361;* two white stripes on side of grayish head; *dark rounded tail white on edges.* **Behavior:** Usually forage on ground but carry on many other activities in bushes. **Voice:** Cheerful *see-tsee-tsee* song ends in a lower or higher-pitched trill.

363. SAGE SPARROW, *Amphispiza belli.* **Range and habitat:** Common resident of inner coast dry hills of central and southern California; common summer visitor at south end and east of Sierra in fairly dense brush such as chaparral, desert scrub and sagebrush. Often found in dry alkaline plains. **Distinguished by:** Dark head with white above and below eye, *dark chin stripe and black spot on whitish breast.* **Behavior:** Often forage on dry substrate around bushes; often jerks tail. **Voice:** Soft *kik-kik* call; thin high jerky song, third note high.

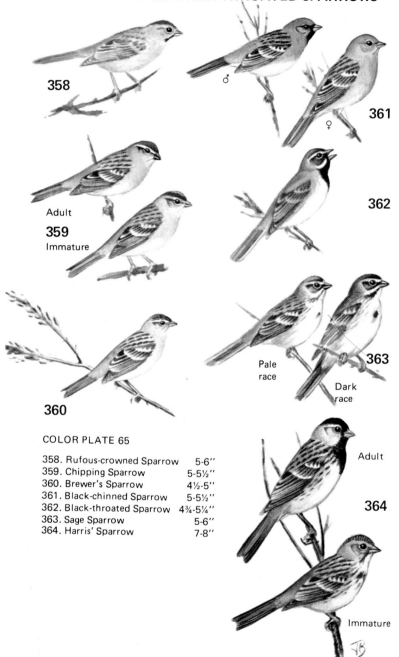

358

361 ♂ ♀

Adult
359
Immature

362

360

Pale
race

Dark
race

363

COLOR PLATE 65

358. Rufous-crowned Sparrow   5-6"
359. Chipping Sparrow   5-5½"
360. Brewer's Sparrow   4½-5"
361. Black-chinned Sparrow   5-5½"
362. Black-throated Sparrow   4¾-5¼"
363. Sage Sparrow   5-6"
364. Harris' Sparrow   7-8"

Adult

364

Immature

TOWHEES

365

367

♀

368

366

COLOR PLATE 66

365.	Rufous-sided Towhee	7-8½"
366.	Green-tailed Towhee	6¼-7"
367.	Brown Towhee	8-10"
368.	Abert's Towhee	8-9"

HOUSE SPARROW

The House Sparrow is not a true sparrow (Fringillid), but a Weaver Finch (Ploceid). It was introduced successfully into the New York area over a century ago and in less than fifty years arrived in San Diego. Its residence in San Francisco began earlier than the continental movement, probably as a result of further introduction. The success of this invasion has made it one of the most familiar species in the United States.

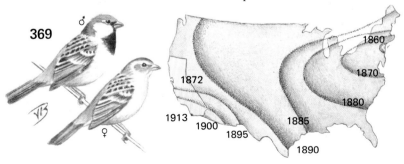

369

♂

♀

364. HARRIS' SPARROW, *Zonotrichia querula*. **Range and habitat:** Widely scattered, occasional winter visitor, except in S.E. and N.W.; habitat as 356 and 357. **Distinguished by:** *Large black-throated black-crowned sparrow*, white on back half of head and neck, brown back with black streaks; conspicuous *pink bill*. In winter the black crown appears more grayish. **Behavior:** Individuals associate with flocks of White and Golden-crowned Sparrows. **Voice:** Song generally three querulous notes, repeated at a different pitch.

365. RUFOUS-SIDED TOWHEE, *Pipilo erythrophthalmus*. **Range and habitat:** Common resident in most areas (except highest mountains and S.E. deserts), in chaparral, streamside thickets, woodland understory and cultivated areas. **Distinguished by:** *Black head; back and wings spotted and barred with white; black tail* with *white outer tail-tips; rufous on sides;* white breast and belly. **Behavior:** Often scratches noisily among dry leaves; most foraging done under brush, with abundant leaf litter. **Voice:** Call an insect-like *to-wheee* or *tay-wink;* also a mewing call; and a loud buzzing trill.

366. GREEN-TAILED TOWHEE, *Chlorura chlorura*. **Range and habitat:** Common summer visitor in high mountains; migrant mainly in central portions of state; winter visitor to the coastal south; favors brushland. **Distinguished by:** *Reddish-brown crown, white throat* with dark streak on either side; grayish face, chest and sides; *greenish back, wings and tail*. **Behavior:** Spends much time on or near ground; avoids danger by running into brush. **Voice:** Soft mew call; churring, burring song, starts with *whee-chrrrrr.*

367. BROWN TOWHEE, *Pipilo fuscus*. **Range and habitat:** Common resident west of Sierra and deserts; in shrubby thickets, open brushland, chaparral edges, streamside thickets, cultivated areas. **Distinguished by:** The only *robin-size plain brown bird with reddish-brown under tail;* throat light-colored and brown-streaked. **Behavior:** When disturbed, flies with jerky flight, not going far before alighting; typically forages on ground. Common in suburban backyards. **Voice:** Metallic *tink* note, repeated rapidly in song, ending in trill.

368. ABERT'S TOWHEE, *Pipilo aberti.* **Range and habitat:** Resident in S.E. deserts in streamside woods and desert scrub. **Distinguished by:** *Black around base of bill; underparts buffy-brown* usually with narrow black streaks on throat; grayish-brown above washed with reddish-brown. **Behavior:** Active in vicinity of a water supply, shy, generally active on or near ground in brush. **Voice:** *Cheep* cry and noisy blustering spluttering notes; song similar to 367.

Weaver Finches: Family Ploceidae. Introduced species from Old World. (See page 50.)

369. HOUSE SPARROW, *Passer domesticus*. **Range and habitat:** Common resident in vicinity of human dwellings and in most cultivated areas. **Distinguished by:** ♂ with *black throat and breast; chestnut band widening into patch behind eye; gray crown;* the ♀ resembles several native sparrows, but has marked buffy band over eye with dark streak back of eye and a streaked brownish back. Legs shorter and bills heavier than in native sparrows. **Behavior:** Aggressive; usually in flocks; hop on ground. **Voice:** Coarse *cheep* note.

ORGANIZATIONS AND CLUBS

American Ornithologists' Union
Museum of Natural History
Smithsonian Institution
Washington, D. C. 20560

California Field Ornithologists
San Diego Natural History Museum
Box 1390
San Diego, California 92112

Cooper Ornithological Society
Chesapeake Bay Center (for Environmental Studies)
Route 4, Box 622
Edgewater, Maryland 21037

National Audubon Society (many local chapters in California)
1130 5th Avenue
New York, New York 10028

National Wildlife Federation
1412 16th Street N.W.
Washington, D. C. 20036

Nature Conservancy, The
Western Regional Office
215 Market Street
San Francisco, California 94105

Point Reyes Bird Observatory
P. O. Box 321 Mesa Road
Bolinas, California 94924

Sierra Club
1050 Mills Tower
San Francisco, California 94104

Western Bird Banding Association
P. O. Box 446
Cave Creek, Arizona 85331

Wilderness Society, The
729 15th Street N.W.
Washington, D. C. 20005

Wildlife Society, The
3900 Wisconsin Avenue N.W.
Washington, D. C. 20016

Wilson Ornithological Club
West Virginia University
Morgantown, West Virginia 26505

BIBLIOGRAPHY

GENERAL

American Ornithologists' Union. *Checklist of North American Birds.* 5th Edition. American Ornithologists' Union, Baltimore, Maryland, 1957.

Austin, Oliver L. *Birds of the World.* Golden Press, New York, New York, 1961.

Bent, Arthur G. *Life Histories of North American Birds.* 21 Volumes. U.S. National Museum, Washington, D.C., 1919-1968.

Booth, Ernest S. *Birds of the West.* Outdoor Pictures, Escondido, California, 1960.

Fisher, James and Peterson, Roger T. *The World of Birds.* Doubleday, Garden City, New York, 1964.

Grinnell, Joseph and Miller, Alden H. "The Distribution of the Birds of California", *Pacific Coast Avifauna.* No. 27. Cooper Ornithological Society, Berkeley, California, 1944.

Hoffmann, Ralph. *Birds of the Pacific States.* Houghton Mifflin Co., Boston, Massachusetts, 1927.

Kortwright, Francis H. *The Ducks, Geese and Swans of North America.* Stackpole Books, Harrisburg, Pennsylvania, 1953.

McCaskie, Guy and Devillers, P., Craig, A.M., Lyons, C.R., Coughran, V.P., Craig, J.T. "A Checklist of the Birds of California", *California Birds.* Volume 1, No. 1, pages 4-28, 1970.

Miller, Alden H. "An Analysis of the Distribution of the Birds of California", *University of California Publication in Zoology.* Volume 50, No. 6, pages 531-644, 1951.

Peterson, Roger Tory. *A Field Guide to Western Birds.* Houghton Mifflin, Boston, Massachusettes, 1961.

Pettingill, Olin S. Jr. *A Guide to Bird Finding West of the Mississippi.* Oxford University Press, New York, New York, 1953.

Pettingill, Olin S. Jr. *Ornithology in Laboratory and Field.* 4th Edition. Burgess Publication Co., Minneapolis, Minnesota, 1970.

Pough, Richard, H. *Audubon Land Bird Guide.* Doubleday, Garden City, New York, 1949.

Pough, Richard H. *Audubon Water Bird Guide.* Doubleday, Garden City, New York, 1951.

Pough, Richard H. *Audubon Western Bird Guide.* Doubleday, Garden City, New York, 1957.

Robbins, Chandler S., Brunn, Bertel and Zim, Herbert S. *Birds of North America, A Guide to Field Identification.* Golden Press, New York, New York, 1966.

Ruth, Ferd S. *Habitat Checklist of the Vertebrates of Contra Costa*

County, California. Diablo Valley College, Concord, California, 1960.

Sams, James R. and Stott, Ken Jr. "Birds of San Diego County, California: An Annotated Checklist", *Occasional Papers of the San Diego Society of Natural History.* No. 10. San Diego, California, 1959.

Saunders, Aretas A. *A Guide to Bird Songs.* Doubleday, Garden City, New York, 1959.

PERIODICALS

American Birds (incorporating Audubon Field Notes). Published by the National Audubon Society, 950 Third Avenue, New York, New York 10022.

Auk, The. Published by the American Ornithologists' Union, Museum of Natural History, Smithsonian Institute, Washington, D.C. 20566.

California Birds. Published by the California Field Ornithologists, San Diego Natural History Museum, Box 1390, San Diego, California 92112.

Condor, The. Published by the Cooper Ornithological Society, Chesapeake Bay Center for Environmental Studies, Smithsonian Institution, Edgewater, Maryland 21037.

Journal of Wildlife Management, The. Published by The Wildlife Society, 3900 Wisconsin Avenue, N.W., Washington D.C. 20016.

Point Reyes Bird Observatory Newsletters and Annual Reports. Published by the Point Reyes Bird Observatory, P.O. Box 321, Mesa Road, Bolinas, California 94924.

Western Bird Bander. Published by the Western Bird Banding Association, P.O. Box 446, Cave Creek, Arizona 85331.

Wildlife Review. Published by the Bureau of Sport Fisheries and Wildlife, Fish and Wildlife Service. United States Department of the Interior, Patuxent Wildlife Research Center, Laurel, Maryland 20810.

Wilson Bulletin, The. Published by the Wilson Ornithological Club. West Virginia University, Morganstown, West Virginia 26506.

RECORDINGS

Laboratory of Ornithology, Cornell University. *A Field Guide to Western Bird Songs.* Houghton Mifflin Co., Boston, Massachusetts, 1962.

INDEX OF COMMON NAMES

The * indicates Color Plates.

(Egret, cont.)

Great, 15, 93, 94*
Reddish, 60
Snowy, 93, 94*
Eider, King, 60

Falcon
  Peregrine, 135*, 136
  Prairie, 135*, 136
Finch
  Black Rosy, 63
  Cassin's, 197, 198*
  Gray-crowned Rosy, 197, 198*
  House, 20, 41, 197, 198*
  Purple, 197, 198*
Flicker, Common, 39
  Gilded, 143*, 144
  Red-shafted, 39, 143*, 144
  Yellow-shafted, 143*, 144
Flycatcher
  Alder, 167*, 168
  Ash-throated, 165, 166*
  Coues', 62
  Dusky, 167*, 168
  Gray, 167*, 168
  Great Crested, 61
  Hammond's, 167*, 168
  Least, 62
  Olive-sided, 167*, 168
  Scissor-tailed, 61
  Vermilion, 167*, 168
  Western, 167*, 168
  Wied's Crested, 62
  Willow, 167*, 168
Frigate-bird, Magnificent, 113, 114*
Fulmar, Northern, 113, 114*
Gadwall, 85, 86*
Gallinule
  Common, 97, 98*
  Purple, 60
Gnatcatcher
  Black-tailed, 169, 170*
  Blue-gray, 169, 170*
Godwit
  Bar-tailed, 61
  Marbled, 18, 107*, 108
Goldeneye
  Barrow's, 83*, 84
  Common, 83*, 84
Goldfinch, 16
  American, 199*, 200

Lawrence's, 199*, 200
Lesser, 199*, 200
Goose, 16, 18
  Cackling, 89, 90*
  Canada, 89, 90*
  Emperor, 60
  Hutchin's, 89, 90*
  Lesser Canada, 89
  Ross', 45, 89, 90*
  Snow, 89, 90*
  White-fronted, 89, 90*
Goshawk, 135*, 136
Grackle, Boat-tailed, 63
Grebe, 16, 18
  Eared, 15, 77, 78*
  Horned, 77, 78*
  Least, 60
  Pied-billed, 77, 78*
  Red-necked, 77, 78*
  Western, 77, 78*
Grosbeak
  Black-headed, 195*, 196
  Blue, 195*, 196
  Evening, 195*, 196
  Pine, 197, 198*
  Rose-breasted, 63
Grouse, 19
  Blue, 153, 154*
  Ruffed, 39, 153, 154*
  Sage, 39, 153, 154*
  Sharp-tailed, 61
Guillemot, Pigeon, 18, 109, 110*
Gull, 5, 16, 22
  Black-headed, 61
  Bonaparte's, 121, 122*
  California, 123*, 124
  Franklin's, 61
  Glaucous, 61
  Glaucous-winged, 123*, 124
  Heermann's, 121, 122*
  Herring, 123*, 124
  Laughing, 61
  Little, 61
  Mew, 121, 122*
  Ring-billed, 123*, 124
  Sabine's, 121, 122*
  Western, 123*, 124
Gyrfalcon, 61

Hawk, 19, 20, 22

INDEX OF SCIENTIFIC NAMES

OTHER NATUREGRAPH PUBLICATIONS

THE CALIFORNIA CHAPARRAL, An Elfin Forest, *by W. S. Head.* A well-illustrated description of the dense and spine-like brush country found in most of California from north to south wherever the climate is too hot and dry to allow much tree growth, but does allow the small leathery-leaved bushes to grow. Fascinating stories of animal and plant life, mindful of the ecology-bent reader. 100 pages.

THE CALIFORNIAN WILDLIFE REGION, Second revised edition, *by Vinson Brown and Dr. George Lawrence.* Covers the greater part of California except for the deserts and coniferous forests. Descriptions and pictures of mammals, birds, reptiles, amphibians, fish and plants. Habitat areas explained.

EXPLORING PACIFIC COAST TIDE POOLS, *by Ernest Braun and Vinson Brown.* Tells not only how to explore for interesting specimens and identify them, but how to find things of beauty and to appreciate and conserve them. Color photographs and good line drawings.

POMO BASKETMAKING, A Supreme Art For the Weaver, *by Elsie Allen.* Shows the ancient art of Indian basketweaving, fully illustrated in a step-by-step method for recreating beautiful and useful baskets. The 68 pages include an interesting story about the life of the author.

THE POMO INDIANS OF CALIFORNIA AND THEIR NEIGH-BORS, *by Vinson Brown and illustrated by Douglas Andrews.* 64 pages, plus a full color map that shows the old trails and villages and paintings of Indian life; 12 photographs and 70 illustrations. All these finely illuminate a simply and interestingly-told text.

REPTILES AND AMPHIBIANS OF THE WEST, *by Vinson Brown and illustrated by Phyllis Thompson.* This guide will be welcomed by those interested in the fascinating array of reptiles and amphibians found in the West. A section on how to catch and care for these animals in captivity is included. Illustrated with line drawings, 16 improved color plates. 80 pages.

ROCKS AND MINERALS OF CALIFORNIA, Third revised edition, *by Vinson Brown, David Allan and James Stark.* 50 rocks and minerals are shown in color along with a good workable key. 51 two color maps of mineral locations. 80 new pages of quadrangle map listings helping to pinpoint rock and mineral locations down to a few acres. 204 pages.

See these books at your nearest bookstore or send for a free catalog to Naturegraph Publishers, P. O. Box 1075, Happy Camp, CA 96039.